D0759630

American
Liberty & Justice

**Gordon Morris Bakken**
Series Editor

**Editorial Board**
Michal Belknap
Richard Griswold del Castillo
Rebecca Mead
Matthew Whitaker

## Also in the series

*A Clamor for Equality:*
   *Emergence and Exile of Californio Activist Francisco P. Ramírez*
      Paul Bryan Gray

*Hers, His, and Theirs:*
   *Community Property Law in Spain and Early Texas*
      Jean A. Stuntz

*Lone Star Law:*
   *A Legal History of Texas*
      Michael Ariens

*Sex, Murder, and the Unwritten Law:*
   *Courting Judicial Mayhem, Texas Style*
      Bill Neal

# The
# Reckoning

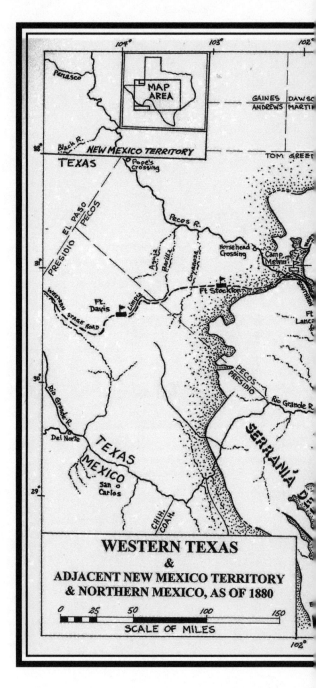

Map 1. Generalized geology of the area of "The Reckoning." Modified from the *Geological Highway Map of Texas* (Renfro and Feray, 1979) and *Lower Cretaceous Stratigraphy, Northern Coahuila, Mexico* (Charles I. Smith, 1970, plate 1), with permission. Stippled pattern is the outcrop of the Trinity Formation (sandy soils); white area adjacent is the outcrop of the Edwards Limestone.

# The Reckoning

## THE TRIUMPH OF ORDER ON THE TEXAS OUTLAW FRONTIER

**PETER R. ROSE**

**FOREWORD BY T. R. FEHRENBACH**

Series editor's preface by Gordon Morris Bakken

Texas Tech University Press

Copyright © 2012 by Peter R. Rose

All rights reserved. No portion of this book may be reproduced in any form or by any means, including electronic storage and retrieval systems, except by explicit prior written permission of the publisher. Brief passages excerpted for review and critical purposes are excepted.

This book is typeset in Monotype Perrywood. The paper used in this book meets the minimum requirements of ANSI/NISO Z39.48-1992 (R1997). ∞

Designed by Kasey McBeath
Cover art by Kasey McBeath; cover photographs courtesy Austin History Center, Austin Public Library, and Frederica B. Wyatt.
Maps by Peter R. Rose

Library of Congress Cataloging-in-Publication Data
Rose, Peter R.
    The reckoning : the triumph of order on the Texas outlaw frontier / Peter R. Rose ; foreword by T. R. Fehrenbach.
        p. cm. — (American liberty & justice)
    Includes bibliographical references and index.
    ISBN 978-0-89672-769-4 (hardcover : alk. paper) — ISBN 978-0-89672-801-1 (e-book)
1. Outlaws—Texas—Texas Hill Country—History—19th century. 2. Peace officers—Texas—Texas Hill Country—History—19th century. 3. Frontier and pioneer life—Texas—Texas Hill Country. 4. Law enforcement—Texas—Texas Hill Country—History—19th century. 5. Texas Hill Country (Tex.)—History—19th century. 6. Texas Hill Country (Tex.)—Social conditions—19th century. 7. Texas Hill Country (Tex.)—Biography. I. Title.
    F392.T47R67 2012
    976.4'31—dc23                                        2012020659

Printed in the United States of America
12 13 14 15 16 17 18 19 20 / 9 8 7 6 5 4 3 2 1

Texas Tech University Press
Box 41037 | Lubbock, Texas 79409-1037 USA
800.832.4042 | ttup@ttu.edu | www.ttupress.org

Library
University of Texas
at San Antonio

**For Virginia—**
because she is my hero; and
because she loves a good story

WITHDRAWN
UTSA LIBRARIES

# Contents

# Maps

# Figures

# Foreword

This book is a microcosm of what was a macrocosmic crime war in Texas. It creates a feel for country, time, people—the dramatis personae in a narrative that no "big picture" can achieve. Many Texans descended from frontier times will find something familiar to their own past. Newcomers may marvel at what Texas was before the state became "civilized."

Overlooked by historians (but not by makers of song and story) is the great cleanup of crime and general disorder in Texas's inner border regions between 1874 and 1881. For two generations Texas's history was dominated by a three-pronged war (Mexicans, Indians, and Yankees), and this violence left anarchy and detritus along what had been the old Indian border and farm-ranch line. Whatever the law was west of the Pecos, little of it existed in the Hill Country and beyond. Rustlers and road agents not only abounded; in some counties they organized and ruled. Sheriffs were hamstrung by both fear and local politics. Security fell to the scattered settlers, and in every central Texas county some sort of militia or minuteman organization was formed. But nothing was really effective until the Rangers came.

The Frontier Battalion, reconstituted in 1874, mustered only a few hundred men—without badges or uniforms, and poorly paid. (However, ammunition expended was replaced.) They were, by modern standards, a brutal bunch. However, they accomplished one of the greatest law-and-order feats in human history by cleaning up the border—arresting hundreds, killing hundreds more, and driving an estimated three thousand bad actors from the state. This effort did not erase crime but reduced it to the kind tolerated by civilization.

The context of the times is often hard to grasp by moderns. As one lawman wrote, the country was populated by men "mean as hell," and shooting was too good for some of them.

More important, I think, beyond whatever historical interest this book may arouse and satisfy, it contains a lesson that, unspoken, should always be as bright as morning: Order must come before law, and civilization cannot exist without the will and power to defend it. This, after all, was what the Old West was all about.

**T. R. Fehrenbach**
San Antonio, Texas

# Series Editor's Preface

Peter R. Rose's *The Reckoning: The Triumph of Order on the Texas Outlaw Frontier* is a most welcome addition to the American Liberty and Justice series. Rose artfully describes the progression from anarchy to the rule of law in Kimble County, Texas. The county was home to an "entrenched confederation of criminals" locked in a five-year struggle with the Texas Rangers and "law-abiding settler-citizens." Rose analyzes the struggle in terms of family history and the quest for order by settlers and crime victims working with the Texas Rangers. This brilliantly executed history marries the best of deep research into documents with a clear understanding of the Texas criminal justice system.

Rose's study of Kimble County adds substantially to a growing literature on criminal justice administration at the local level and questions whether state and regional studies of criminal justice administration have sufficient factual foundation.[1] Rose also questions recent revisionist interpretations of the role of the *Texas Rangers*.[2] This work focuses upon people in action.[3] This behavioral approach to historical analysis harkens back to James Willard Hurst's insistence that law worked out at the local level told far more about law's reach than law in books.[4]

This book also resonates powerfully with John Phillip Reid's *Law for the Elephant: Property and Social Behavior on the Overland Trail* (1980) and *Policing the Elephant: Crime, Punishment, and Social Behavior on the Overland Trail* (1997). Reid demonstrates that law learned and practiced in local communities found behavioral reality outside of the institutions of formal law in matters of crime and punishment. Private property and life were critical ingredients in the procedural mix when property crimes or violence occurred in the wagon train. The behavior of overland trail emigrants demonstrated "that the sanctification of property was accepted by a far wider social spectrum than merely the wealthy and their lawyers. To know and respect rights to personal ownership, nineteenth-century Americans needed guidance of neither trained bar nor legislature."[5] Reid's 1997 work demonstrated that "a majority of emigrants expressed popular acceptance—if not actual approval—of overland punishments, including the penalty of death." Emigrants expressed this sentiment with "silent acquiescence" yet "an impressive number expressed support by active participation."[6] Even more certainly, as the Kimble County Confederation spread its net into adjacent counties, stealing cattle and horses, civilians and the Texas Rangers took action in a very American way out of respect for private property and personal security.

Further, Rose goes beyond the single criminal story, resonating with other scholarly works, such as Ronald Lansing's *Nimrod: Courts, Claims, and Killing on the Oregon Frontier* (2005) investigating the legal travail of Nimrod O'Kelly in real estate transactions, criminal proceedings, and executive politics in frontier Oregon. Rose also analyzes Texans' views of emigrants. The Potters arrived from Mendocino County, California, and the Dublins were rootless outlaws. Kevin J. Mullen's *Dangerous Strangers: Minority Newcomers and Criminal Violence in the Urban West, 1850–2000* (2005) found a strong immigrant animus in San Francisco that focused upon the Chinese. Rose's work is far more nuanced. Rose asks whether the Potter boys of the 1870s could be seen as counterparts of urban gang members of today. *Dangerous Strangers* readers will be able to see linkages in crime family history in both California and Texas.

Rose's work on property crimes and incarceration adds another dimension to studies of criminal penalties. Readers will be interested to compare this aspect to three other studies: Ronald Woolsey's "Crime and Punishment: Los Angeles County, 1850–1856" (in *Southern California Quarterly*, vol. 61 [1979], 79–98); John Joseph Stanley's "L.A. behind Bars, 1847 to 1886: Establishing a Secure Institution" (in Gordon Morris Bakken, *California History: A Topical Approach* [2003], 42–62); and Joseph W. Laythe's *Crime and Punishment in Oregon, 1875–1915* (2008). Rose, like Laythe in particular, makes clear that generalizations about crime must be local, and each community forges a unique composition of order and the rule of law.

Readers will be impressed with Rose's meticulous evaluation of historical evidence and reasoned interpretation of context. In his point-by-point consideration of facts, geographical circumstance, and probative evidence, Rose's work closely resonates with Bruce Thornton's *Searching for Joaquin: Myth, Murieta, and History in California* (2003). Thornton argues that the search for truth that made the discipline of history great should not end in printing the legend when the truth is known. The truth about Murieta resides in "the slit throats and bullet-riddled chests of his victims."[7] Moreover, "postmodern relativism thus undergirds multicultural history, which focuses on the oppression and exclusion of minorities on the part of a dominant white society that shapes history to serve its own pretensions to superiority."[8] In outlining the relevant Texas historiography, particularly on the Texas Rangers, Rose, like Thornton, substantiates his interpretation through the historical evidence.[9]

Rose's work, though focused on specific histories of Texas violence, is rich in themes resonating throughout western legal history, particularly in the role of the

Texas Rangers in forging order and establishing rule of law. The events in Kimble County had counterparts in other places in Texas. Settlers, as those in Scyene, Dallas County, who organized to help the military identify the raiders of their herds, played no small part. Necessarily settlers took the theft of livestock seriously, and trials of the enemy deviants drew large crowds. In congratulating Scyene's citizens for saving the region from "robberies, horse stealing, murder, etc.,"[10] Judge A. B. Norton underscored what hung in the balance in post–Civil War Texas.[11] Yet for posterity, no one to date has laid it out more plainly than Peter Rose in his examination of the struggle between criminal families and the forces of order in Kimble County.

**Gordon Morris Bakken**
California State University, Fullerton
2012

# Author's Preface

It is partly true that Kimble County, Texas—isolated by nature and passed over by unfolding events of the 1870s—was founded by outlaws. It is wholly true that a few dozen mostly law-abiding settler-citizens, supported by Texas Rangers, struggled against an entrenched confederation of criminals for more than five years before a lawful, functioning local government was finally established in the eastern Edwards Plateau country.

At first, Texas Rangers of the Frontier Battalion spearheaded the fight against the extortionary criminal element that populated the forks of the Llano River, the region where the east-flowing North Llano River joins the northeast-flowing South Llano. Gradually, however, fearful citizens organized and asserted themselves, taking on increasingly responsible and dangerous roles, assisting in apprehending and eventually helping to eliminate the outlaws. They understood that before the rule of law could exist, order must first be established.

Frontier communities might endure ongoing criminal depredations with forbearance for a time. Long-suffering, however, they were likely to eventually rise up and exact a grim reckoning from their tormentors. In the closing years of the Kimble County struggle, an exasperated state finally and imperfectly imposed its punishment on the leading outlaws. The adjacent community then wreaked a grim and lawless final reckoning on the last of the renegades, cloaking the deed for public view in the accoutrements of legality.

One purpose of this book is to document how order—followed by its handmaiden, the rule of law—finally came to Kimble County, Texas, and to the adjacent counties around the eastern margins of the Edwards Plateau. It reinforces some of the timeless verities concerning the establishment and maintenance of law-abiding civil societies by their citizens. Many of these principles are as applicable today as they were 135 years ago.

The other purpose is simply to tell a fascinating, heroic, and tragic tale, one with many twists and turns, about contending people—settlers and Indians, lawmen and outlaws—in a time of great change near the end of the Texas frontier period.

Following the 1977 reprinting of Walter Prescott Webb's classic, *The Texas Rangers: A Century of Frontier Defense*, originally published in 1935, a number of excellent books have been written about the Texas Rangers, especially during the last decade: Frederick Wilkins's *The Law Comes to Texas: The Texas Rangers, 1870–1901* (1999); Charles M. Robinson III's *The Men Who Wear the Star: The Story of the Texas Rangers* (2000); Robert M. Utley's *Lone Star Justice: The First Century of Texas Rangers* (2002); Chuck Parsons and Donaly Brice's *Texas Ranger N. O. Reynolds, the Intrepid* (2005); Mike Cox's *The Texas Rangers: Wearing the Cinco Peso, 1821–1900* (2008), a modern reprise of Webb's original, *The Texas Rangers*; and Bob Alexander's *Winchester Warriors: Texas Rangers of Company D, 1874–1901*, (2009).

Although all these fine books used a variety of historical sources, they depended primarily on the remarkable body of primary source material—Monthly Returns, correspondence, rosters, and administrative papers of the Texas Rangers, particularly of the Frontier Battalion—preserved in the archives of the Texas State Library. These books are mostly about the men and deeds of the Texas Rangers, and they tend to present generally favorable perspectives of this venerable law-enforcement organization. Other recent works have presented more negative views about the Rangers, before 1874 when the Frontier Battalion was established, especially in relation to their treatment of Indians, blacks, and Mexicans, such as revisionist historian Gary C. Anderson's *The Conquest of Texas: Ethnic Cleansing in the Promised Land* (2005) and Michael Collins's *Texas Devils: Rangers and Regulars on the Lower Rio Grande* (2008).

The present book, too, draws extensively on the Texas Ranger files, but it is not primarily about the Texas Rangers. It relates and explains how a unique region in the western Hill Country of Texas—long delayed in its settlement because it lay isolated between east-reaching lobes of the Edwards Plateau[1]—struggled to evolve into an organized county governed by its citizens and the rule of law. It traces the civil evolution of a nascent frontier society still visited by Indian raiders to an emerging, still-fragile civil community. It is about the settlers of Kimble County, law-abiding citizens as well as members of the outlaw confederation, and their counterparts in neighboring counties.

In integrating the story from the Texas Ranger historical records with the histories of individual Kimble County settlers (as they are preserved in sometimes less-than-objective essays in county historical collections, or available through variably disciplined descendants engaged in family genealogy), I have tried to discern the reliability of material and communicate my confidence to the reader with such phrases as "may have," "family tradition maintains," "it is possible," and so on. Generally, I have taken dates of births, deaths, or marriages as reliable—depending on the source—but have qualified other unverified claims or opinions.

This book is also unique in that it relates the previous history of the principal families at the heart of the outlaw organization, and where they settled along the forks of the Llano. It explores why they may have embraced criminal ways in Kimble County, follows their misdeeds and punishments, and tracks their fascinating subsequent histories. Here I have been fortunate to obtain extensive, carefully documented records of the Potter and Dublin families, as provided by their descendants.

Not to have made use of the wealth of existing family historical material—imperfect as much of it may be—would have resulted in just another book about Texas Rangers and one-dimensional outlaws, a historical picture that would have been superficial and one-sided, indeed.

---

Unraveling the now-tangled and time-faded threads of the larger story has been a fascinating, long-pursued inquiry—a historical detective investigation. As much as possible, I have tried to let the unfolding story tell itself, through the words of those involved, or of contemporary observers, simply arranging the historical record to tell the story, and minimizing interpretive commentary. My intent is to take the reader back; to involve the reader in the attitudes, values, and language of the frontier times; and to share in the emerging insights that attend a dramatic and complex story as it unfolds.

The integrated history reveals recurrent themes that still resonate across the years, across a societal and technological gap whose breadth would have been unimaginable in 1880, and which may tempt the more presumptuous of us to dismiss their relevance today.

- The influence of geology on patterns of frontier settlement was profound.

- The importance of, and loyalty to, the extended family was the dominant social and commercial force in the region during the 1870s, amounting to frontier tribalism.

- Tribalism is the mortal enemy of the progressive, representative, commercial, legal state.

- The open ranges, a vague cattle law, clandestine livestock markets, and scarce law officers encouraged behaviors ranging from merely aggressive to criminally violent.

- Prolonged criminal enterprises require sustained clandestine markets.

- The establishment of civil society requires from its citizens individual sacrifice and personal risk.

- The police power of the state is a blunt and imperfect tool.

- Before the rule of law can function in a community, order must first be established.

In the face of the violence and criminality, and individual and family struggles for survival, it has been heartwarming to identify continuing examples of forbearance, perseverance, and courage, especially among the officers and men of the Frontier Battalion of the Texas Rangers as well as the citizens they were assisting. It has been reassuring to see that, after all the dust had settled, many individuals could put the old violent ways behind them and thereafter lead productive lives.

---

My maternal grandfather, Peter Paterson, the Scotsman for whom I was named, came to Kimble County, Texas, in 1891, and began ranching with his brother James Paterson on the uplands of the Edwards Plateau. In 1898 he married the Englishwoman who was governess of his brother's children. They founded Little Paint Creek Ranch, headquartered in the valley of the South Llano River, fifteen miles upstream from its confluence with the North Llano, at Junction City.[2]

The Indians and the outlaws were long gone from the South Llano valley by 1898, except for a few local bad actors and the occasional horse thief who was just passing through. The local sheriff kept things tolerably under control. Once in a while a solitary Texas Ranger made a cautionary visit.

Early Kimble County records being largely incomplete—the courthouse having been burned down in 1884[3]—the history of the coming of order and law to the forks of the Llano was buried at that time in various files of the State of Texas, twenty-year-old newspapers, private family journals, and the fading memories of those who had lived it. It was, however, alive in oral tradition, passed down from still-surviving pioneer settlers to their descendents. Unfortunately, my British grandfather and grandmother were not intimates of that original Kimble County pioneer community, so the stories were never transmitted to my mother and her siblings, or on to me.

By the time I was a young man, however, many stories about the early years had made it into print: fascinating episodes by historians such as O. C. Fisher and Walter Prescott Webb, and memoirs of Texas Rangers D. W. Roberts and J. B. Gillett.[4] Many of the adventures they related had occurred in the South Llano valley, because that is where the most notorious of the outlaws—the Dublins and the Potters—had lived.

The stories were fragmentary, mostly unconnected, and incremental. There were large gaps and unexplained details. But I was interested to learn that the Dublins and the Potters had settled less than three miles north of my grandparents' Little Paint Creek headquarters, where my mother was born in 1903. She professed to have heard nothing from her parents about the Dublins or the Potters, but she did relate a pertinent story:

> In 1906, Father and Mother moved our family to an upland homestead on the divide, about six miles west, to satisfy residency requirements to acquire four sections of school land. Once or twice a month, Father would stop by the Little Paint Creek headquarters to be sure the place was secure. On the Fourth of July, 1907, he went to Junction City for supplies, where he was told that a stranger had recently hired a hack from the livery stable, inquiring about the Little Paint Creek Ranch, but returned later without further comment and left town. Father went out to the Little Paint headquarters, and as he was driving up the road that led to the house, he noticed a fresh mound of dirt beside the road, opposite a bluff on the far side of Little Paint Creek. Peering into the empty hole, he could see the clear imprint of a round-bottomed pot, freshly lifted from its burial place. God only knew what it had contained, and how long it had been buried.[5]

Today, having gathered voluminous facts about those early outlaw years and "connected the dots" into a continuous narrative, I do not find it hard to believe that one of the Dublins or Potters may have returned to the confluence of Little Paint Creek and South Llano River to recover a stash of stolen money that had been buried many years before.

My roots go deep in the region for additional reasons as well. Early in my geological career, I carried out the definitive stratigraphic investigation and geological mapping of the eastern Edwards Plateau, an area covering more than four thousand square miles of west-central Texas.[6] I became intimately familiar with its rocky creeks and canyons, its ledgy hills and hollows, its thick-turfed divide tablelands. I came to understand how the geology of the Edwards Plateau influenced the distribution of springs and grazing lands and alluvial terraces, where the people settled and the roads ran, shaping the lives of those who lived there.[7] I came to know many of the present inhabitants, many of them direct descendants of the original settlers.

Today my family ranches on the plateau, on land my grandfather settled more than one hundred years ago. Every time we drive southwest, up the South Llano valley, we pass beside the old homestead sites of the Dublins and the Potters, and three miles farther on—and a generation later—Peter and Mary Paterson's old home site at the mouth of Little Paint Creek, the birthplace of my mother.

---

The story of "The Reckoning" spans more than thirty years and involves many characters. They fall into eight general categories: (1) Native Americans, primarily Kickapoos, Lipan and Mescalero Apaches, and Seminoles, raiding from their sanctioned settlements in Mexico; (2) U.S. Army officers; (3) officers and men of the Texas Rangers; (4) outlaws of the Kimble County criminal confederation, primarily the Dublins, Potters, and their relatives, friends, and neighbors; (5) Kimble County settlers who resisted the outlaw faction; (6) the tragic James Dowdy family; (7) a few county sheriffs and their deputies; and (8) two judges, one long-tenured and influential, the other an appointed "one-time" judge. Because the land exerts such a profound influence on the story, a number of reference maps have been prepared to help illuminate the action.

The story begins with a historical overview, followed by a review of the region's geology, geography, and hydrology and how they influenced settlement history.

# Acknowledgments

My first thanks must go to Frederica Wyatt, the director of the Kimble County Historical Commission in Junction, Texas, and a superb historian. Her remarkable memory for names, relationships, and events greatly facilitated my research, provided informed insight into the community that grew around the forks of the Llano, and prevented or corrected many of my errors. Ms. Wyatt also supplied rare photos of the Dublin brothers, her great-uncle Rube Boyce, and other early-day Kimble County settlers. Frederica Wyatt's continuing interest in the project was very important and greatly appreciated.

I am also deeply grateful to Kit Fuller of Los Angeles, California, who generously provided voluminous and well-documented information about her relatives, the Potter family, especially in California and Texas, which allowed a major advancement in understanding their part in the early history of Kimble County.

Through Ms. Fuller, I was able to meet John and Bob Midkiff of Midland, Texas, whose great-grandfather was William Potter, and whose great uncles included Mack and Bill Potter, as well as the Indian sons of Tom Potter—Frank, John, and "Indian Jim" Potter. Through the marriages of their great-aunts Lizzie and Doodie Potter, they also connect to Dell and Roll Dublin, respectively. Mary Lou Midkiff, John's wife, kindly provided photos of Potter forebears, and Toni Midkiff, Bob's wife, supplied much useful information and documentation about the Potter family in the Midland area after 1900, for all of which I am truly appreciative.

I am also indebted to my old friend Tom Syfan of Mountain Home, Texas, who showed me around the Mountain Home area, discussed various aspects of its colorful history, and introduced me to his friends in the area, most of whom agreed to be interviewed.

W. C. (Billy) Dowdy of Mountain Home, Texas, spent an entire day with me in May 2008, touring the key Dowdy sites in Kerr County, discussing his own extensive research into his family's history, and diplomatically challenging—and changing—some of my assumptions and conclusions. He also gave me copies of his photographs of his Dowdy ancestors. Thanks, Billy.

I am grateful to Charles Evans, manager of the Fred Burt Ranch, about eight miles southwest of Junction, Texas, who kindly took me to the "Potter Waterhole" on Chalk Creek, and to his mother, Jo Fred Burt Evans, who shared her knowledge of the history of that site in particular and of the Kimble County area in general. Chuck Parsons of Luling, Texas, offered experienced encouragement, useful information, and publication guidance as well as access to his superb collection of vintage photographs, for all of which I am most appreciative. Steve Grimes of San Angelo, Texas, the grandson of Kimble County's first historian, O. C. Fisher, granted permission to use the photo of Judge W. A. Blackburn.

The staff of the Texas State Library and Archives Commission, Austin, helped me locate obscure materials and showed me how to pursue various research interests over a one-year period commencing in September 2007. They also granted permission to use photos and images of materials from their collections. I am particularly grateful to Donaly Brice, whose knowledge about the materials contained therein, especially those pertaining to the frontier period, is encyclopedic. John Anderson, TSL photo curator, helped to locate the long-missing photo of Corporal R. G. Kimbell and his horse, and reunite it with Kimbell's memoirs in the Texas Rangers papers.

The Texas General Land office maintains an extraordinary collection of historic maps, including all the land records and maps of early Texas; in addition, these materials are preserved and accessible with remarkable efficiency by very helpful and knowledgeable staff. I am grateful for their help.

The staff of the Center for American History at the University of Texas at Austin provided access to important newspapers of the 1874–83 period, rare books about the Edwards Plateau, Trans-Pecos Texas, and northern Mexico, and their photo collection covering the area during the frontier period. I thank them for their cheerful and effective assistance.

Other photographs were kindly provided by the Institute of Texan Cultures, San Antonio, Texas; the Noah H. Rose Photo Collection of the Western History Collections at the University of Oklahoma, Norman, Oklahoma; the Kimble County Historical Commission; and the Austin History Center. I am most grateful for the inspiration to preserve these windows into our past, and to these institutions and individuals for organizing, maintaining, and housing them.

Federal District Judge Lynn Hughes of Houston, Texas, and Linda Uecker, district court clerk in Kerrville, Texas, gave useful perspectives on state court practices, and Mike Bowlin of the Kerr County Historical Commission, provided additional materials and insights, especially the tape of the 1971 interview of Mr. and Mrs. Solon Dowdy by Meryl Doyle of the Butt-Holdsworth Library, Kerrville, Texas. O. B. Shelburne of Austin and Patrick Dearen of Midland provided useful counsel about the route of the old San Antonio–El Paso stage road. Thanks, Lynn, Linda, Mike, O. B., and Patrick.

I am indebted to Eric Potter, Joel Lardon, and Amanda Masterson of the Bureau of Economic Geology, University of Texas at Austin, for expert counsel and thoughtful assistance regarding geologic and physiographic maps. David Stephens performed miracles in digitally enhancing some of the old photographs in the book as well as some of my hand-drafted maps. David, you are amazing.

Many thanks to Virginia Rose, Kit Fuller, Deb Karpuk, and Chuck Parsons, who read the first draft and offered sage counsel. I'm grateful to Marvin Womack and Dwight Cassell, who provided important connections at critical times, and to Ted Fehrenbach, who gave insightful advice about placing the manuscript.

Kathy Clayton and Linnea Fredrickson edited the notes and bibliography, and Lee Gable prepared the index. Judith Keeling, Joanna Conrad, and Kasey McBeath of Texas Tech University Press expertly saw the book through production and publication and were a pleasure to work with.

Elizabeth Ethridge Sherry, my "good right arm" for the past twenty years, provided constant and essential guidance regarding computers, software, layout, editing, and preparation of figures and captions, and prepared the final draft. Well done, Elizabeth.

Finally, my ever-patient wife, Alice, experienced being a "widow for a year" while this book was being written and continued to provide cheerful encouragement, loving support, emotional sustenance, and profound tolerance throughout its over-long gestation period. Words cannot adequately express the depth and value of her contribution. My dear, thank you.

I am profoundly grateful to all these good people who have been so interested in this project as it evolved, so generous with their time and knowledge, and so steadfast in their encouragement and support. Any errors that remain are entirely my responsibility.

# The
# Reckoning

# 1 :: Oasis of Outlaws

The word was out: the U.S. Army was finally doing something about the Indian raiders who had for years plagued the western Hill Country of Texas. Comanche raids from the north and Mexican Indian raids from the southwest would be eliminated, or at least greatly curtailed. Now the wide apron of vacant, well-watered lands that bordered the vast, empty Edwards Plateau—west of the Hill Country counties that had organized before the Civil War—lay waiting, inviting, open for settlement.

The new arrivals started trickling in during 1873 and 1874. Most were of southern origin and outlook: some battle-scarred Confederate veterans who had returned to their Texas homes and families, now grown accustomed to violence. Others came destitute from the war-ravaged Deep South, dispossessed by Reconstruction, looking to make a new start. Some were of rougher stripe—criminals, troublemakers, and ne'er-do-wells who had been run out of eastern Texas counties that were becoming civilized.[1]

They congregated along the North and South Llano Rivers, following those sparkling, clear-water streams and tributaries to their respective headwater springs, building cabins for their families and sheds for their livestock. Gradually, a community began to nucleate at the forks of the Llanos.

Settlement of the Texas Hill Country was already well underway before the Civil War. U.S. Army posts, such as Fort Martin Scott in Gillespie County (established 1848), Fort Croghan in Burnet County (1849), Fort Mason in Mason County (1851), Fort McKavett in Menard County (1852), and Camp Verde in Kerr County (1855), served as marginally effective centers of protection for early settlers as well as the basis for an embryonic road network, which facilitated transportation, communication, and development of nascent communities.[2]

The nearest supply centers were San Antonio and Austin. Goods were shipped in wagons or carts drawn by mules or oxen, or carried by pack animals.

Whenever army posts were established in the Hill Country, county governments were organized soon thereafter—Gillespie (1848), Burnet (1852), Llano, Kerr, and Bandera (1856), Mason and Blanco (1858)—usually around towns that would become county seats.[3] Imperfect order was established. Agriculture and commerce took root. The rule of law began to take effect.

When the Civil War began, federal troops abandoned the frontier forts. Confederate Texas, short of recruits, did not regarrison the vacated posts during the war; makeshift squads of local militia occupied them only periodically. The western frontier in Texas retreated eastward under increased Indian forays. With Reconstruction, federal troops returned to the frontier forts; the Texas frontier recovered lost ground and began to resume its westward march.[4]

The western fringe of the Hill Country, merging with the eastern margins of the Edwards Plateau, was sparsely settled, populated by nomadic cattle drovers and widely scattered, courageous—or desperate—homesteaders. Before 1874 Indian raids were frequent, by Comanches and Kiowas from the north, and Kickapoos, Lipan Apaches, and Seminoles from Coahuila, Mexico. To try to control such raiders, an important new military post was established in 1867, Fort Concho, at the forks of the Concho River, just north of the northern edge of the Edwards Plateau. Many of the enlisted men were ex-slaves—"buffalo soldiers"—commanded by white officers.[5] The presence of black troops did not sit well with many settlers.

Menardville, located on the road connecting Forts Mason, McKavett, and Concho, sprang up in 1867. The next year the regular mail service connecting San Antonio and El Paso was routed through on the military road, and three years later the village became the county seat of Menard County, which was protected by Fort McKavett twenty miles to the west. Civil order was established—after a fashion—and the process of settlement and civilization began around Menardville.[6]

Kimble County lay south of Menard County, southwest of Mason County, west of Gillespie County, and northwest of Kerr County. It had been created from Bexar County in 1858 but remained unorganized until 1876, roughly twenty years after the adjoining counties had come into being. The first settlers had located in the eastern end of the county during the early 1860s. Following upon a short-lived settlement established by James Bradbury and his large extended family in the late 1860s, a village began to grow at the forks of the North and South Llano Rivers, which eventually became the county seat, Junction City.[7]

Kimble County was different, for reasons that were primarily geological (see map 1). The western half of the county lay on the Edwards Plateau, an immense limestone tableland, a waterless wilderness stretching 150 miles farther west, to the Rio Grande and Pecos River and beyond. The numerous clear-water tributaries of the Llanos were fed by permanent springs issuing from deep rocky canyons carved into the periphery of the plateau, veritable oases in a semiarid landscape, but there was no reliable water on top of the plateau.[8]

The high, dry divides of the plateau, like east-reaching bony fingers, isolated the forks of the Llano from settlements that lay to the north, east, and south. But swift-moving Indian marauders, raiding southward from the high plains and eastward from Mexico, regularly used the flat prairies atop the plateau as wilderness pathways for lightning raids that struck without warning the vulnerable settlements marginal to the Edwards Plateau. Until about 1874, the continued threat of such raids deterred all but the boldest settlers from locating in the well-watered, verdant valleys of the Llano and its tributaries.[9]

Clandestine markets developed in Mexican border towns, where Kickapoo, Lipan, and Seminole raiders could dispose of cattle, horses, booty, and even captives stolen in Texas. Mexican officials fostered, profited from, and protected such markets, which encouraged further cross-border raiding by resident Indians who had received official sanction from the Mexican government.[10]

Because of this geology, geography, and recent history, Junction City was isolated from neighboring communities. It lay on no through road, as did towns in adjoining counties; on the contrary, it lay at the end of the road. The nearest troops were thirty miles to the northwest at Fort McKavett. To the south, the nearest soldiers were stationed at Fort Clark, near present Brackettville, one hundred miles across the plateau.

The main route for trail herds bound north for Kansas railheads was the Western Beef Trail, located about one day's horseback ride east from Junction City. Avoiding rough terrain, it skirted the plateau's eastern margins. The Western Beef Trail provided tempting opportunities to sell stolen cattle and horses to trail herds passing through, as well as to pick up strays and stragglers that could be disposed of to later herds in transit.[11]

So the forks of the Llano, vulnerable to Indian attacks and isolated from adjacent Hill Country communities, was late to be settled. Among those who were originally attracted to Kimble County, many were freebooters and outlaws, attracted to the area by the coincidence of seven attributes: (1) suppression of Indian raiding by the U.S. Army, (2) sparseness of permanent inhabitants, (3) existence of furtive markets where stolen livestock could be disposed of, (4) ample free open range on which they could run their own cattle and horses as well as livestock they had stolen in neighboring counties, (5) absence of organized county government—and thus law, (6) abundant hiding places provided by the dark, well-watered coves and hollows in the tributary canyons of the plateau, and (7) the adjacent wilderness of the vacant plateau, into which they could readily vanish when lawmen did venture into their domain. Sensing territory in which they could safely operate, the word spread among those inclined to favor lawless surroundings. Beginning in 1873 and 1874, a rough crowd began to congregate around the forks of the Llano and to prey on adjacent communities.[12]

In the absence of law, the prevailing structure of the frontier community that grew at the forks of the Llano was fundamentally and stubbornly tribal, ruled by loyalty to extended family and friends. Strangers, especially state officials, were enemies. Like a malignant cancer, a substantial criminal confederation took root and spread through the nascent community, dominated by men of the Dublin and Potter families. Dark rumors spread that they sometimes raided disguised as Indians, or that they had Indian connections. The lawless element seized control of the first Kimble County government, formed in 1876. Outnumbered law-abiding citizens were intimidated. Brazen livestock raids on neighboring counties increased. Complaints flowed in to state officials in Austin.[13]

Starting in the spring of 1877, civil order began slowly to be established, primarily by Texas Rangers of the Frontier Battalion, assisted by regional law officers. Local citizens, vulnerable to threats by the outlaws, were slow to lend their support. Jurors and witnesses were routinely threatened and coerced, and convictions by Kimble County juries were rare. Much hard and dangerous work by elected law officers and Texas Rangers was negated. Backed up by the presence of Texas Rangers, however, citizens gradually began to organize and assert themselves against the criminal element.

It took about five more years for order to be established and the rule of law to finally take root. But settlers in neighboring counties, many of them long-suffering victims of the Kimble County thieves, finally wreaked their vengeance on the surviving criminal element, in a brutal exercise of flawed frontier justice. Order and law were finally imposed—imperfectly—on the community at the forks of the Llano, and on the settlements and societies that adjoined it.

The unvarnished history of this extended campaign provides stark reminders that tribalism is the mortal enemy of representative commercial societies operating under the rule of law. Further, the establishment and sustenance of orderly, lawful self-government requires determination, sacrifice, and action by ordinary citizens as well as the police power of the state. However, once aroused by ongoing predatory criminal activities, it is all too easy for communities to embrace vigilante justice, which may be facilitated by bias, manipulation, collusion, and the desire for revenge.

# 2 :: The Country

The geology of west-central Texas, especially the presence and geological attributes of the Edwards Plateau, profoundly influenced the settlement history of the region. It controlled where reliable water was, and wasn't, which governed where settlers located and what remained uninhabited wilderness. It controlled the natural distribution of arable soil, necessary for subsistence corn patches and kitchen gardens. It influenced the occurrence of timber, necessary for construction of frontier buildings and fences. It influenced the placement of early roads that connected frontier military establishments and towns, or left them unconnected and isolated. To understand post–Civil War settlement patterns in west-central Texas, the historian must grasp that the vast Edwards Plateau, because there was reliable water around its serrated periphery but not on its flat top, because its ragged margins were rough and rocky, and because it reached westward clear into northern Mexico, was a formidable physical and environmental barrier that retarded frontier settlement by about twenty years.

## The Edwards Plateau

Covering more than thirty thousand square miles, the Edwards Plateau dominates the landscape of west-central Texas (see map 2). Along its northern and eastern margins, the plateau stands one hundred to three hundred feet above the adjacent rolling prairies; on its southern margins, it stands five hundred to fifteen hundred feet higher than the adjacent coastal plain of the Rio Grande embayment. It extends westward across the Pecos River, where it is sometimes called the Stockton Plateau, and to the southwest, across the Rio Grande, into northernmost Coahuila, Mexico, where it is known as the Serranía Del Burro. To the northwest it merges imperceptibly with the high plains (or Llano Estacado) of West Texas and the Texas Panhandle.[1]

The plateau is the topographic and geomorphic expression of a thick, widespread, flat-lying geological formation of early Cretaceous age known as the Edwards Limestone.[2] This formation ranges from about four hundred feet thick on the north to about eight hundred feet thick along the southern edge of the plateau. Its limestone strata are generally harder and more resistant to weathering and erosion than the softer sandy and clayey formations that lie just beneath, assigned to the Trinity Formation, which is why the Edwards Plateau is a high-standing,

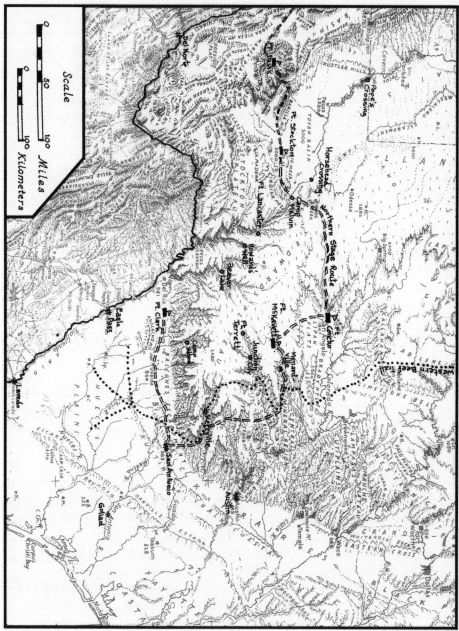

Map 2. Physiography of the area of "The Reckoning." Modified from Erwin J. Raisz landform maps (1957, 1964) with permission.

rough-edged geomorphic feature. Moreover, Edwards Limestone strata are susceptible to dissolution by water, hence they are, like many limestone formations, porous and permeable, and honeycombed with caves.

Rainwater that falls on the plateau, rather than running off, tends to sink into the fractured, cavernous limestone, where it accumulates in the lower part of the Edwards Limestone simply because the sands and clays of the underlying Trinity Formation are much less permeable and transmissive. So, blocked from further downward movement, the down-trickling rainwater accumulates in the honeycombed lower Edwards limestones, thus forming a widespread unconfined aquifer at the base of the formation.[3] It is this aquifer that is the source of copious permanent springs that constitute the headwater springflow of all the region's rivers, and also the source from which most of the region's windmills draw water.[4]

Headward-cutting streams dissect the periphery of the Edwards Plateau from the east and south. Clockwise from the north, they are the Concho, San Saba, Llano, and Pedernales (all tributaries of the Colorado River), Blanco, Guadalupe, Medina, Sabinal, Frio, East and West Nueces, and Devils Rivers. This headward dissection creates deep canyons and rugged topography around the margins of the plateau, with intervening high interfluvial divides. Strong permanent springs issue from the head of each tributary. These headwater springs are all located where the headward-cutting tributary canyons intersect the permanent groundwater table just above the base of the Edwards.[5]

This distinctive dissected landscape occupies an arcuate swath across central Texas, east and south of the main mass of the Edwards Plateau, and west and north of the Balcones Escarpment, known as the Texas Hill Country (see map 3). It began to be settled in the 1850s, and permanent towns soon began to be established to serve developing agriculture and commerce.

To the west, the vast, flat-topped mass of the Edwards Plateau was a wilderness savanna, uninhabited precisely because there was no permanent water, no reliable streams—and no law. That changed in the 1880s with the advent of cable-tool drilling and windmill-powered deep wells that could reliably lift life-giving pure water to the surface, for use by settlers and their livestock. Another new technology, barbed wire, enabled early ranchers to control their livestock.[6]

The historical pattern of Hill Country settlement, from 1850 on, was simply for frontiersmen and their families to locate adjacent to the region's rivers or creeks, farming the soils that had developed on the soft Trinity-age sands and clays as well as the alluvium in the stream valleys, and running their cattle on the adjacent unfenced range. Successively, newcoming settlers moved steadily upstream, west and north, until they arrived finally at each respective stream's headwater spring, in narrow coves and canyons bounded by confining bluffs of

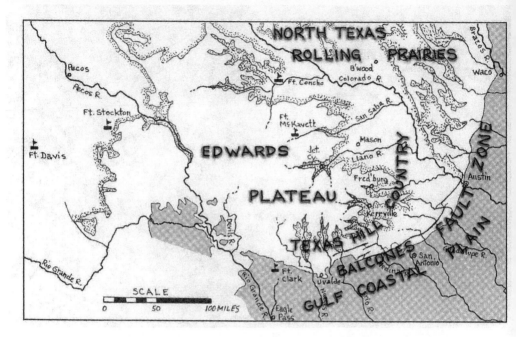

Map 3. Geologic provinces of Central Texas. Modified after Rose, "Regional Perspectives" (2004, fig. 5), with permission.

Edwards Limestone. Then and there, the progress of their homesteading necessarily stopped, until deep-well drilling, windmills, and barbed wire opened up the Edwards Plateau to permanent settlement in the 1880s.

## Springs

There is something primordial about a living limestone spring, a haunting sense of magic that resonates in the human spirit, in the same way that a night-time campfire arouses archetypal feelings. The effect is partly visual, to be sure: the sparkling, crystal rush emerging from a mysterious, cavernous, cliffy gloom, then tumbling downslope, channeled amid vividly verdant ferns and mosses and watercress, dancing in and out of the mottled shade of overhanging trees, contrasting starkly with the adjacent sere landscape. Where the newly emergent stream pauses in linked limpid pools, the water is stunningly clear, yet it conveys a distinctive grayish-green hue, transmitted and filtered from the clean-washed pebbles on the bottom. Special small creatures congregate there—dragonflies and scooters and midges, hummingbirds and dippers and swallows.

Springs also have magical sounds that touch us: the primeval chuckle of a steadily flowing brook, and here and there, the variable faint punctuations of dripping ancillary springs. Special trees, such as sycamores and cottonwoods and pecans, grow around springs in the Texas Hill Country, and breezes moving through their leaves impart familiar whispers and flutters characteristic of the setting.

But the most memorable and evocative attribute of living springs is their natural fragrance, a cool freshness of air that is palpable, and the unforgettable clean, hovering, nose-wrinkling astringency of wild horsemint.

The Spanish word for spring is *nacimiento*; it also means birth. The duality of meanings is apt.

### Hostile Indians and Military Posts

Two different groups of Native Americans frequented the Edwards Plateau–Hill Country region after the Civil War. From the north, Plains Indians raided regularly. They included Comanches—Penatakas, the southern group, whose ancestral hunting ranges lay just north of the plateau and Hill Country, and the even fiercer northern Comanche, especially the Kwahadis and their Kiowa allies—who raided southward and southeastward from the high plains, and after 1867, periodically from government-sanctioned safe-havens in southern Oklahoma.[7]

Raiding eastward and northeastward into Texas from northern Coahuila were disparate groups of tribal remnants including Kickapoos, Lipan Apaches, Seminoles, and Mescalero Apaches, all of whom bore implacable hatred for Texas and Texans. These Indians had the official sanction of Mexico. Some had intermarried with Mexican citizens as well as with some blacks, who had gone to Mexico as fugitive slaves.[8] Such renegades, in parties of up to forty or fifty men, raided aggressively and frequently in the upper Rio Grande plain, Texas Hill Country, and Edwards Plateau regions up until the early 1880s, when continuing pressure from both U.S. and Mexican troops finally brought an end to their attacks.[9]

In 1852 the U.S. Army had established a north-south line of military posts across frontier Texas that was intended to protect the westward-advancing settlements from Indian raiders.[10] Those pertinent to the Edwards Plateau area were Fort Chadbourne, in northwest Coke County; Fort McKavett, at the headwaters of the San Saba River in far western Menard County; and Fort Clark, just south of the Edwards Plateau at Las Moras Spring in Kinney County. Fort Terrett, near the headwater spring of the North Llano River, just west of the Kimble County line, was permanently abandoned in 1854, only a year and a half after it had been established. In retrospect, it seems likely that the extended turbulent history of Kimble County and surrounding areas during the late 1870s would not have occurred if Fort Terrett had continued to operate as a permanent military post.

Three other military posts were established later in the 1850s to protect the San Antonio–El Paso mail route: Fort Davis (1854), in the volcanic highlands of the Davis Mountains; Fort Lancaster (1855), a small outpost at the western edge of the plateau on the Pecos River; and Fort Stockton (1858), about eighty miles west of the western margin of the plateau, at Comanche Springs in Trans-Pecos Texas.

All these posts were abandoned by federal troops at the beginning of the Civil War and were only lightly and periodically garrisoned by state and local militias during the war years 1861–65. They were, however, reoccupied by federal troops by 1867, and an important new post, Fort Concho, at present-day San Angelo on the Concho River, was established as well.[11] Other posts were occupied only periodically, such as Fort Duncan, near present Eagle Pass; Camp Hudson, on the Devils River in northwestern Val Verde County, protecting the southern route of the San Antonio–El Paso stage road; and Camp Melvin, on the northern stage route, guarding the Pontoon Crossing of the Pecos River, also known as Pecos Station.[12]

Indian raiding parties were stealthy, mobile, and unpredictable. Despite regular and far-reaching patrols by the U.S. Army and (after 1874) the Texas Rangers, the number of Indian raids into the Texas Hill Country only gradually subsided. But decimated by disease; the progressive destruction of their dietary mainstay, the southern bison herd; and unrelenting pressure from frontiersmen, Texas Rangers, and the U.S. Army, the Comanches and Kiowas gradually gave up their raiding into the Edwards Plateau–Hill Country region during the time period 1872 to 1875. Ranald Mackenzie's destruction of Comanche and Kiowa winter camps, supplies, and horse herds at Palo Duro Canyon in the fall of 1874, followed by the winter campaign known as the Red River War, was the effective coup de grâce to further serious raiding by Plains Indians southward into the Edwards Plateau–Hill Country region.[13] But Indian marauders from Mexico continued to raid frequently into Texas for another eight years.

Both groups of raiders—Plains Indians from the north, and Indians from the west, in Mexico—utilized for their raiding the vacant expanse of the Edwards Plateau, especially its high, serrated, interfluvial divides that projected eastward into the Hill Country. These flat, easily traveled but waterless divides served as wilderness pathways that gave ready access into the settlements that sprang up in the river valleys. From 1850 to the early 1880s, rapidly moving raiders could travel undetected into areas of developing Hill Country ranches and farms, descend suddenly and violently upon unsuspecting settlers, and make off with horses, cattle, and other plunder, including captives for ransom. Oftentimes such raids turned bloodthirsty, leaving brutally murdered victims in their wake. And the same wilderness pathways used for ingress into the settlements also provided ready routes for escape, back whence the raiders had come.

### Edwards Plateau as a Frontier Barrier

The simple presence of the vast, rugged, waterless Edwards Plateau, coupled with the frequent Indian raids on settlements around its margins, constituted a barrier to the westward spread of civilized settlers in west-central Texas, delaying the establishment of permanent towns and organized counties by as many as twenty to thirty years (see map 4). Civil disorder and criminal organizations further retarded settlement.

The main "highway" network during the 1855–80 period also demonstrates the isolation of the Edwards Plateau region (see map 5). The main westward route from San Antonio to El Paso and California traversed the upper Rio Grande coastal plain, skirting the plateau on the south. At San Felipe Springs (near present Del Rio), it veered northwest for a hundred dangerous miles across the western edge of the plateau to Fort Lancaster on the Pecos River, and then turned west again toward Fort Stockton and El Paso. Attacks, mostly by Indians raiding from Mexico, became so frequent and deadly that the San Felipe–Fort Lancaster segment was abandoned as an official mail route after 1868.[14]

The only other main westward road was the military supply route connecting San Antonio with U.S. cavalry establishments to the northwest. That road passed through Boerne, Comfort, Fredericksburg, Mason, Menardville, and onward to Fort McKavett and Fort Concho. It then veered west, following the middle fork of the Concho River, then southwest to Camp Melvin, guarding the Pontoon Crossing of the Pecos River, then on to Fort Stockton, where it rejoined the main westward route to El Paso and on to California. This more northerly route was used from 1868 on, thus avoiding the deadly San Felipe–Fort Lancaster segment.[15]

Otherwise, there were no east-west or north-south through roads across the Edwards Plateau. There were, of course, preferred routes for more local travel: to get from Austin to Fredericksburg, travelers went west, through what later became Johnson City, staying mostly in the valleys of east-draining rivers and creeks. The road connecting San Antonio and Kerrville utilized the military road northwest to its crossing of the Guadalupe River, and then followed the Guadalupe valley westward to Kerrville. The main road connecting Junction City to the outside world followed the Llano River valley fifty miles northeastward to Mason.

### The Western Beef Trail

By 1876 the main route for northbound cattle herds was the Western Beef Trail, which also mostly avoided the plateau.[16] It passed west of San Antonio, skirting the east-reaching high divides of the plateau through Bandera and Kendall Counties, and then veered northwestward across Kerr County, up the valley of the Guadalupe River. It then crossed a dry twenty-mile divide, leaving Johnson Creek near the headwaters and arriving at the Llano River in western Mason County.

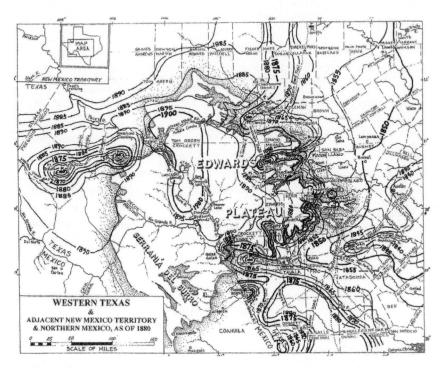

Map 4. Edwards Plateau, a barrier to westward settlement. The "civilization contours" are based on establishment of permanent settlements or organized county governments. Modified after Rose, "Regional Perspectives" (2004, fig. 9), with permission.

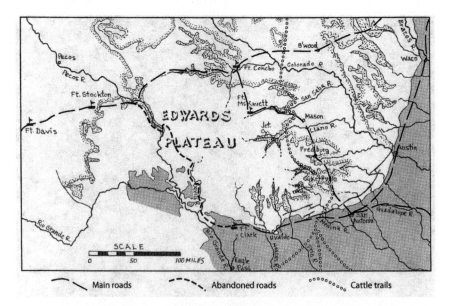

Map 5. Area frontier roads and trails, which mostly skirted the Edwards Plateau. Modified after Rose, "Regional Perspectives" (2004, fig. 8), with permission.

From there, the Western Beef Trail bore generally northward along the eastern margin of the Edwards Plateau, fording the San Saba River at Pegleg Crossing, and then swinging northeast to traverse the northernmost Edwards interfluve through Cow Gap, in western McCulloch County, whereupon it continued northward across the rolling prairies of the Colorado and Brazos drainages, leaving the Edwards Plateau behind.

The advent of the range-cattle business contributed to the lawlessness of the 1870s. Free-ranging livestock were gathered on the open unfenced range for eventual shipment to Kansas railheads. A vague, lenient, and often unenforceable state range law actually promoted conflict by making theft easy within the course of routine gathering, branding, and droving.[17] Cattle have strong herd instincts, and local animals frequently fell in with passing trail herds. Also, many settlers and cowboys made it their business to provide incremental supplies of cattle to the entrepreneurs who amassed the trail herds and drove them north to market—and many of the early trail bosses were not too particular as to where such livestock came from. Besides, by the time their legal owners discovered their losses, the trail herds that had absorbed the cattle were far away.

### Requirements for Settlers

Aspiring frontier farmers and ranchers had three main requirements in the Texas Hill Country. They required at least some arable soil. They required a reliable source of fresh water. And they required some modicum of security against Indian raiders and other renegades. Although security was enhanced by frontier military posts, Texas Rangers, and local militias, increasing numbers of settlers and the growth of early towns also provided some safety in numbers.[18]

The 98th meridian passes through Austin and about twenty miles west of Fort Worth. It coincides closely with the contour marking thirty inches of average annual rainfall, the recognized effective difference between moisture surplus and deficiency.[19] Westward from the 98th meridian, annual rainfall diminishes regularly, by approximately four inches every one hundred miles. At the 100th meridian, about thirty miles east of San Angelo, average annual rainfall is about twenty-two inches. At Fort Stockton, on the 103rd meridian, annual rainfall averages about thirteen inches. Thus the region known as the Texas Hill Country may be described as semiarid: natives recognize that they live at the edge of a desert, and drought is always a threat. The western edge of the Edwards Plateau impinges on the northern extension of the Chihuahuan Desert, where average annual rainfall is less than ten inches.[20]

This climate mandated that active, full-time farming was a chancy business in the region of the Hill Country and eastern Edwards Plateau. It naturally encouraged cattle raising on the open rangeland, endowed by centuries of migratory buffalo herds with their cyclical grazing patterns as well as periodic wildfires, so as to present to arriving settlers impressive vistas of climax grassland. Little did they realize how thin were the underlying soils and how fragile those grasslands really were.[21]

For the most part, arable land in the Hill Country was confined to valleys containing perennial streams where riparian soils could be plowed, planted, and in a few cases, irrigated. Timber, useful for building cabins and fences, was also concentrated in such valleys. New settlers could locate upon an alluvial terrace, plant corn patches and kitchen gardens, draw water from nearby springs or streams, build stake cabins and corrals from local timber, and graze their cattle in the adjacent hills. In time they could sink a shallow well into underlying alluvial gravels, and set up stake-and-rider fences or stone walls close by the homestead. Otherwise there were no fences until the 1880s. Divide areas between streams were bereft of surface water, so cattle could graze there only within walking distance of live water. The unclaimed land, diverse tall range grasses, and mild climate appeared to make the country ideally suited for the raising of beef cattle.[22]

As rivers flowed radially out of the plateau, their valleys widened. Some of the most attractive open-range areas in the region were the open, gentle valleys of the Llano and San Saba Rivers, in eastern Kimble and Menard Counties. Constrained by bounding high bluffs of Edwards Limestone, fine mature grasslands had developed on the deep, sandy and clayey soils derived from the Trinity Formation, well watered by a network of spring-fed streams flowing out of narrow canyons and coves cut into the margins of the Edwards Plateau. These open valleys were the first lands taken up by the earliest settlers, just before and just after the Civil War.[23]

Because of their proximity to the plateau, these rangelands, and the settlements that were beginning to nucleate, organize, and grow there, were also attractive targets for frequent raids by marauding Indians, moving eastward undetected across the high, vacant tableland from their villages in northern Coahuila and Chihuahua, in search of cattle, horses, plunder, captives—and revenge against the hated Texans.

# 3 :: Indian Raiders from Mexico

L ike dried leaves accumulating in an eddied bywater, disparate and broken remnants of different Native American tribes began to settle in northern Coahuila after the Texas Revolution, seeking refuge from the recurring storms of the American westward movement. All of them bore a grudge against Texas and Texans.

### The Kickapoos

The first to arrive were a small band of Kickapoos that had been kicked out of the Republic of Texas in 1839. They settled around the town of Morelos, about forty miles southwest of Eagle Pass.[1] Mexico was happy to have them, employing them to defend against Comanche, Kiowa, and Mescalero raiders preying on the northern settlements of Coahuila. They were skillful and effective warriors.

More Kickapoos came in 1849, along with the Seminole chief Coacoochee and a contingent of his tribesmen. Coacoochee, also known as Wild Cat, had fought U.S. troops during the Seminole Wars. Rather than move to Indian Territory under the jurisdiction of the U.S. government, he elected to go to northern Mexico. About 250 Kickapoos followed him, with some Seminoles and fugitive black slaves as well. The next year Coacoochee visited Indian Territory, soliciting additional recruits; another 250 Kickapoo Indians also agreed to join his group in Mexico.[2] But about half of the Kickapoos returned to Indian Territory in 1851.

Those who stayed continued to serve the Mexican army as guides and supplemental troops, protecting Mexican citizens and property from marauding Apaches coming down into Coahuila from the northwest. But the Kickapoos also began to raid eastward, into frontier settlements in southern Texas and the Hill Country.[3]

In Mexico, they lived in villages such as Zaragoza, El Remolino, and Santa Rosa, all located about forty to seventy miles southwest of the Rio Grande, opposite Eagle Pass (see map 1). In time, the Mexican government formally recognized them as Mexican citizens and granted them lands in the area. Eventually, some of the Kickapoos moved as far west as Muzquiz, to a settlement called Nacimiento.[4]

### The Lipan and Mescalero Apaches

Pushed southward by the Comanches and Kiowas after 1750, the Lipan Apaches frequented the southern reaches of the Edwards Plateau and upper coastal plain, impinging on the Rio Grande. As the Lipans became fewer and weaker during the early nineteenth century, they affiliated with other Apache bands in New Mexico and Arizona, especially the Mescalero Apaches. Beginning in 1848, the Lipans in Texas came under increasing pressure from Texas settlers, state forces, and the U.S. military.[5] By 1858, the last Lipans had been driven out of Texas.[6] Lipans and Mescaleros also took up residence in northern Mexico, where some became hispanicized; many cooperated with the Kickapoos on raids into Texas. Some Lipans lived near El Remolino and Zaragoza, close by Mescalero villages. Other Lipan bands that affiliated with Mescalero Apaches lived in remote scattered villages in the vicinity of San Carlos, about fifty miles southeast of present Presidio, Texas, and about eighteen miles south of the Rio Grande, in extreme northeastern Chihuahua, Mexico.[7]

### The Kickapoos Return to Mexico

By 1861, relatively few Kickapoos remained in Mexico, many having returned to the United States, lured to Indian Territory by the promise of substantial reservation lands and government protection. Those who remained lived primarily at Morelos and Allende, under the leadership of a "Captain Tobaco," who visited the United States that year to encourage U.S. Kickapoos to come back to Mexico. His solicitations bore fruit.[8]

In December 1862 Chief Machemanet led a band of six hundred Kickapoos on their emigration from Kansas to Mexico. To avoid confrontations with Texas settlers and militias on their southward journey, the Kickapoos swung west of the existing frontier. Nevertheless, a Confederate patrol encountered them in western Tom Green County, about fifteen miles southwest of present San Angelo. Intent on taking the Kickapoos' substantial herd of horses, the Confederates shot three peace emissaries sent out to treat with them and then attacked the migrating village. The Indians held their ground, however, retook their horses, and "sent the patrol reeling, with 16 cavalrymen shot out of their saddles."[9] Afterward the Kickapoos continued their southward march and rejoined their relatives in Coahuila, where they were welcomed and protected by the Mexican government. Encouraged by Mexican markets for stolen livestock and booty, they resumed their profitable raiding into Texas.

Hearing of this new-found prosperity, other Kickapoo bands in Kansas and Indian Territory decided to move to Mexico. Seven hundred Kickapoos under Chiefs Pecan, Papequah, and Nokoaht began to emigrate in September 1864. Once again, their migration routes were kept well west of Texas frontier settlements. But on January 8, 1865, a band of 120 Kickapoos under Chief Nokoaht, which had camped near the headwaters of Dove Creek along the northern breaks of the Edwards Plateau near present Mertzon, were gratuitously attacked by Confederate scouts and militiamen.[10] The Kickapoos were well armed and organized, and they directed a withering fire on the charging Texans. The fight lasted all day. By nightfall, the Texans had lost twenty-six men killed, sixty wounded, and sixty-six horses killed. The survivors were lucky to escape during the night. The Kickapoos lost fifteen warriors killed; they resumed their southward journey to Mexico without further interference.[11]

Once the Kickapoos arrived in Coahuila and settled in their new and protected Mexican home, they resolved to take revenge on Texas and Texans for the two unprovoked attacks. Over the next two decades they extracted a heavy retribution from Texas settlers across the Rio Grande. Their raids covered an arcuate swath, from Laredo on the southeast, to San Antonio on the east, into the western Hill Country and Edwards Plateau on the northeast and north, and even into the Trans-Pecos region to the northwest, nearly to Fort Stockton.[12] Although such raids were primarily focused on horses, cattle, and booty, they often turned bloody as well, with settlers murdered, scalped, and otherwise mutilated, women raped and killed, and children abducted. Such acts were in keeping with their tribal traditions of raiding, and they further aggravated the already seething and indiscriminate hatred of the Texans for all Native Americans.

**Mexican Markets**

The Kickapoos also had a long trading history. The goods they stole were the merchandise they exchanged. In the 1850s, Kickapoos raiding on the high plains in present western Kansas and Colorado brought "great stores of plunder and huge herds of livestock" to Fort Scott, Kansas, where they were offered for sale.[13] Once arrived in Mexico, the Kickapoos soon found a Mexican citizen, one Jesus Galán, to represent them as their official business agent. By 1877 their raiding prowess in Texas had become so daring and capable that they were taking commercial orders from interested parties in Mexico for particular types and numbers of animals, such as "a pair of large black mules." The standard rate for return of a white captive at Nacimiento by Kickapoo war parties was $250. Negotiations proceeded from local political *jefes* through the middleman Jesus Galán to the Kickapoo captors.[14]

Mexican merchants, supported by their politicians, continued to provide ready markets for stolen livestock and goods.[15] Such markets operated openly at several locations in northern Mexico: Garza Galán (present Ciudad Acuña), Zaragoza, Santa Rosa, El Remolino, Muzquiz, and about two hundred miles farther northwest, at San Carlos and Del Norte (present Ojinaga), Chihuahua (see maps 1 and 2).[16] Mexico supplied de facto protection and immunity for the Kickapoos and their other Indian allies, who could mount swift raids into Texas and then retreat back across the Rio Grande into their Mexican safe haven before effective pursuit could be organized by the U.S. Cavalry, Texas Rangers, or local militiamen.

By 1865 the Indians living in Mexico had been exposed to European ways and weapons for several decades. They had moved back and forth across the border several times. They had become skillful in the use of firearms. They knew the habits of frontier American settlers. Some had become hispanicized in Mexico. It is no wonder that many Anglo survivors of their Texas raids could not be sure whether their attackers had been Indians, Mexicans, or white men disguised as Indians.

Raids by Indians from Mexico into Texas were frequent and costly: Kickapoo raids between 1865 and 1872 were estimated by a U.S. government commission to have resulted in the loss of five hundred thousand cattle and fourteen thousand horses, driven to Mexican markets. No official count was provided of the number of settlers killed, women and children taken captive, or ranches burned, but a petition to the U.S. Army from a Uvalde County grand jury in 1868 claimed that marauding Kickapoos had killed at least sixty-two persons, wounded many others, and driven off livestock worth thousands of dollars over a three-year period. And by 1870, the raiders had virtually wiped out the formerly flourishing horse-raising—or horse-gathering—business in southwest Texas.[17]

**Official Responses**

Because the occupying U.S. Army tended to discount the seriousness of these attacks, Governor E. J. Davis was authorized by the Texas Legislature, effective June 13, 1870, to reestablish a state frontier force to protect the westernmost settlements of Texas. In December 1870, Captain H. J. Richarz was dispatched with his Company E to station themselves at old Fort Inge, near Uvalde, on the upper gulf coastal plain, south of the Edwards Plateau.[18] During a series of fierce encounters with Mexican Indian raiders, three of Richarz's militiamen were killed.

State funds were limited, however, and this frontier force was gradually disbanded over the next eighteen months. In substitution, the state legislature authorized the creation of local militias, called "minute companies," on November 25, 1872. These continued at a low level of activity and effectiveness through 1873.[19]

Texas citizens exerted increasing pressure on the U.S. Army to take action during the years 1869 to 1873. On August 2, 1872, General McCook reported "that the Mexican system of cattle stealing on the frontier threatened disaster to the stock-raising interests of Texas and was causing a local war which might eventually result in an international conflict."[20]

A U.S. Congressional commission, appointed in May 1872, recognized that Mexican authorities were complicit in these raids:

The Mexican local authorities, as a rule, civil and military, have been cognizant of these outrages, and have [with one or two honorable exceptions] protected the offenders, defeated with technical objections attempts at recovery of the stolen property, assisted in maintaining bands of thieves, or directly and openly have dealt in the plunder or appropriated it to their personal uses.[21]

As a consequence of their investigation, the commission recommended an increase of U.S. cavalry forces along the southwestern frontier.[22] In January 1873 President Ulysses S. Grant announced that military forces along the Mexican border would be redistributed and that Mexico would be held accountable for the depredations. The 4th Cavalry Regiment, judged to be a more efficient scouting unit under the command of Colonel Ranald S. Mackenzie, would replace the 9th Cavalry at Fort Clark. By early May 1873, most companies of the 4th Cavalry Regiment were in place, fully equipped, trained, and ready.[23]

### Mackenzie's 1873 Raid

On the night of May 17, 1873, Mackenzie led a column of 360 cavalrymen, 17 officers, 24 scouts (mostly Mexican black Seminole Indians under the command of Lieutenant John L. Bullis), and 14 civilians across the Rio Grande at El Moral, located at the mouth of the San Rodrigo River, about eighteen miles northwest of Eagle Pass (see map 1).[24] They were bound southwest, for three Indian villages about two miles west of El Remolino, and about thirty miles inland from their fording place on the Rio Grande.[25]

At about eight o'clock on the morning of May 18, Mackenzie's troopers fell on the largest of the three villages, a Kickapoo settlement, without warning. Most of the warriors had ridden off west the morning before, so the village was primarily occupied by women, children, and old men. Then the troopers went on to the other two villages, one a Lipan Apache settlement, the other a Mescalero community. The destruction was total—all three villages were burned to the ground, crops and food supplies destroyed, at least nineteen Indians killed, sixty-five stolen horses recovered, and forty Kickapoo women and children captured. Costilietos, a principal Lipan chief, was taken captive, lassoed by one of the Seminole scouts. While the cavalrymen were razing the Kickapoo village, most of the Lipans and Mescaleros were able to escape westward, into the Santa Rosa Mountains.[26]

Mackenzie's command suffered only light casualties: one trooper killed, two wounded, four horses killed. By 1:00 p.m. they headed for the United States, riding back through the village of El Remolino, and then turning northeasterly, toward the mouth of Sycamore Creek, where it empties southward into the Rio Grande about fifteen miles downstream from Garza Galán. This route covered about forty miles—they rode all night with their prisoners, detouring around the potentially hostile town of San Carlos before midnight, and crossing back into Texas, exhausted but in good order, early on the morning of May 19.[27] Mess wagons awaited their arrival. During that day, a crowd of angry Mexicans and Indians gathered across the river from the bivouacked troopers. Anticipating such a reaction, however, Mackenzie had already deployed his sharpshooters so as to cover the ford, and put his horses under close guard. No further border incident occurred that day or the next. The column arrived back at Fort Clark at midday on May 21.[28]

In the public and political furor that followed, it became apparent that Mackenzie had no formal orders for conducting the El Remolino raid but was acting on his own initiative. It was just as apparent, though, that General Philip H. Sheridan, Secretary of War William W. Belknap, and President Grant were complicit in the action and fully sympathetic with its results. Texans were delighted.[29]

At last, the gauntlet had been thrown down: Indian raiders could no longer expect sanctuary in their settlements across the Rio Grande. American diplomacy now began to work. Representatives of the U.S. Bureau of Indian Affairs began negotiations to persuade the Kickapoos and their allies to move back to reservations in Indian Territory. The forty prisoners Mackenzie had captured at El Remolino were sent to Indian Territory and held there, as an inducement for the Mexican Kickapoos to accept the proposals of the bureau. A group of 317 Kickapoos and Pottawatomies left Mexico on August 28, stayed well west of Texas frontier settlements on their northward return journey, and arrived at Fort Sill on December 20, 1873, when they were reunited with their families. Negotiations continued, but only 115 additional Indians could be persuaded to go to Indian territory—the rest chose to stay in Mexico.[30]

After dithering for eight months, the Mexican government decided not to make Mackenzie's raid an international issue. Finally, in mid-January of 1874, Mexico sent a mild official protest to Washington, objecting to Mackenzie's entry into Mexico, promising no reciprocal raids into the United States by Mexican troops, and indicating future willingness to cooperate in joint actions against other border offenders.

However, it is noteworthy that almost no cross-border raids into Texas by Indians were conducted between the time of Mackenzie's raid and the delivery of Mexico's official note. Raids during the first seven months of 1874 were also greatly reduced. It is probably no coincidence that Mackenzie's 4th Cavalry continued its active patrolling in the area along the Rio Grande (even making one more brief incursion into Mexico) through August 1874, when they were transferred to northwest Texas to deal with the Comanches.[31]

## Implications for Settlers

There can be no doubt that the adoption by the U.S. military, from late 1873 onward, of more forceful operations against Indians marauding from Mexico or Indian Territory into Texas reduced—but did not eliminate—the number and impact of such raids. The change in military policy was understood by frontier settlers to signal that border regions formerly vulnerable to such attacks were likely to be more secure in the future, which had the effect of opening them up for settlement.

As soon as Indian raiding from Mexico into Texas was being actively countered by the widely publicized actions of the U.S. military along the Mexican border, Anglo-Celtic frontiersmen and their families began to migrate into the western Hill Country, around the margins of the Edwards Plateau. One such family consisted of two brothers named Potter, who together brought their families to Texas from northern California, drawn by the promise of free land and open range, looking to make a new start.[32]

# 4 :: The Potters

**N**ew settlers William and Thomas Potter, together with their large families, arrived at the forks of the Llano in early 1874. They came from Mendocino County, northern California. According to family tradition, the two brothers made the two-thousand-mile, three-to four-month journey by wagon, bringing with them a sizeable herd of good horses.[1] Even though they were southern sympathizers, they were not typical Kimble County settlers—they were not veterans of the Civil War, they were not from the Deep South, and they were not destitute.[2]

Will Potter had married Mary Evaline Gordon in California, and they had raised a large family. In early 1874, Will was about forty-nine years old; Mary Evaline was about eight years younger. He brought his wife, their five sons, and three youngest daughters all to Texas.[3] Two elder Potter daughters, both married, stayed behind in Mendocino County.

Figure 1. William and Mary Evaline Gordon Potter, mid-1870s. Courtesy of Mary Lou Midkiff. (Images digitally enhanced, with permission.)

Figure 2. Looking southwest up the South Llano River valley, Kimble County, Texas, about eleven miles southwest of Junction (City), near the mouth of Bailey Creek, a western tributary. The location of the old James Dublin homestead is just off the lower left corner of the photo. Cajac Creek is the farthest line of trees crossing the floodplain in the distance. Photo by the author, 2008.

The Will Potter family settled about twelve miles southwest of, and upstream from, the forks of the Llano, adjacent to the valley of the South Llano River, a perennial, clear-water stream that runs in an open, bluff-bound valley about one mile wide. Tributary creeks, all spring fed, enter the river from either side. The river road, a wagon track that crossed the river repeatedly, ran down the valley floor toward the young settlement that was forming at the confluence of the two streams.

Will Potter located his family in the narrow, cliff-walled, alluvium-floored valley of Cajac Creek, about a mile west of the main valley of the South Llano River. This site was concealed from passersby on the river road because Cajac Creek hides, curving between two offsetting limestone ridges, and then rises westward through a narrow rocky pass before opening up into a long sheltered cove less than a quarter-mile wide, perfect for confining loose horses and cattle. Deep soil had developed on the alluvial bottom, ideal for a corn patch. Regular access would have been gained only by traveling—either by horseback or wagon—up the flat-rock bed of the creek, covered usually by a few inches of clear water. It was not a location that encouraged casual visitors, and it was easy for the Potters to be

Figure 3. Tom Potter home site on Cajac Creek, a western tributary of the South Llano River, Kimble County, Texas, looking north. The Potter cabin was probably located in the small open space surrounded by trees immediately adjacent to the creek in the left center of the photo. A strong spring is located in the dense grove of trees at the mouth of the south-draining gulch at center. Photo by the author, 2008

quickly away from home, up onto the adjacent vacant Plateau, if they believed approaching visitors might not be friendly.[4]

Thomas Potter, about forty-three years old in early 1874, brought with him six sons, all offspring of their father's serial unions with two Indian women in Mendocino County. The mother of the four oldest boys was dead; the mother of the two youngest boys had remained in California with a third son.[5]

Tom Potter chose an even more secluded place to live, a mile farther back up Cajac Creek from his brother Will, on a narrow, tree-lined alluvial bench on the north bank of the creek. At the east end of the bench, a strong spring tumbled out of a small cave in the rocky wall of a tributary gully; at the west end, Tom and his sons built a one-room cabin. Giant native pecan trees provided a canopy of shade, and massive cottonwood trees grew along the sloping banks of Cajac Creek, their leaves constantly rustling in the summertime breezes. To the west rose the ledgy slopes and vast expanses of the plateau, allowing immediate access and swift flight when warranted. It was a dark, secretive home site, one that also did not welcome company.[6]

## The Potters in California

William and Thomas Potter were authentic California pioneers, men who were involved in the formative events that attended the birth of a great state. They came to California from Missouri in 1845 with their parents, John and Nancy Anderson Potter, and four sisters, traveling by wagon with the Grigsby-Ide party. Will was twenty; Tom was fourteen.[7]

The family settled in northern California, in what is now Butte County, and purchased half a league of land (about 2,200 acres) near the present town of Chico. Here the Potters "built a cabin, planted fig trees and a garden . . . had cattle, and employed local Indian helpers."[8] A third son, James Knox Polk Potter, was born in 1846. His mother, Nancy Anderson Potter, died sometime before September 30, 1850.[9]

John Potter learned early of John Marshall's discovery of placer gold at Sutter's Mill in 1848 and began mining periodically, with a company of other settlers, on the middle fork of the Feather River, at "Potter's Bar," where he reputedly made a fortune. It was reported "that in two years [Potter] collected $40,000 to $50,000 worth of gold. As there were no banks, Potter reportedly cached his fortune near his home. . . . He died in January, 1851; his neighbors provided a crude coffin and buried him on his ranch. . . . The family never found his supposed cache."[10]

Although Potter's ownership of one large tract of purchased land, descended from a Spanish land grant, was disputed and subsequently disallowed by the newly formed California Land Commission, his ownership of a counterpart tract was confirmed by the commission. Upon his death, John Potter left a substantial estate that was in probate for twelve years before finally being settled and divided among his seven children.[11]

Will Potter participated in the abortive Bear Flag Revolt of 1846 that took place just before the onset of the U.S. war with Mexico, 1846–47. Presumably, young Tom Potter looked after his mother, sisters, and baby brother Jimmy during the times when his father and older brother were adventuring elsewhere in California.

Sometime in 1848, Will Potter moved to Sonoma County, near present Healdsburg, where he courted and married Mary Evaline Gordon in 1849. After their father's death, all the Potter offspring moved to Sonoma County, living with or near their elder brother, who by now was "running the only store for miles around, out of an adobe [building] built by [his future brother-in-law and business associate] Lindsey Carson, brother of Kit Carson."[12] Will and Mary Potter soon started a family, beginning with Louisa J. (born 1851) and Thomas H. "Mack" (1852), which eventually numbered five sons and six daughters.

Meanwhile, in Butte County, Tom Potter, not yet twenty years old, began keeping company with a Maidu Indian woman, "Juley," by whom he eventually had six surviving children—four sons and two daughters. It was a life choice that would bring him and his children profound tragedy.

The marriage was eventually recorded on March 24, 1854; by then, Tom Potter had moved his family to Sonoma County, where he was running cattle on the open ranges. After Juley died, about 1863, Tom took up with "Molly Metock," a Pomo Indian woman, by whom he had three more sons. This union was never formalized. Apparently Tom's brothers and sisters, while they did not approve of Tom's domestic arrangements, tolerated them, continued to live nearby, and interacted together with their unconventional brother.[13]

### Potter's Valley

Searching for grazing space, Will and Tom Potter, together with their sister Elizabeth's new husband, Moses Carson Briggs, and neighbor James Lowe Anderson (who would later marry their sister Mary Jane), began exploring the upper reaches of the Russian River, perhaps following up on counsel received from Kit Carson, who had traversed the area when it was inhabited only by Native Americans.[14] In the fall of 1852, they first rode into a lovely small intermontane valley on the north fork of the Russian River, in Mendocino County, where they remained, exploring, for about three weeks, deciding on the best sites for their future ranches and locating their respective claims. "Clover, ready for the scythe, was spread over thousands of acres of valley land . . . [and] wild oats . . . stirrup-high . . . waved in abundance on every hillside, looking like vast fields of cultivated grain."[15] This valley became known as Potter's Valley.

In 1852 Potter's Valley was inhabited by three separate communities of Pomo Indians, each of which contained about five hundred people. The Pomos were placid and sedentary hunter-gatherers, not given to raiding traditions.[16] With the coming of the white settlers, the lives of the Pomo residents, as with most northern California Native Americans, would undergo wrenching and tragic change.[17]

The next spring, Will Potter and Moses Briggs returned to Potter's Valley in a wagon. Potter stayed, claiming a homestead and founding a prosperous ranching establishment in the fertile northern part of the valley, to which he soon brought his family. Reports from Indians and whites alike indicate that Potter got on well with the Pomos and came to be familiar with their customs and language.[18]

Moses Briggs also located a land claim but returned to his existing ranching operation in Sonoma County. He passed back and forth for several years before finally bringing his cattle and settling his family in Potter's Valley in April 1857. Tom Potter came permanently with his cattle in 1856, locating his family on his earlier claim.[19] Eventually, they were joined by two sisters—Ruth Ann and Mary Jane—and the youngest Potter sibling, James K. P. Potter, all living on adjoining three-hundred- to six-hundred-acre farms and running their cattle on the unfenced meadows of the pristine valley.[20] In 1860 Will Potter indicated real estate valued at $1,000 and personal property worth $7,500; his brother Tom showed real estate valued at $1,000 and personal property worth $8,700. Times were good for the Potters.[21]

But not for long—other white settlers soon followed, in droves.[22] Other issues, involved with the northern California Indians, would become even more pressing. The Potters' paradise would be short-lived.

### The Round Valley Indian Persecution

In their rush for land ownership and the free use of unfenced public land, American settlers in northern California, and especially in Mendocino County, unconscionably exploited, persecuted, abused, and exterminated the original Native American inhabitants. This campaign could only be described, in today's terms, as ethnic cleansing, and it was generally condoned by the Anglo-Saxon community.[23]

Beginning in late 1865 and early 1866, and continuing for some years thereafter, all Native Americans in Mendocino County were forced to move to a reservation in Round Valley, another intermontane valley about fifty miles northwest of Potter Valley, populated in 1856 by an estimated ten thousand Yuki Indians. U.S. Superintendent of Indian Affairs for California Thomas J. Henley had set up a reservation there in 1856, which became known as the "Nome Cult Farm." In 1858 Indian Agent Simmon Storm recommended that all of Round Valley be set apart for a reservation, pointing out that the existing claims of the twenty resident American settlers could be purchased for about fifteen thousand dollars.[24]

Even though the U.S. secretary of the interior, following the recommendations of General J. B. McIntosh, had designated Round Valley as one of four California Indian reservations, President Grant did not sign the necessary declaration, and the uncooperative General McIntosh was replaced in July 1870. Resident white settlers refused to abandon their Round Valley homesteads and by early 1873, most of Round Valley had been opened for public preemption.[25]

Meanwhile local militias engaged in a campaign of extermination, killing and capturing resident Native Americans of many tribes, and forcibly delivering them to the Round Valley reservation. A particularly reprehensible example was Walter S. Jarboe's Eel River Rangers, which engaged in repeated raids on northern California Indians: between July 1859 and June 1860, when they were officially disbanded, Jarboe's Rangers killed an estimated three hundred Indians and captured another five hundred.

Under such pressures, indigenous Native Americans moved to the Round Valley reservation, beginning in 1856. By 1871, 793 Indians lived there; another 685 Indians were moved there from the Potter, Redwood, Walker, and Little Lake Valleys in May 1872, "forced out by white laboring classes who did not want their competition on farms and ranches."[26]

But the Nome Cult Farm was no safe haven. Rape of Indian girls and women on the reservation by white men was commonplace and casual, as were the abduction and forced servitude of Indian men and women. In the winter of 1874–75, northern California Congressman J. K. Luttrell visited the Nome Cult Farm and reported a dismal picture of Indian life there: "Indians were living in bark, slab, or grass huts, with little clothing; two-thirds suffered from advanced syphilis, worked for very little return, and all were poorly fed." Congressman Luttrell concluded that the Round Valley reservation system represented little more than slavery.[27]

### Tom Potter in Round Valley

Tom Potter had been living in Potter Valley with his five minor children by his late wife Juley. He took up with Molly Metock, under Indian custom, in 1864. Molly presented him with three sons, William (born 1865), Sam (1866) and Tom Jr. (1868).[28] Potter Valley Indians were ordered to the Round Valley reservation in 1865, and forcibly driven there in late 1865 and early 1866. Cohabitation with a white man did not exempt an Indian woman from living on the reservation, and children having any Indian ancestry were included in the edict. So Tom Potter, if he wanted to keep his family intact, would have been forced to accompany his five minor children by Juley—Frank, John, Rebecca, Jim, and Moses—to the Round Valley reservation.[29] Molly Metock and the three youngest boys would have gone, too. Presumably, Tom's status as an early white settler and a man of some means would have allowed his family to delay their move and to be spared much of the abuse and starvation experienced by less well-connected reservation Indians.[30]

By July 26, 1870, Tom Potter had left Potter Valley and was living in Round Valley township with his five children by his late wife Juley.[31] One can only speculate about the emotional impact on Tom's children (then aged seventeen, thirteen, twelve, eleven, and seven) from the routine brutal treatment of reservation Indians by white settlers, which they must have witnessed—and perhaps suffered—repeatedly.

Tom Potter did not acknowledge his union with Molly Metock in the 1870 federal census, even though she had almost certainly been forced to go to the Round Valley reservation with her three young children by him, along with other

Potter Valley Indians.[32] Nevertheless, it appears likely that by 1870, Tom Potter was looking after his second family there as well. Perhaps these wrenching moves and family responsibilities may account for the evident decline in his financial assets: in the 1870 census, Tom showed no real estate ownership and personal property worth just two thousand dollars.[33]

The same 1870 federal census indicates that Tom's brother Will stayed behind, in Potter Valley, with his family. Will indicated no real estate ownership and personal property worth one thousand dollars.[34] He had already sold his Potter Valley land holdings by 1863. In 1872–73, he declared personal property worth $808.[35]

## The Decision to Leave California

Large numbers of new settlers arrived in Potter Valley during the late 1850s and early 1860s, exerting inevitable and increasing pressures on the land.[36] By 1860 the valley began to experience overgrazing, which would only intensify with time and additional immigrants.[37]

By the late 1860s, the fortunes of Will and Tom Potter were turning bad in California. Times were changing, and the Potter brothers weren't changing with them. Neither brother owned his original land. They had seen their lovely valley become overcrowded and overgrazed, and the old free ways vanish in the onrushing tide of land-greedy immigrants. Tom must have been heartsick over what had happened to his family, what his sons and daughters must have experienced as Indian children, what his Indian consort, Molly Metock, had been forced to endure at the hands of California settlers.

Sometime, probably in 1872, Will and Tom Potter decided to pull up stakes and start over, in Texas. Somewhere, they had heard that unincorporated Kimble County, 140 miles west of Austin, offered good water, abundant free grazing, few settlers, and maximum freedom.[38] Perhaps they could re-create the early good years of northern California in Texas.

Molly Metock told Tom Potter that she was not going to Texas; their son Sam stayed with her in Mendocino County. Tom's daughters Mandy and Rebecca also stayed in Mendocino County. Probably in the fall of 1873, Tom Potter, then forty-two years of age, set out for Texas with six Indian sons, Frank (twenty), John (fifteen), Jim (twelve), Moses (ten), William (eight), and Tom Jr. (five).[39]

Aside from his daughters Louisa and Margaret Ann, both of whom were now married, Will Potter, then forty-eight, took his entire family: his wife, Mary (age forty), Thomas H. "Mack" (twenty-one), Bill (seventeen), Joseph (fourteen), Jeff Davis (twelve), John H. (nine), Elizabeth (six), Mary Ellen (five), and Roberta M. (one).[40]

Will and Tom Potter were repeating a migration with their children that they

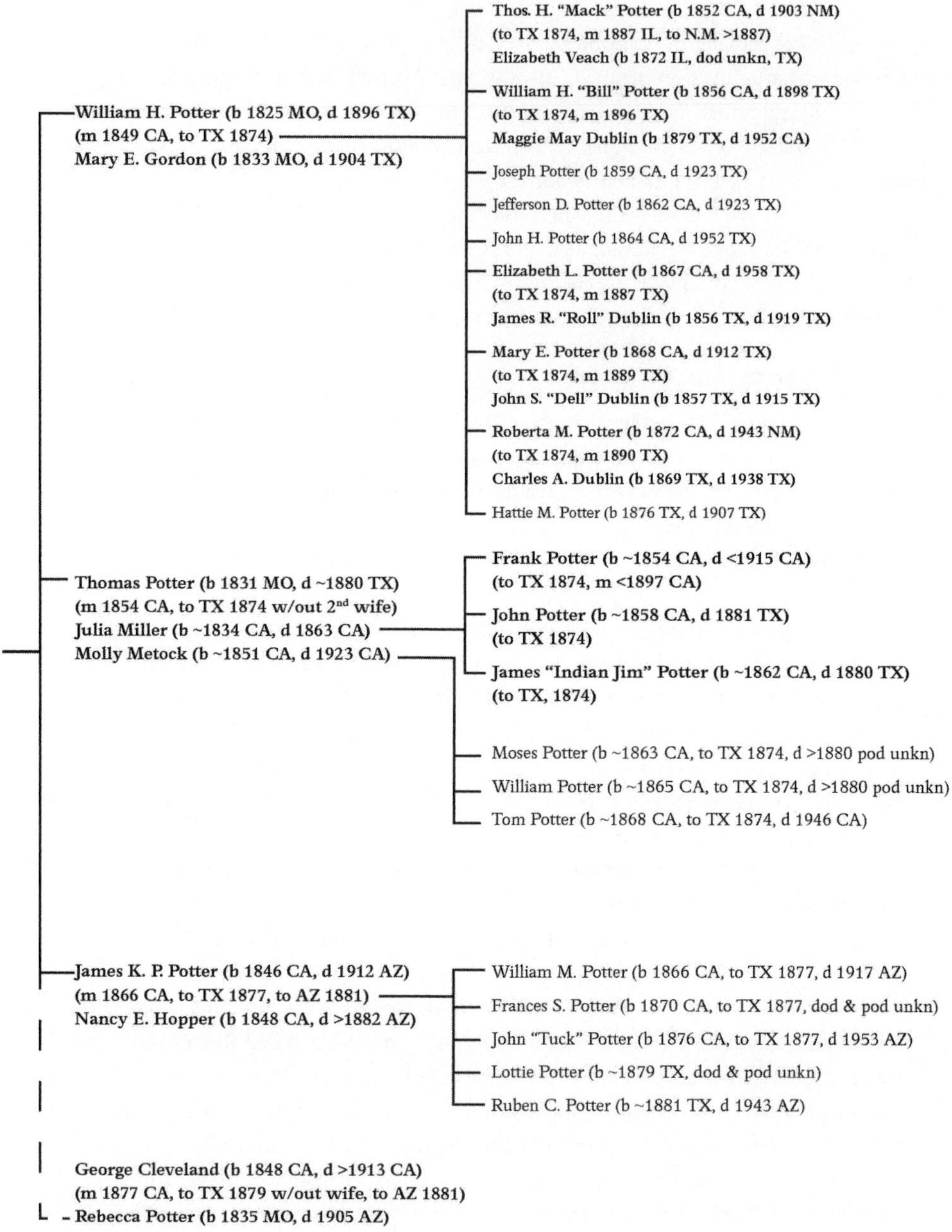

William H. Potter (b 1825 MO, d 1896 TX)
(m 1849 CA, to TX 1874)
Mary E. Gordon (b 1833 MO, d 1904 TX)

- Thos. H. "Mack" Potter (b 1852 CA, d 1903 NM)
(to TX 1874, m 1887 IL, to N.M. >1887)
Elizabeth Veach (b 1872 IL, dod unkn, TX)

- William H. "Bill" Potter (b 1856 CA, d 1898 TX)
(to TX 1874, m 1896 TX)
Maggie May Dublin (b 1879 TX, d 1952 CA)

- Joseph Potter (b 1859 CA, d 1923 TX)

- Jefferson D. Potter (b 1862 CA, d 1923 TX)

- John H. Potter (b 1864 CA, d 1952 TX)

- Elizabeth L. Potter (b 1867 CA, d 1958 TX)
(to TX 1874, m 1887 TX)
James R. "Roll" Dublin (b 1856 TX, d 1919 TX)

- Mary E. Potter (b 1868 CA, d 1912 TX)
(to TX 1874, m 1889 TX)
John S. "Dell" Dublin (b 1857 TX, d 1915 TX)

- Roberta M. Potter (b 1872 CA, d 1943 NM)
(to TX 1874, m 1890 TX)
Charles A. Dublin (b 1869 TX, d 1938 TX)

- Hattie M. Potter (b 1876 TX, d 1907 TX)

Thomas Potter (b 1831 MO, d ~1880 TX)
(m 1854 CA, to TX 1874 w/out 2nd wife)
Julia Miller (b ~1834 CA, d 1863 CA)
Molly Metock (b ~1851 CA, d 1923 CA)

- Frank Potter (b ~1854 CA, d <1915 CA)
(to TX 1874, m <1897 CA)

- John Potter (b ~1858 CA, d 1881 TX)
(to TX 1874)

- James "Indian Jim" Potter (b ~1862 CA, d 1880 TX)
(to TX, 1874)

- Moses Potter (b ~1863 CA, to TX 1874, d >1880 pod unkn)

- William Potter (b ~1865 CA, to TX 1874, d >1880 pod unkn)

- Tom Potter (b ~1868 CA, to TX 1874, d 1946 CA)

James K. P. Potter (b 1846 CA, d 1912 AZ)
(m 1866 CA, to TX 1877, to AZ 1881)
Nancy E. Hopper (b 1848 CA, d >1882 AZ)

- William M. Potter (b 1866 CA, to TX 1877, d 1917 AZ)

- Frances S. Potter (b 1870 CA, to TX 1877, dod & pod unkn)

- John "Tuck" Potter (b 1876 CA, to TX 1877, d 1953 AZ)

- Lottie Potter (b ~1879 TX, dod & pod unkn)

- Ruben C. Potter (b ~1881 TX, d 1943 AZ)

George Cleveland (b 1848 CA, d >1913 CA)
(m 1877 CA, to TX 1879 w/out wife, to AZ 1881)
Rebecca Potter (b 1835 MO, d 1905 AZ)

Figure 4. The Potter family in Texas. Bold font signifies characters who were prominent in the events related herein.

themselves had experienced with their own father and mother a generation before. They had known a magical time as young men in a golden new world that
was pristine, yielding, rich, and adventuresome beyond their wildest dreams. Others had become rich as California grew and developed. They, who were there at
the beginning, who had every expectation of growing prosperous and influential
as strong young settlers in a new land, had been bypassed by events, the consequences of their own choices, and fate.

Perhaps they could do it over again in Texas, and this time get it right.

### New Paradise on the South Llano

The fertile floodplains and alluvial terraces of the South Llano valley were composed of good soil, and springs were ubiquitous, flowing from every tributary
creek and gully. Timber along the river provided logs for cabins, and flagstone
rock from the adjacent limestone hillsides provided abundant material for walls,
chimneys, and flooring. Native range grasses grew tall and lush on the valley flats,
reaching up the slopes of the unfenced hills marginal to the valley, providing superb grazing for settlers' cattle. Game abounded. To Will and Tom Potter, and
their families, it must have looked like paradise.

Although a few settlers had started locating at the forks of the Llano after the
end of the Civil War, they tended to avoid the narrow upper valleys of the Llanos
because of their vulnerability to Indian attacks.[41] But by the middle of 1874, perhaps a half-dozen homesteads were strung up and down the South Llano valley.[42]
The river road ran just a mile to the east of Will Potter's Cajac Creek location, and
the alluvial terrace on which the Potter house was built provided land for a corn
patch, kitchen garden, and home pasture for saddle horses and captured cattle.
Little or no fencing was required.

Once the Will Potter family had begun settling in and starting their improvements, Will Potter himself set about making his way in the new community. He
got acquainted with his neighbors, and he transferred his Masonic membership
to the nearest Masonic lodge, in Mason, Texas, sixty miles to the northeast, down
the Llano River.[43] Almost certainly, he began to develop a friendship with Jimmy
Dublin, patriarch of a large clan that had located a mile to the north on the west
side of the South Llano valley, where the river road crossed Bailey Creek. The
Jimmy Dublin and Will Potter families, new arrivals and nearby neighbors in a
new land, developed increasingly close ties. Their futures would be closely linked
in the coming years.

Tom Potter's secluded location farther up Cajac Creek did not welcome company. Perhaps his choice of such a dark, isolated home site may also have been
an acknowledgment of his family's ambivalent status with respect to his brother

Will's family, as well as their new Dublin neighbors: the Indian cousins were separate and different but still family, and therefore still connected.

Tom Potter's sons, Frank, John, Jim, Moses, William, and Tom Jr.—the Indian cousins—would follow their own stars.

# 5 :: Responding to the Indian Threat

### General Ord's Policy of Pursuit

By 1875 Indian raids into Texas from Mexico had resumed, with even greater frequency and damage than before.[1] One of the worst raids targeted Corpus Christi, on March 26, during which many settlers and their families were killed. This raid raised regional tensions to such a level that they gained the attention of the U.S. government.[2]

On June 3, 1875, General Edward O. C. Ord assumed command of U.S. military forces constituting the Department of Texas. He immediately dispatched troops to scattered posts along the Rio Grande. Ord believed the only way to protect Americans and their property was to follow Indian raiders back into Mexico whenever their fresh trails were found—and federal troops thereafter began to carry out Ord's unofficial policy.[3] Serving under Ord was Colonel William R. ("Pecos Bill") Shafter, who carried out cross-border raids into the rugged country opposite the present Big Bend National Park of west Texas, beginning in the summer of 1876, mostly against Lipan and Mescalero Apaches. Shafter also ordered raids against Kickapoo, Lipan, and Mescalero Indians in the lower settlements, opposite Eagle Pass.[4] The Ord policy mandating the pursuit of raiders into Mexican territory was adopted officially by the U.S. government on June 1, 1877.[5]

First Lieutenant John L. Bullis was the primary instrument implementing General Ord's policy, through his commanding officer, Colonel Shafter. Bullis commanded the Seminole Scouts, a small, highly mobile scouting force of Seminole black Indians employed by the army against Mexican Indian raiders. Bullis reported that he carried out sixteen scouts and raids into northern Mexico between June 1876 and November 1877.[6] Many of these sorties ended in sharp fights with hostile Indians. Bullis was cited for gallant service in four engagements with Indians: in 1873 at El Remolino with Mackenzie; in 1875 on the Pecos River; in 1876 near Zaragoza, Mexico; and in 1881 in the Serranía del Burro of northern Coahuila. Three of his troopers were awarded the Congressional Medal of Honor for gallantry in action. On April 7, 1882, the Texas Legislature adopted a resolution thanking him for his service against Indians and other enemies on the frontier.[7] By the 1880s, Bullis had become a military legend and a Texas hero.

Between 1873 and 1883, at least twenty-three such raids were mounted by

U.S. troops into Mexico, over a three-hundred-mile length of the Rio Grande, seeking to capture or kill primarily Kickapoo, Lipan, and Mescalero raiders and to destroy their villages and horses.[8]

### The Diaz Policy

In a constitutional coup, Porfirio Diaz assumed the presidency of Mexico in November 1876.[9] He recognized the need for internal stability if Mexico was to attract Western capital for economic development, and he perceived that continued marauding by Indians from Mexico tended to suppress such investment. He also sought U.S. diplomatic recognition for his regime. For its part, the United States wanted assurance that Mexico would prevent its residents from raiding Texas settlements.[10]

Both Ord and Diaz played their political cards shrewdly. Ord cultivated influential Texas politicians who could help him persuade the U.S. War Department to approve a more aggressive policy toward raiders from Mexico into Texas, and he initiated contact with Diaz through U.S. diplomats in Mexico to encourage the placement along the border of Mexican troops led by capable Mexican army officers. Generals Falcon and Trevino not only began to exert control over Indian raiders in northern Coahuila and Chihuahua but also started cooperating quietly with General Ord, in an international gentlemen's agreement.[11] The Mexican Army generally did not challenge U.S. troops on their frequent forays into Mexico in pursuit of Indian raiders, and American officers "looked the other way" on a few occasions when Mexican troops crossed over in pursuit of renegade Indians fleeing into Texas.

President Rutherford B. Hayes ordered the official recognition of the Diaz government in Mexico by the United States on April 9, 1878; the Ord doctrine was officially revoked on February 24, 1880.[12]

### Lieutenant Bullis's Testimony

It is one thing to review the pattern of cross-border raiding by Indians from Mexico in terms of international diplomacy, U.S. relations with Native Americans, and U.S. military history. It is quite another to understand such marauding (and counterattacking against it) in personal terms, as experienced by those who were directly and personally involved.

In Congressional testimony on January 12, 1878, First Lieutenant John L. Bullis shared some of his experiences regarding Mexican Indian raiders:

> There are five [six] bands of Indians on the Mexican shore, none or very few of whom have ever been on reservations. I have followed them for

years and years and fought them and know their chiefs. The name of the present chief of the Lipan Indians is Washa Lobo. This Indian and his people reside most of the time near Saragossa [Zaragoza] in Mexico. They steal constantly on the American side and have done so for years. They came over and made two raids in 1876. On one of these raids they killed 13 men and one woman. That was in September and October, 1876, and in the months of April and May of the same year the same party of Indians came over and killed 12 men. Washa Lobo is a cunning fellow . . . [whose] party of men does not exceed 30.

Bullis identified the other five Indian groups in northern Mexico. A band of marauding Mescalero Apaches resided at Del Norte, Mexico (present Ojinaga), under a chief known as Magnus Colorado, with forty to sixty raiders. There were also three parties of Indians living around San Carlos, an Indian town about eighteen miles southwest from the Rio Grande, in the state of Chihuahua, and about fifty miles downriver from Del Norte. One party followed a chief by the name of Tejano. One band of Mescalero Indians lived near San Carlos under a chief named Leon and another under a chief named Cheno. The fifth group lived about sixty miles south of San Carlos, in the Sierra Carmel, under a chief known as Alsate. Bullis stated that all of these Indians, totaling some 225 men, depredated on the American side of the river.[13]

The Indians cross the Rio Grande in parties of two up to 35 or 40 . . . invariably [coming] in on foot, wearing moccasins, although I have known one or two instances where they have brought in one horse carrying their packs. They work east from the Rio Grande through the rough, broken country, through cedar-breaks [sic].[14] . . . During the daytime they hide or stay on the top of the highest peaks or mountains, and when the moon is . . . full they come down. I have known them to gather up within one or two nights 200 head of horses. Then they put out [westward], driving night and day, and [recrossing] the Rio Grande within four days and nights. . . . They change from one horse to another . . . riding bare-back. . . . They take a piece of rawhide from cattle which they kill while on the Texan side, put a string of it over the head of a horse and pass a piece of wood through the horse's mouth for a bit, and use a strip of rawhide for a bridle-rein, and in this way they will travel 60 to 80 miles in a day and night.[15]

Bullis recommended to the congressional committee that an additional army post be established on the Rio Grande to fill in the 200-mile uninhabited stretch between San Felipe (present Del Rio, Texas) and Del Norte. He pointed out that Indian raiders crossed invariably above the mouth of Devils River and passed through that uninhabited country, making for the settlements. He testified that he had known them to steal within twenty-five miles of San Antonio during the previous year. Bullis claimed that it would not be possible to eliminate them entirely

> because they are too cunning. They can hide their families in the rocks and fastnesses of the mountains, and it is almost impossible to get at them. . . . They are broken up into small bands, and the country is so very rough . . . that it is very difficult . . . to strike them.[16]

Bullis went on to relate the particulars of a sortie, pursuing Indian raiders returning to Mexico from a foray into Texas. While on a patrol in late June 1877, two of Bullis's men found an Indian trail between the Pecos and the Rio Grande, about seventy miles from the mouth of the Pecos. On June 30 Bullis and thirty-five Seminole Scouts followed it to the Rio Grande and crossed the river. The next day they followed it for thirty miles before camping for the night. The next morning, July 2, they saddled up before daylight, continued on the trail, and discovered the Indians a few miles farther on. Bullis and his troopers attacked, captured twenty-three horses, killed one Indian and wounded three, then returned to the American side on July 4. Bullis claimed that this party of Indians, composed of Lipans and Mescaleros, had been stealing stock in Kerr County, Texas, and had wounded one boy, who was placed in the post hospital in Fort Clark, Texas.[17]

Another experienced frontier officer, Colonel H. B. Clitz, stationed at Fort McKavett, also testified before the same congressional committee on December 7, 1877:

> I suppose that almost every alternate moon, at certain seasons, there has been some sort of raid in there from either the Lipans or Mescalero Apaches, accompanied by some Mexicans. . . . They generally cross the Rio Grande above the mouth of the Pecos, cross Devil's River and enter into the settlements between the forks of the Llano and go toward Kerr County, or toward Fredericksburg and Mason.[18]

If lightning-quick strikes by Bullis and his Seminole Scouts were the 1870s equivalent of today's U.S. Special Forces, Colonel William R. Shafter and his

Figure 5. Major John B. Jones, commander, Frontier Battalion, Texas Rangers, about 1875. Courtesy of Texas State Library and Archives Commission, Austin.

mounted columns represented a ubiquitous hammer, heavy and mobile reinforcements backing up Bullis wherever he was, along the Texas border as well as deep into Mexico.[19]

### The Frontier Battalion

Pressure maintained by the U.S. military was largely responsible for the gradual demise of Indian raiding from Mexico into Texas from 1875 to 1881. Control was only gradually achieved, however, and the Frontier Battalion of Texas Rangers also played an important, if secondary, role in eventually bringing a modicum of security to western Texas.

During the post–Civil War occupation, Texas citizens had become increasingly aggravated by the perceived indifference of U.S. military forces to the frequent Indian attacks on frontier Texas—southerly raids by Comanche and Kiowa marauders from their reservation sanctuaries in Indian Territory as well as easterly forays by Kickapoo and Apache Indians from northern Mexico.[20]

In early 1874, more than two months after Texans had voted the hated do-nothing Republican carpet-bagger government out of office, Democrat Richard Coke finally assumed the governorship. One of Coke's first acts was to urge establishment of the Frontier Battalion of the Texas Rangers, whose primary task would be to defend the frontier against Indian raiders.[21]

New Governor Coke appointed Major John B. Jones to establish and command the Frontier Battalion, Texas Rangers. Jones reported to the adjutant general of Texas, William Steele. Six companies of about seventy mounted policemen each were to be recruited and organized. By early July, Jones had positioned his ranging companies in a north-south line west of the existing frontier, the northernmost being Captain E. F. Ikard's Company C, positioned in southwestern Clay County about twenty miles southeast of present Wichita Falls. Next was Captain G. W. Stevens's Company B, located about forty miles farther south, in eastern Young County between Graham and Jacksboro; Captain John R. Waller's Company A, stationed another fifty miles southwest, in southwestern Stephens County between present Breckinridge and Abilene; Captain W. J. Maltby's Company E, positioned about sixty miles farther south-southwest, in southwestern Coleman County; Captain Rufus Perry's Company D, located another seventy miles south, in western Mason County; and Captain Neal Coldwell's Company F, stationed about seventy-five miles south of Company D, in southern Edwards County (see map 1).[22]

The primary responsibility of all six companies was to intercept, pursue, and destroy Indian raiders preying on Texas frontier settlements.[23] As events and budgets dictated, companies moved about and were reorganized over the next five years. A major reduction in force at the end of 1874 reduced the average company roster to thirty to forty mounted policemen; some officers resigned; others were reduced in rank. Despite their reduced numbers, the Frontier Battalion continued to give substantial attention to the detection, pursuit, and punishment of Indian raiders. The Ranger records reveal clearly just how frequent such raids were, how fearful frontier settlers were of the Indian marauders—and how very difficult it was to engage and apprehend them.

### 1875 Indian Encounters and Patrols

In early 1875 the state's western line of defense in the eastern Edwards Plateau and western Hill Country consisted of two Ranger companies. Lieutenant Dan Roberts's Company D, then stationed on Big Saline Creek in southern Menard County, and Lieutenant Neal Coldwell's (later Lieutenant Pat Dolan's) Company F, stationed on Johnson Creek of the Guadalupe drainage, were charged with defending the frontier against Indians marauding from Mexico. Five or six raids had been reported in the area of the Johnson Fork of the Llano River between May 7 and June 1. Two raiding parties were Indians; one was believed to be white men.[24]

Throughout 1875, both companies carried out repeated wide scouting sweeps to the west, usually involving eight to twenty men, searching for Indian trails, watering holes, or stopping places. Such scouts often covered several hundred miles, consuming one to two weeks. Although they actually encountered Indians only rarely, the Rangers' frequent penetration of the vacant western Edwards Plateau region acted as a warning to raiding Indians that they might, at any time, run into squads of well-armed, well-mounted state police. The Rangers also responded to reports of Indians from settlers in the western Hill Country. Usually, by the time the Rangers arrived at the place of a reported sighting, the Indians had a substantial head start, which prevented realistic expectations of being overtaken. Many reports of Indians also turned out to be false.[25]

Major Jones, with Coldwell's Company F Rangers, conducted an uneventful scout of the North and South Llanos watershed during the first week of July 1875, and planned a more extensive scout farther west, to the Devils and Pecos Rivers in September, under Sergeant N. O. Reynolds.[26] This patrol had to be postponed because of urgent law-enforcement demands on the Rangers associated with the Mason County War.[27] In August, Lieutenant Roberts and fourteen men pursued Lipan raiders led by "Old Magoosh," who had stolen horses in Kimble, Mason, and Menard Counties, and fled westward out the South Concho watershed, where the Rangers caught up with them, killed one Indian, wounded several, killed four of their horses, and recovered one captive boy.[28]

By late 1875, the threat of southward raids by Comanches and Kiowas had diminished substantially, primarily because of Mackenzie's destruction of their horses and goods at Palo Duro Canyon in September 1874, followed by continuing pressure on remnant plains Indians through the following winter and spring, known as the Red River War.[29] Now most Ranger companies began to shift their priorities to address rampant civil lawlessness on the Texas frontier. In mid-November, Lieutenant Coldwell was sent with a large squad of Rangers on an eleven-day scout to investigate rumors that a strong band of outlaws was operating around the headwaters of the Llano River. Coldwell encountered no such men.[30] Subsequent events suggest that a confederation of outlaws did exist on the upper Llanos, and that it maintained an active system of spies and lookouts to warn of incursions by the Rangers.

However, the menace of Indians raiding from Mexico remained substantial in the upper Rio Grande Plain, Edwards Plateau, and western Hill Country. Lieutenant Dan Roberts's Company D continued to focus on the western Concho, San Saba, and Llano River valleys, and Lieutenant Pat Dolan took over Company A, stationed most of the time at Camp Wood, along the East Nueces River in present Real County, Texas.[31] Dolan's area of responsibility comprised the severely dissected southern margins of the Edwards Plateau and the upper Rio Grande coastal plain, from the Pecos River on the west to the Medina River on the east, and from the crest of the divide on the north to the coastal-plain prairies along the southeast-flowing Nueces River on the south (see map 2). This was the area most frequented by Indian marauders from 1875 to 1881.

Figure 6. Captain Pat Dolan, commander, Company F, Frontier Battalion, Texas Rangers, about 1874. From the Noah H. Rose Collection, courtesy of the Western History Collection, University of Oklahoma, Norman.

**1876 Indian Encounters and Patrols**

Dolan's monthly returns for 1876 indicate that he and his command were in-volved in the unsuccessful pursuit of Washa Lobo's Lipan raiders, in April–May, and September–October, as reported by Lieutenant Bullis. Dolan's reports also show almost continual scouting through the year, and reports of Indian raids al-most every month.

Lieutenant Dan Roberts's Company D reported five substantial patrols during 1876, scouting for Indian raiding parties. In May, responding to recent signs of Indians going west, three different patrols went to the heads of the Llanos; in late June, Sergeant Reynolds and twenty men conducted a scout to the west under Major John B. Jones; and in August, Company D's Sergeant Hawkins and twenty men went out to the heads of the Llano, South Concho, and Devils Rivers, search-ing for trails of Indians returning to Mexico from raids in Uvalde County.[32] Dan Roberts resigned in September, and Frank M. Moore replaced him as lieutenant, commanding Company D.[33] Two months later, responding to increasing reports of civil disorder in Kimble County, Moore moved Company D from its camp on the San Saba River in Menard County to a new headquarters location, where Bear Creek empties into the North Llano River, six miles west of Junction City.[34]

A Ranger camp was located there for the next three years, and intermittently for three years after that.

Raids by Mexican Indians during 1876 claimed the lives of at least thirty Texas settlers, including Isaac Kountz and Sam Speer, killed by a party of eight to ten Indians on a horse-stealing raid at Junction City, at the forks of the Llanos, on December 24, 1876. The raiders were reported to have long hair but were dressed like white men. They were pursued by a party of Kimble County settlers and six Texas Rangers, commanded by Lieutenant Frank Moore. The raiders traveled east along the main Llano, then turned south toward Kerrville in the Guadalupe River valley, where they stole more horses, then turned southwest up the south fork of the Guadalupe, over the divide into the drainage of the Medina River and then on to the Frio River. There they were pursued by local settlers so closely that they finally abandoned their horse herd and headed back west, across the coastal plain, for the Rio Grande. Lieutenant Moore and the Kimble County posse exhausted their horses and gave up the chase on the divide between the Guadalupe and Medina Rivers.[35]

### 1877 Indian Encounters and Patrols

During 1877, heightened border activity by General Ord's U.S. Army forces continued, as did repeated westward scouts by Texas Ranger Companies A, C, and D. Nevertheless, cross-border raids by Indians into southwest Texas did not diminish during that year. The following summaries provide perspective on the character and frequency of such raids:

On March 24, word came to Lieutenant Dolan of Indians stealing horses from ranches north of Camp Wood; Dolan and 12 men followed their trail toward Kickapoo Springs on the West Nueces River, but could not overtake them.[36]

On March 31, Lieutenant Dolan and 12 Company A Rangers overtook a party of Indians on the head of Devils River near Beaver Lake, in far northeastern Val Verde County, where they captured all their equipment and 13 horses.[37]

On April 22, a raiding party of 20 Indians killed E. Wehrmann in Kinney County, stole 28 horses in Uvalde County, 30 horses in Dimmitt County, then crossed back into Mexico.[38]

In two engagements in early May, in the area between Eagle Pass and present Del Rio, Texas [probably across the Rio Grande River in Coahuila], Captain P. L. Lee's Company G, 10th Cavalry, killed four Indians and wounded six, recovered 69 head of stock and destroyed 15 lodges.[39]

On June 22, 13 Indians from Mexico wounded two men near Camp Wood and stole 14 horses in Uvalde County.[40]

On June 22, Lieutenant Moore and 12 men from Company D followed an Indian trail from the South Llano valley eastward for 40 miles, whereupon about 15 raiders circled back to the upper South Llano watershed, where they scattered.[41]

On July 26, Lieutenant Dolan and seven Company A Rangers searched for Indian trails in Kerr County, where reports of marauding Indians were received; none found.[42]

In fall, 1877, Indian horse thieves raided eastern Kimble County near the ranches of Tobe Joy [on the James River], and Jerry Roberts, on Johnson Fork of the Llano River. Roberts and his men pursued the Indians and recaptured their horses, plus two Indian ponies.[43]

In November, 20 Indians from Mexico stole 5 horses in the Nueces Canyon and killed one man; next, they stole 26 horses near Uvalde, then turned and crossed back into Mexico.[44]

### Effects of Indian Raids on Frontier Settlements

In the 1870s, the Texas Hill Country was a wholly rural region given over to the raising, gathering, and driving of cattle and horses. Ranching establishments were isolated. Farming was secondary, more common in older settlements to the east. Indian raids on frontier settlements were the equivalent of modern terrorist attacks but with different purposes and consequences. The chief source of terror fed on settlers' fears of indiscriminant murder, rape, and the abduction of women and children. To be sure, such horrific attacks did take place, and frontier families learned to live with the perpetual threat of sudden, devastating Indian attacks.

But the most common motivation for Indian raids was the theft of livestock, principally horses. Human targets of opportunity were, of course, seized upon. Frequent Indian raiding seriously disrupted the most common form of business in the region, generating substantial financial losses and significant inconvenience to ranchers, freighters, and farmers. Even when horses were recovered from the Indians who stole them, they were frequently so broken down and worn out that they were useless afterward.

# 6 :: The Confederation

From the forks of the Llano, the nearest towns—Kerrville, Fredericksburg, and Mason—lay fifty to sixty miles away, to the southeast, east, and northeast, respectively. In 1875 all had existed as organized, lawful communities for at least twenty years. Fort McKavett, only thirty miles to the northwest, had been an active military establishment since 1852, except for the Civil War years.

With a history of frequent Indian raids, neighboring Kimble County had remained isolated, legally unorganized, and sparsely settled. But there was boundless open range, virgin soil, and plenty of water. Land was cheap. The full import of the toughened new federal Indian policy and aggressive military control sank in. That lured enterprising new settlers from many states who sensed opportunity. It also drew indigent refugees from the ravaged South, intent on making a new start, and, of course, the usual fringe of raggedy frontier riffraff, many of whom no doubt envisioned a new land of lemonade springs, honey ponds, and fritter trees. Many settlers were desperately, miserably poor, squatting along rivers and creeks, living hand-to-mouth off the land, building makeshift, soon squalid shelters of logs and brush, and scrambling for any transitory advantage that offered itself.[1]

There were no churches or schools, but they could be built. There were no towns or stores or trade markets, but they could be established. There were virtually no roads, but they could be laid out.

There was also no law. That attracted the criminal element, from Texas and beyond, to the newly opened country around the forks of the Llano, likely imagined as a place of untrammeled freedom and license, where they might live opportunistically, preying on the fruits of other settlers' labor.

**The Dublins**

About a mile northeast from Will Potter's, on the west side of the South Llano valley, was the homestead of another large frontier family, headed by James "Jimmy" Dublin. Henry Dublin, Jimmy's older brother, lived nearby.[2]

The Dublins were rootless, fiddle-footed—they had been in Texas since before 1857 but had moved repeatedly, the last time from Coryell County, probably arriving in Kimble County about the same time as did the Potters. They settled at the mouth of Bailey Creek, beside the river road. James Dublin, age fifty-four in

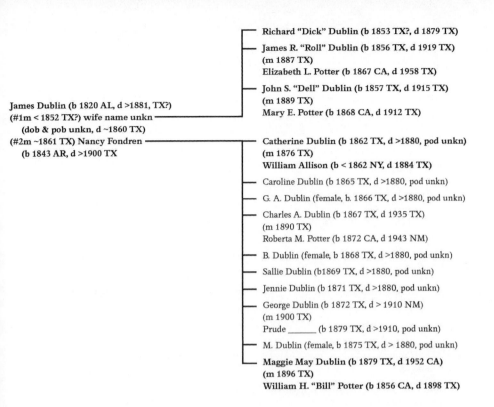

James Dublin (b 1820 AL, d >1881, TX?)
(#1m < 1852 TX?) wife name unkn
   (dob & pob unkn, d ~1860 TX)
(#2m ~1861 TX) Nancy Fondren
   (b 1843 AR, d >1900 TX

Richard "Dick" Dublin (b 1853 TX?, d 1879 TX)

James R. "Roll" Dublin (b 1856 TX, d 1919 TX)
(m 1887 TX)
Elizabeth L. Potter (b 1867 CA, d 1958 TX)

John S. "Dell" Dublin (b 1857 TX, d 1915 TX)
(m 1889 TX)
Mary E. Potter (b 1868 CA, d 1912 TX)

Catherine Dublin (b 1862 TX, d >1880, pod unkn)
(m 1876 TX)
William Allison (b < 1862 NY, d 1884 TX)

Caroline Dublin (b 1865 TX, d >1880, pod unkn)

G. A. Dublin (female, b. 1866 TX, d >1880, pod unkn)

Charles A. Dublin (b 1867 TX, d 1935 TX)
(m 1890 TX)
Roberta M. Potter (b 1872 CA, d 1943 NM)

B. Dublin (female, b 1868 TX, d >1880, pod unkn)

Sallie Dublin (b1869 TX, d >1880, pod unkn)

Jennie Dublin (b 1871 TX, d >1880, pod unkn)

George Dublin (b 1872 TX, d > 1910 NM)
(m 1900 TX)
Prude _____ (b 1879 TX, d >1910, pod unkn)

M. Dublin (female, b 1875 TX, d > 1880, pod unkn)

Maggie May Dublin (b 1879 TX, d 1952 CA)
(m 1896 TX)
William H. "Bill" Potter (b 1856 CA, d 1898 TX)

Figure 7. The James Dublin family in Texas. Bold font signifies characters who were prominent in the events related herein.

1874, was born in Alabama; his second wife Nancy (Fondren), then age thirty-one, was from Arkansas.[3] The Dublin offspring were numerous: Richard (Dick) Dublin, then about twenty-one years of age; James Roland (Roll), about seventeen; and John Sheldon (Dell), about sixteen—all sons by Jimmy Dublin's first wife. Then there were three consecutive Dublin daughters by Nancy, ranging in age from about twelve to eight, followed by son Charles, age seven, and then three more daughters, ages six to two. Brother George Dublin was born in 1873, followed eventually by two more daughters by 1879.[4]

As "down-the-road" neighbors and new arrivals in a raw, unsettled land, with active sons and daughters of similar ages, it was perhaps inevitable that the Jimmy Dublin and Will Potter families would form strong and lasting interfamilial bonds—bonds that led the older Dublin sons to establish and lead a notorious criminal confederation, and later, long after they had been driven out of Kimble County, to intermarry with the daughters of Will and Mary Potter.

In retrospect, it is clear that from the beginning the Dublins were at the heart of the substantial lawless confederation among early Kimble County settlers. Dick Dublin and a friend, Ace Langford, had killed two men in Coryell County in January 1873 over a horse race, for which crime Dick was indicted in April 1874 and a warrant issued on June 20, 1874, for his arrest.[5] The State of Texas and Coryell County offered rewards of five hundred and two hundred dollars, respectively, for his arrest and return for trial. In the fall of 1873, according to James B. Gillett, both fugitives worked as cowboys for cattleman Joe Franks in Menard and Kimble Counties:

> [They] were always armed and constantly on watch for fear of arrest. Dublin was a large man, stout and of dark complexion, who looked more like the bully of a prize ring than the cowman he was. . . . [Dublin was] often heard to say that he would never surrender. While cow hunting with [the Franks outfit], he discovered that the brushy and tangled region of Kimble County offered shelter for such as he, and [he] persuaded his father to move out into that county.[6]

Kimble County historian O. C. Fisher, who interviewed many old-timers who had settled in Kimble County during the 1870–80 frontier period, offered these insights into the Dublin family:

> Jim Dublin, accompanied by his family, including his son-in-law, William Allison, moved to Kimble County about 1874. Dick, Role, and Dell, the sons, were "outlaws in the rough." The family moved in by way of Mason . . . from Coryell County, and settled on the wild slashes of South Llano. At the time Dick Dublin was wanted for murder in Coryell County, and the other two brothers soon made themselves "wanted" for crimes of major import. The Dublins trailed cattle to Kimble, and Lou Walton remembers them passing the Rance Moore ranch on Big Saline. There [they] committed their first Kimble County offense. Coming out of the soft sandy-land belt, their [unshod] horses became tender-footed as they trampled against rocky hillsides. Rance Moore had a number of freshly-shod saddle horses in his horse trap on the creek, and it was quite a coincidence that Moore's horses came home that day sans shoes—and there had been nobody through those parts except the Dublins![7]

## A Tribalistic Criminal Network

In the America of the early twenty-first century, it is difficult to grasp how powerful and pervasive was the influence of family relationships among Anglo-Celtic American settlers of the eighteenth and nineteenth centuries. As with the clustering of the extended Potter relatives and in-laws in Potter Valley, California, familial interrelatedness was even more prevalent among early settlers in Kimble County. This led to a tribal social structure in the community that generated fierce loyalty to patriarchs, appointed leaders, extended family members, and friends, and stubborn resistance to duly elected community governance and law enforcement in general, and interference of any kind with their own nefarious activities in particular.

Questionable characters began to filter into Kimble County during 1874 and 1875, such as Bill Allison, Rube Boyce, Stark Reynolds, Tom Doran, J. A. "Black" Burt, Caleb Hall, Lewis (Luke) Cathey, Jim Deaton, Matthew Wilkins, John Elliott, James Polk Mason, and many others. They formed a veritable criminal network, centered around the home of Jimmy Dublin.[8] In one way or another, many of their families were, or became, interrelated—for example, Bill Allison married Catherine Dublin about 1875, thus becoming Jimmy Dublin's son-in-law.

Given that this clannish, lawless contingent of the general population of Kimble County had about three years (1874–77) in which to incubate and take root without substantive interference from the law, it is no wonder that another four years (1877–81) would be required to eradicate the outlaw element from Kimble County, even with growing numbers of law-abiding new arrivals and repeated interventions by the Texas Rangers.

As the threat of Comanche and Kiowa raiders diminished in early 1875, the Frontier Battalion could begin to change its priorities, to give more attention to the problem of lawlessness on the Texas frontier. By early spring 1875, Major John B. Jones was aware of rumored large-scale livestock-rustling operations in western Kimble County. He conducted an uneventful scout of the Llano watershed in early July but failed to locate such outlaws, possibly because inside word of his plans had arrived in time for them to disperse. Another more extensive patrol, planned for September 1875, had to be postponed because of other priorities.[9]

The outlaw confederation entrenched at the forks of the Llano was becoming recognized as the continuing primary cause of rampant livestock theft in the region, as well as being a receiver and purveyor of stolen livestock,[10] a particular threat to the citizens of adjoining Kerr, Gillespie, Mason, and Menard Counties, and an obstacle to the establishment of a stable and lawful community in Kimble County.

Sometime, probably in late 1876, another member of the Potter family arrived. Jimmy Potter, Will and Tom Potter's baby brother, showed up with his wife and three young children, come to join the clan.

### James K. P. Potter Arrives

James Knox Polk Potter was the youngest of Will and Tom Potter's siblings. Born in 1846 shortly after the Potters arrived in California, he was orphaned by the age of five. The little boy went to live in Sonoma with his older siblings, who had congregated around oldest brother William, now married and the leader of the surviving Potter family. William became his legal guardian.[11]

In 1866, having received his share of his late father's estate, Jimmy Potter married Evaline Hopper in Calpella Township, Potter Valley. He was nineteen; she was seventeen. By 1870 they had two children, William (two years old) and Frances (four months). Their father was shown to be a stock raiser, declaring a net worth of five hundred dollars. A third child, John "Tuck" Potter was born in the first half of 1876 in California.[12]

Shortly after the birth of Tuck Potter, James K. P. Potter, then thirty years old, took his wife Evaline and three children to Texas, probably arriving in late 1876 or early 1877. He joined his brothers, William and Tom, in the South Llano valley. After becoming acclimated to the new country, he settled his family, probably on Chalk Creek, on the east side of the South Llano from his brothers, and about five miles distant. Like his older brothers, Jimmy Potter chose a secluded home site more than two miles south of, and hidden from, the river road, in a narrow, shadowy canyon under towering limestone cliffs, just downstream from a crescent-shaped pool now known as the "Potter Waterhole." The young family lived at first out of their wagon, but Potter built a log house on an elevated alluvial floodplain beside the creek sometime in early 1878, planted a corn crop that harvested three hundred bushels that fall, and claimed to own "a few cows, hogs, and horses." A fourth child, Lottie, was born in 1878 or 1879 (see fig. 4).[13]

Such activities may have suggested that Jimmy Potter had adopted the life of an industrious and productive stock farmer. Inspired, however, by the activities of his brothers and nephews, as well as their new friends, it didn't take any time at all for Jimmy Potter to pick up the ways of the confederation of thieves that was accumulating around the forks of the Llano. But he did not run with his white nephews, Mack and Bill Potter, or with their pals, the Dublin boys. Instead, James K. P. Potter hung out with other members of the confederation, and starting in late spring 1879, an old pal newly arrived from California, George Cleveland.[14]

### Clandestine Livestock Markets

An important and enduring question, perhaps self-evident but never addressed in the pertinent contemporary literature, concerns the destinations of livestock that were stolen by outlaws operating in Kimble and Menard Counties. Certainly, some of these stolen cattle and horses must have been supplied to none-too-particular trail bosses of herds "making up" in the spring of each year for departure to Kansas markets, and moving north along the Western Beef Trail, which crossed the Llano River about twenty miles east of Junction City.

Frequent reference in Ranger correspondence to outlaws operating at the headwaters of the North Llano River—westwardly remote from the wide valleys of the main Llano and San Saba Rivers—begs the question of what markets such livestock were destined for.[15] In addition to springtime deliveries to passing trail herds, the nearest markets were in Mexico, 100 to 150 miles southwest, in towns such as Garza Galán (present Ciudad Acuña), Piedras Negras, Zaragoza, San Carlos, and Del Norte (present Ojinaga).

That insight leads naturally to the next question: what was the nature and extent of the relationship between the Kimble County outlaw confederation; the Kickapoo, Lipan, and Mescalero Indian raiders who supplied those border markets with stolen livestock, plunder, and captives; and the Mexican nationals who served as receivers, purveyors, and protectors of the markets? At least one generally accepted version of this trade involved a regular traffic in horses stolen in Texas and driven to the Mexican border, to be exchanged there for cattle, which were driven back and delivered to herds being made up for trailing to Kansas railheads.[16]

It seems logical to suspect that some agent or agents of the Kimble County confederation probably interfaced with those who controlled and administered the Mexican markets. Moreover, given the persistent and widespread rumors that the Dublins and their accomplices often conducted raids disguised as Indians (see chap. 9, p. 98, "Indians, Mexicans, or White Men?"), and the polyglot composition of the Indians living along the Mexican border, one is tempted to speculate—since there is not one shred of independent evidence to confirm it—that the grown Indian sons of Tom Potter may have served the confederation as such agents.

Scrutiny of the Monthly Returns and correspondence files of the Frontier Battalion suggests which of the various Kimble County outlaws were frequent accomplices, wanted and sought after by the Rangers as suspects in various criminal enterprises. It is clear that the older sons of Will Potter—Mack and Bill—ran with the elder sons of James Dublin—Dick, Roll, and Dell—and their relatives, and also that their uncle, James K. P. Potter, hung out with other white members of the confederation.[17]

It is also clear that Tom Potter's Indian sons, John Potter and—after spring 1877—John's older brother Frank, stayed out of the way of the law.[18] This may have reflected the parental efforts of their father, who knew all too well the profound animosity held against Indians by most Anglo-Texans, and therefore may have tried to protect his sons by keeping them close to home, away from their lawless cousins and errant uncle. The third son, Jim ("Indian Jim") Potter, does not certainly appear as a person of interest in Ranger records or correspondence until late July 1880, when he was about nineteen years old.[19]

Or were the Spanish-speaking young Indians Frank, John, and Jim Potter ordinarily not in Kimble County during the years 1877–80? If they were not in Kimble County, then where were they? Could one or more of them instead have been frequently in northern Mexico, serving as middlemen between the confederation, the polyglot Indian raiders, and the Mexican traders?

The names of Tom Potter's three youngest sons—Moses (fourteen in 1877), William (twelve), and Tom. Jr. (nine)—also do not appear in any Ranger records as persons of interest, presumably because they were too young to be involved in any livestock rustling activities.

### Patrolling the Llanos

Ranger squads from Lieutenant Dan Robert's Company D, stationed about thirty miles north on the San Saba River, began periodic patrols into Kimble County, beginning in June 1875, focused on the outlaw element. Roberts investigated "the troubles existing on South Llano, [but] failed to meet with any of the marauding party" between June 11 and 13. Sergeant N. O. Reynolds and ten men "left 25th [June] for the South Llano with capiases for the arrest of different parties. Failing to make any arrests, or of learning anything of their whereabouts, [they] returned the 27th instant." Such patrols continued on about a monthly basis throughout the rest of 1875.[20] Acting on instructions from Major Jones, Lieutenant Neal Coldwell led a substantial detachment of Company F Rangers on a patrol to scour the Llano headwaters area in late November, again looking for cattle rustlers, again without making any arrests.[21]

### Kimble County Organizes

The settlers of Kimble County formally organized the county on January 3, 1876, and elected their county officers on February 15, six weeks later. Will Potter was elected as the first county judge (in Texas, the head of county government), and Jordan A. "Black" Burt, the county's first hide inspector.[22] Frank Latta was elected as the first sheriff, but he resigned on October 4, 1876, probably under intimidation by the confederation, the first of many later resignations by elected county officers. As subsequent events demonstrated, when J. M. Reynolds was appointed by the county officers to succeed Latta as sheriff two weeks later, the criminal element had achieved effective control of the new county.[23]

In a spirited election, the citizens chose the new county seat to be at Kimbleville, a flood-prone site on the west bank of the Llano, about two miles downstream from the confluence of the North and South Llanos. But before the year was out, another election rejected Kimbleville, and the plat of the eventual county seat, Junction City, was laid out in the summer of 1876.[24] It was an attractive place for a town—a triangular alluvial terrace covering about eight hundred acres, at

Figure 8. Frank Latta, first sheriff of Kimble County, elected in February 1876. He resigned eight months later, probably intimidated by threats on him and his family, the first of many early Kimble County officials during the first three years to resign their offices. Photo taken about 1880. Courtesy of Kimble County Historical Commission.

the confluence of two small limpid rivers, confined by shelving slopes beneath buff and gray high bluffs of stratified limestone. Majestic pecan, elm, and live-oak trees crowded the river bottoms. The town site "was owned by one William McLane, who donated alternate lots for the beginning of the town. County Surveyor M. J. "Sel" Denman and the county officers laid out the town in the summer of 1876. A public square was set aside and dedicated."[25] The even-numbered lots were conveyed to County Judge Will Potter on August 29, 1876.[26]

The establishment of a new county government, and the founding of Junction City, however, did not bring order to Kimble County. In fact, the opposite effect resulted, especially after J. M. Reynolds took over as sheriff in mid-October.

### The Law and Order Contingent

A law-and-order contingent was also present among the new county officials, especially E. K. Kountz, clerk; N. Q. Patterson, treasurer; W. F. Gilliland, assessor; and Felix Burton, commissioner.[27] Despite their ongoing personal vulnerability to intimidation by members of the confederation, these courageous men formed the necessary critical nucleus around which organized criminal activity would be gradually suppressed over the next few years, and Kimble County settlers led toward stable county government.

Ezekiel K. Kountz was a physician, forty-eight years old in 1876. His wife, Harriet Lindamood, the daughter of Dutch immigrants, was then age forty-six. They were both born and raised in Virginia, where they married and raised six of their eight children. Kountz served as a Confederate physician during the Civil War. After the war, the Kountz family left Virginia, living in West Virginia, Minnesota, and Kansas before arriving in Kimble County in 1874. They settled at the old abandoned Bradbury settlement two miles southwest of the forks of the Llanos. Their eldest son, John C. Kountz, born in Virginia in 1850, was also active in forming and serving the new county government.[28]

Nicholas Q. Patterson was born in Tennessee in 1827. His wife, Luvania Cross, was born in 1829, also in Tennessee. He was a captain in the Confederate army. The Patterson family emigrated to central Texas by covered wagon in 1869, finally arriving in Kimble County in 1875. They had four children, three of whom were born in Tennessee.[29]

William F. Gilliland was born in Missouri, in 1841. His wife, Rosetta Moore, was born in 1851 in Illinois. They married in Brown County, Texas, in about 1871, and came to Kimble County in about 1874.[30]

Felix Burton was a wandering stockman, born in 1826 in Missouri, who was in central California in 1860, and Silver City, New Mexico, in 1870. He married Mrs. Adeline Ford, a woman thirty years his junior, with two young children, in Menardville, Texas, in 1875. In Kimble County, Burton lived with his wife and four children on Bear Creek, near where Company D set up its first camp late in 1876. He was a charter member of the Junction City Masonic Lodge.[31]

Another strong supporter of law and order in the early days of Kimble County was Ben F. Pepper. He was born in West Virginia in 1821; his first wife, also born in West Virginia, died in 1866 in Missouri. The next year, Pepper married Sally Ann Coyle, born in Missouri in 1847. Ben Pepper first came to Kimble County in 1874, and shortly thereafter moved his extensive family from Missouri to his new land on the South Llano River, about five miles southwest of Junction City.[32]

Except for John C. Kountz, these were mature, seasoned family men, ranging in age from thirty-five to fifty-five. All of them—and all but one of their wives—had come to Kimble County after living in other states—mostly the border states of the Civil War as well as some northern states. Even the two men who succeeded E. K. Kountz in the county judge's office, J. J. Ramsey and George E. Stewart, were from Iowa and New York, respectively.[33] Previously, all these men

Figure 9. Ben F. and Sally C. Pepper, early settlers in the South Llano valley, about 1890. Ben Pepper, an influential citizen, was one of the first to farm the river floodplains, and he built the first two-story stone house in the area. Courtesy of Kimble County Historical Commission.

had lived in post-frontier American communities in which a functioning rule of law existed. From their own life experiences, they had a model for how a civil community should operate, and they were willing to take personal risks to protect their property, their own lives, and the safety of their families, and, in the process, help establish a lawful society in the region around the forks of the Llano.

For each of them, the first task was to protect their families, homes, and property by fostering the establishment of an orderly community in Kimble County. Their next task was to try to survive the animosity of the confederation while doing so. That there were so many resignations among the county officers during the county's first three years suggests that some stepped down in fear for their personal health as well as the safety of their wives and children.

Given that most members of the criminal confederation were from the southern states, or—like the Potters—were southern sympathizers, it might be expected that the conflict between the law-and-order contingent and the outlaw community would have been aggravated by residual animosities from the Civil War. Surprisingly though, surviving records (including informal family histories) contain no references to such conflicting political attitudes.

Figure 10. Lieutenant Frank Moore, commander, Company D, Frontier Battalion, Texas Rangers, 1876–77. Courtesy of Institute of Texan Cultures, University of Texas at San Antonio.

### Increased Scrutiny from the Rangers

From January through August 1876, patrols and arrests by Texas Rangers in Kimble County became more frequent. Company D, under Lieutenant Roberts, mounted thirteen sorties from their headquarters in Menard County into the Llano valleys. When Roberts resigned in September, Frank M. Moore, forty-three years old, took over command. He was well qualified for the job, with Civil War service in the 32nd Texas Cavalry and later as a lieutenant in Neal Coldwell's Company F of the Frontier Battalion.[34]

On October 30, Moore went to Junction City with ten men to assist District Judge W. A. Blackburn in holding the first term of court in the new county. But Judge Blackburn did not appear, so no court was held.[35] In a subsequent letter to Major Jones, Blackburn wrote:

> I have not been in Kimble County, but from parties recently there, I have learned that from forty to one hundred men can be raised in a few hours to resist the execution of legal process, and that they declare their determination to resist the holding of any court in that county. . . . It is the home of a gang of the most desperate characters from all parts of the state, who are depredating upon all the adjacent counties. . . . I am anx-

ious to hold court in Kimble and will do so, unless prevented by force, which is threatened, I am credibly informed.[36]

It may be confidently surmised that the good judge, having heard of the bold and violent Kimble County outlaw confederation—and perhaps even having received one or more direct or indirect threats against his person—decided that discretion was the better part of valor and postponed his planned October 30, 1876, visit until the next term of district court, scheduled for May 1877.[37]

In late November, Lieutenant Moore moved Company D to a new camp, in western Kimble County, at the juncture of Bear Creek and the North Llano River, about six miles west of Junction City. On December 18, a local resident reported to Moore that "there was a party of four or five armed men on South Llano who would stop passers-by and force them to tell their business, etc." Lieutenant Moore, with a detachment of twelve Rangers, went there on the night of December 19 and surrounded the house of W. H. "Bill" Ratliff, where the troublemakers were reported to be, and searched the house but found no one.[38] Ratliff lived a mile or so southwest of William Potter in the South Llano Valley.[39]

Operating from their base in western Kerr County, Lieutenant Coldwell's Company F Rangers carried out seven extensive patrols of the Kimble County region during the first eight months of 1876, making several arrests. Their most frequent destinations were the upper Llano valleys, with two longer scouts into the divide areas farther west. In late September, Lieutenant Pat Dolan took over Company F and relocated it to Camp Wood, on the upper East Nueces River, where he concentrated on the southern breaks of the Edwards Plateau and the upper Rio Grande plain adjacent to the Mexican border.[40]

Sometime in 1876, probably in late summer or fall, the stagecoach running between Mason and Fort McKavett was stopped by unknown highwaymen while the team labored out of a gulch about a mile west of Pegleg Station on the south bank of the San Saba River in eastern Menard County. It was the first of a series of stage robberies at this location that would loom large in the future affairs of the Dublins, Potters, and their Kimble County accomplices.[41] The main targets were doubtless the tempting military payrolls destined for Forts McKavett and Concho.

In the late fall or early winter of 1876, Major Jones sent a spy into Kimble County to gather intelligence about the outlaw establishment at the forks of the Llano. Ranger Private H. B. Waddill, detached from Lieutenant Sparks's Company C, stationed then in Burnet County, was a courageous man who faced probable death if he were found out.[42]

**Worsening Conditions**

On January 19, 1877, the San Antonio–Fort McKavett stagecoach was robbed again, near Pegleg Crossing. Two weeks later the robbers struck again, in the same vicinity.[43] The identities of the highwaymen remained unknown.

Events began to accelerate in Kimble County. On February 4, Sergeant L. P. Sieker, with six men, accompanied Richard Tankersley and a group of cattlemen from Tom Green County to J. A. "Black" Burt's ranch on Gentry Creek, where they found twenty head of cattle, some of which belonged to them and some to their friends. They penned all the animals, but Kimble County Sheriff Reynolds came back at night and cut them out of the pen without the consent of anyone. The Rangers were thus placed in an awkward position, as they were bound by law to cooperate with county law officers—and the Kimble County sheriff seemed to be in league with cattle rustlers.[44]

This set the stage for what could have been an incendiary confrontation averted only through great forbearance by Tankersley and the Ranger officers. The next day Lieutenant Moore, with Sieker's detachment, went with the Tom Green cattlemen to the mouth of Johnson Fork of the Llano to recover more of their stolen cattle. They discovered 235 head, all freshly branded with the original brands blotted out. The Tom Green party cut out 46 head that could be identified, whereupon three men, accompanied by thirty armed cowboys, rode up and demanded that the cattle be returned to the main herd. Kimble County Sheriff J. M. Reynolds and his posse then came up to the pen and took possession of the cattle, which were claimed by Burt and his partner Ike Baker, who said they had bought the cattle. In the end, only 16 of the cattle could be personally sworn to by the Tom Green cattlemen actually present, the rest of the brands being too badly burned and blotched to be positively identifiable.[45] Frustrating and dangerous as it was, this incident eventually led to the exposure of the corrupt county officers and the forced resignation of Sheriff Reynolds.

On February 22, settler Felix Burton wrote to Major Jones, commending him for stationing Company D in Kimble County but urging him to move it to the forks of the Llano, where it would be more effective. Burton expressed his desire to talk personally with Major Jones during the coming spring, to help him more fully grasp the magnitude of the lawlessness and crime that was going on. Burton went on to describe the high level of criminal activity that was going on in the county, which he characterized as being "everything from Murder down to the lowest grade of thief that you can think of—this county seems to be the great headquarters for men loaded with crime from all other parts of the state."[46]

Events in neighboring Menard County during the last week of February 1877 demonstrate just how bold the Kimble County confederation had become. Bill Rice, a McCulloch County stockman, and two neighbors trailed horse thieves Ben Anderson and Jim Love to the camp of J. A. "Black" Burt in northeastern Kimble County with help from Menard County Deputy Sheriff Dick Godfrey. With assistance from Company D Rangers, they captured Anderson and Love. The next morning, Deputy Godfrey took custody of the two outlaws, and with the help of Rice and his friends, escorted them to the Fort McKavett guardhouse for safekeeping.

On the afternoon of February 27, shortly after Anderson and Love had been placed in the guardhouse, Dick Dublin and a band of Kimble County men arrived and attempted to rescue them. A pitched gun battle broke out along the San Saba River, during which two of Dublin's men, including Jim Deaton, were wounded.

Newly appointed Menard County Sheriff J. H. Comstock and a posse of citizens soon arrived at the site of the gun fight, surrounded Dublin and his men, and demanded their surrender. Under Dublin's leadership, the Kimble County men refused to give up their weapons, and Sheriff Comstock's possemen were unwilling to risk injury by enforcing the sheriff's order during a night action. The standoff was finally resolved when Dublin agreed to report the next morning, with his men, to a Menard County justice of the peace, whereupon Sheriff Comstock's posse disbanded and went home to bed. Dublin and his men did not show up the next morning at the justice of the peace court.[47]

### Major Jones's Spy

In the meantime, Major Jones's spy, H. B. Waddill, had slipped away to Mason, from where he wrote a letter to Major Jones on February 27.[48] Waddill described Kimble County as a "thief's stronghold, the two forks of the Llanos being lined with them." They were organized, expert, and bold, making forays into adjoining counties and obliterating legal cattle brands by burning them out. "Every one that is not known is looked upon as an enemy. . . . [T]he county is unsafe to travel through."

He named residents who harbored outlaws, such as Tom Doran and County Judge [William] Potter. "Old Man [Jimmy] Dublin's may well be called the thieves' house." He identified County Brand Inspector J. A. "Black" Burt as the head man of the cattle rustlers, and went on to identify other prominent settlers who were involved in the outlaw confederation: Justice of the Peace Robert "Squire" Anderson, Robert McIver, and even the widow of deceased rancher Rance Moore, Black Burt's mother-in-law.

Ranger Waddill named wanted fugitives living in the area: "Coburn . . . who wants to kill every stranger who comes into the neighborhood, fearing he is a detective"; Dick and Dell Dublin; "Black" Burt and Tom Doran; Frank Burk, John

Burleson, Caleb Hall, Bill Deal, Bill Allison, Bob and John McIver, and "numerous others that I could name are in the county."

He informed Major Jones that County Commissioner Felix Burton and several other citizens were fearful for their lives, having received threats from "Black" Burt and his cohorts. Further, that Sheriff Reynolds was acting as cattle inspector, and would "tally any brand you give him . . . and accept anyone as bondsman." And that the sheriff had written a note alerting a member of the confederation "to stay out of the way," as he had a warrant for his arrest, but that the wanted man lost the note, and Felix Burton now had it in his possession.

Waddill closed his letter by listing other citizens who could be trusted: W. F. Gilliland, E. K. Kountz, J. E. Temple, and Ben Pepper.[49] He assured Major Jones that Deputy Sheriff Denman was reliable and was cooperating with Lieutenant Frank Moore, who was commanding Company D, Frontier Battalion, now stationed on Bear Creek, six miles west of Junction City. He passed along Felix Burton's recommendation for a Ranger Company to be stationed at the forks of the Llano, or just downstream, at the mouth of the Johnson Fork of the Llano, "as their presence in the immediate neighborhood was necessary for the protection of life and property."[50]

### First Stirrings of Citizen Resistance

On March 14, Company D Rangers arrested three men in the South Llano valley, charged with cattle theft; one of the men was Tom Potter. Then they went to the Jimmy Dublin homestead at night, where they attempted to arrest the wanted fugitive Dick Dublin. Dublin was fired upon four times as he made his break, without effect, and he escaped.[51] On March 19, they arrested Tom Doran on the South Llano on suspicion of harboring thieves.[52]

On March 22, Lieutenant Frank Moore wrote to Major Jones:

> The good citizens of the county have organized themselves to assist us in getting out the bad ones. The thieves of the county have taken up arms [in the night] against those that assisted, and have been making strong threats, but I don't think there will be any killing done, though some are considerably excited over the matter . . . two men came to camp, saying their lives were threatened.[53]

Moore's March 22 letter provides the first indication that some law-abiding citizens of Kimble County were beginning to line up with Moore's Company D Rangers. To assist the Rangers and oppose the confederation they had secretly organized a resistance party that could provide intelligence and support. The problem was that there were not enough of them.

On April 5, Sergeant Sieker and seven Company D Rangers had arrested Kimble County Sheriff J. M. Reynolds at Junction City, charged with fraudulent inspection of cattle, and delivered him to the sheriff of Menard County. The arrest of Sheriff Reynolds may well have emboldened long-suffering Kimble County citizens to openly demonstrate their opposition to the confederation: on April 8, thirteen settlers assisted Lieutenant Moore's detachment of *Texas Rangers* in capturing three fugitives, all wanted for livestock theft.[54]

It was the first time individual citizens had openly taken a stand against the confederation.

### Jones Decides to Act

Major Jones received another alarming letter, from Kerr County Justice of the Peace M. A. McFarland in late March, attesting to the lawless conditions as well as to impending violence between aroused citizens from neighboring counties—bent on vigilante justice—and the Kimble County outlaws.[55] McFarland urged prompt action. On March 31, Jones wrote Mason County Attorney Henry M. Holmes:

> Please write me at Junction City . . . and give me the particulars of the information you have in regard to the letter written from Concho jail to the County Judge of Kimble [County] about the rebranded cattle[,] and then I can prove the contents of it, if you know. Also any other information or suspicions you may have of his or the Sheriff's complicity with the thieves of that county, as I wish to have them both investigated when District Court meets there. . . . I have a letter written by the Sheriff which I think will convict him.[56]

Holmes responded on April 7, indicating his information came through one "Murray" secondhand:

> Black Burt had a fellow inmate in the Concho guard house write a letter for him [Burt could not write] to [C]ounty Judge Potter of Kimble County, alerting him to warn "the boys" that Tankersl[e]y was coming down and to get certain brands of cattle and horses out of the way, [and] change brands. . . . Suggest Jones communicate directly to Murray at Lipan Springs.[57]

On March 30, District Judge W. A. Blackburn asked Major Jones for a Ranger escort so he could hold court in Kimble County, starting the fifth Monday in April. On April 2, Jones promised Blackburn the escort, indicated that he would have three companies in that county by the fifteenth of April and would "scour it thoroughly before the time for your court," and advised that it was imperative that court be held. Jones went on: "Sheriff Runnels [Reynolds] and County Judge Potter should both be removed [as] they are beyond doubt in league with the thieves." Blackburn responded four days later: "I will be very thankful indeed for an escort. I do not think it safe for me to travel through that country without one—and I know I cannot hold court without your assistance"[58]

Having already learned by experience that the confederation maintained an active network of lookouts and spies, Major Jones took precautions to avoid alerting anyone of his impending invasion. On April 11, Jones ordered supplies from Faltin and Schreiner's store in Kerrville to be delivered to Junction City on April 20 or 21, "not earlier or later," and he instructed that the teamsters were not to know their destination until they left Kerrville.[59] The same day he wrote Lieutenant Frank Moore, commanding Company D, then camped on the North Llano:

> I wish you to send 3 men who know where everybody lives on both Llanos and Johnson Fork, to meet me at Paint Rock [at the head of] South Llano next Wednesday evening of the 18th inst. Let them bring rations enough for two days after they get there and *remain there until I arrive.*
>
> You will move the balance of your company, except two or three to keep camp, with 10 days rations, to Junction City, on the evening of the 20th and remain there until you hear from me. I expect to reach there on that day. Do not let anyone know of my coming, except the three men you send to Paint Rock, and charge them not to mention it to anyone.
>
> I will bring Coldwell's and Dolan's Companies with me and will make a general "roundup" of Kimble County, but want it kept secret until we are ready to make the break.[60]

On April 12, in anticipation of his Kimble County operation, Jones asked Adjutant General Steele to ship thirty improved Winchester carbines and sufficient cartridges to Fort McKavett, in care of William Lehne, general merchant. He had learned that the Kimble County outlaws had already bought all the available ammunition in the area, "and have not yet as much as they want."[61]

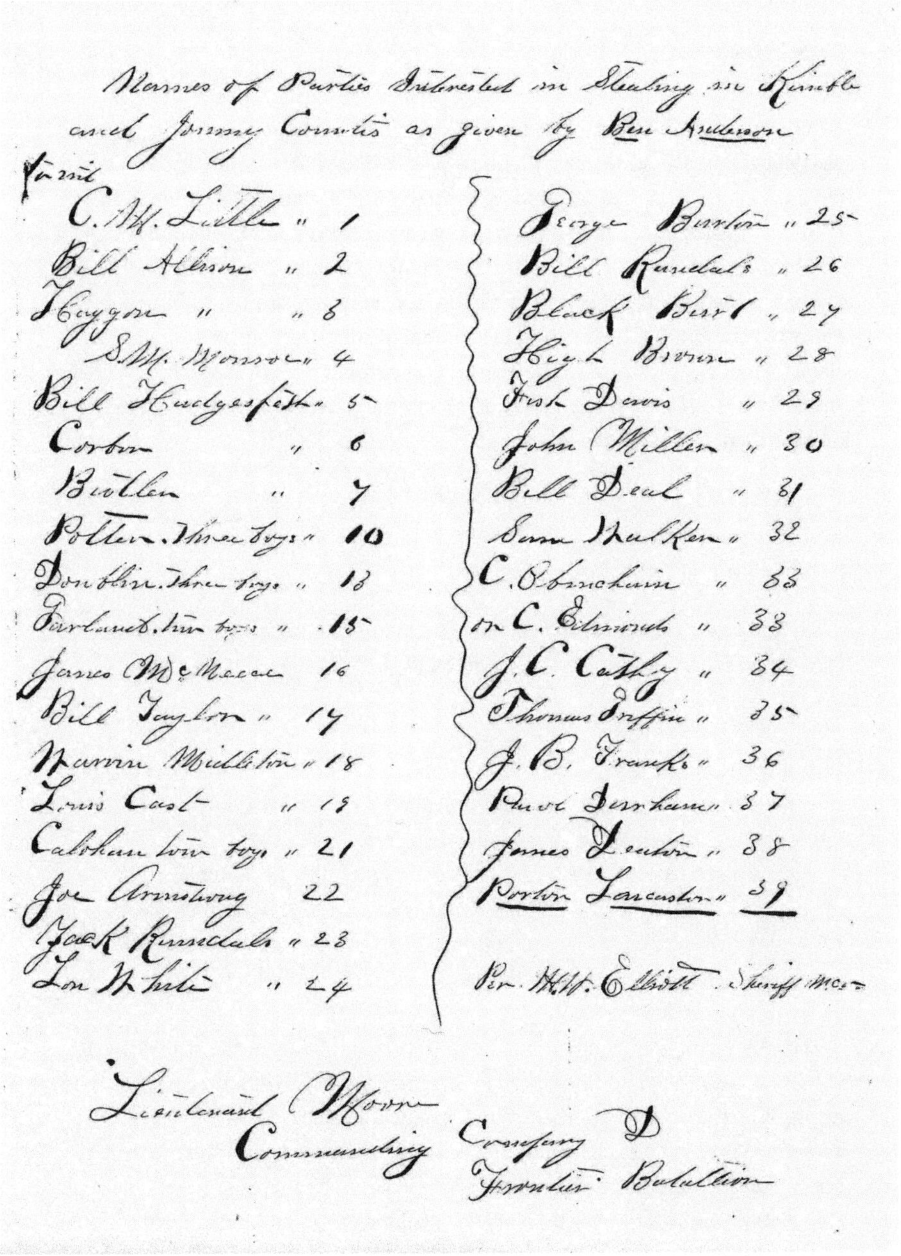

Names of Parties Interested in Stealing in Kimble and Menard Counties as given by Ben Anderson

C. M. Little " 1
Bill Allison " 2
Haggon " " 3
S. M. Monroe " 4
Bill Hudgespeth " 5
Corbin " 6
Butler " 7
Potter. three boys " 10
Doublin. three boys " 13
Parland. two boys " 15
James McMeans 16
Bill Taylor " 17
Marvin Middleton " 18
Louis Cast " 19
Calbhun two boys " 21
Joe Armstrong 22
Jack Rundals " 23
Lon White " 24

George Burton " 25
Bill Rundals " 26
Black Bird " 27
High Brown " 28
Josh Davis " 29
John Miller " 30
Bill Deal " 31
Sam Walker " 32
C. Robinson " 33
on C. Edmonds " 33
J. C. Cathy " 34
Thomas Griffin " 35
J. B. Franks " 36
Powel Denham " 37
James Denton " 38
Porter Lancaster " 39

Per W. W. Elliott - Sheriff Mc—

Lieutenant Moore
Commanding Company D
Frontier Battalion

Figure 11. Suspect list given to Major John B. Jones, commander of the Frontier Battalion, Texas Rangers, by Lieutenant Frank Moore, commander of Company D. This "hit list" was provided by prisoner Ben Anderson to Menard County Deputy Sheriff W. W. Elliott, who passed it on to Lieutenant Moore, probably in April 1877, for use in the Kimble County Roundup. In the left column of names, note "Potter, three boys" followed by "Doublin [sic], three boys." Courtesy of Texas State Library and Archives Commission, Austin.

Other useful inside intelligence was garnered by Lieutenant Moore, through the deputy sheriff of Menard County, W. W. Elliott, from one Ben Anderson, whom Moore's men had arrested in February 1877, charged with horse theft.[62] Before being sentenced to five years in prison, Anderson provided Moore with an extensive list of outlaws in the Kimble County criminal confederation, "Names of Parties Interested in Stealing in Kimble and Joining Counties as given by Ben Anderson, to wit."[63] The list contained a total of thirty-nine names, most of them already frequently present in the Rangers' Reports of Scouts, Records of Arrests, and Monthly Returns in Kimble County over the previous two years. Among the thirty-nine names were the following:

> Bill Allison
> Potter—three boys
> Doublin [*sic*]—three boys

Major Jones was about to cast his net. It would envelop most of the Kimble County confederation, including—eventually—the Potters and the Dublins.

### The Murder of Jim Williams

Before Jones and his Rangers could arrive, however, the confederation carried out a brutal murder, which sent an unmistakable message, warning Kimble County settlers of the dangers of resistance.

Jim Williams was the second son of an early pioneer family that had lived in the North Llano valley since before 1870. In 1875, at age twenty, he married; by 1877 he and his wife, Margaret, and infant daughter Cora were living at their ranch establishment about two miles southwest of the Dublins, in the South Llano valley on the east side of the river.

On April 16, Dell Dublin and Luke Cathey, probably accompanied by Roll Dublin, Bill Allison, and Mack Potter, rode up to the Williams ranch. Dell Dublin, having heard that Williams had slaughtered and butchered a beef—presumably an animal that Dublin claimed—then picked a quarrel with Williams and shot him down. Williams's two younger brothers were helpless onlookers; one, probably Harry, age fifteen, picked up his dead brother's gun and shot at Dublin as he rode out through the corral, narrowly missing the murderer.[64]

The ramifications of this murder intimidated many Kimble County settlers into subsequent fearful silence about the confederation for more than three years.

(Above) Figure 12. Roll (*left*) and Dell Dublin, about 1875. Courtesy of Kimble County Historical Commission. (Image digitally enhanced, with permission.)
(Below) Figure 13. Roll (*left*) and Dell Dublin, about 1879. Courtesy of Kimble County Historical Commission. (Image digitally enhanced, with permission.)

# 7 :: The Roundup

**P**aint Rock Spring, so-called for Native American pictographs on adjacent limestone cliffs, was a lonely and remote place in northeastern Edwards County. It was also an important place because it was the headwater spring of the South Llano River, providing the first reliable water for riders on the trail from Fort Clark and Camp Wood northward to Fort McKavett. Once northbound travelers left Hackberry Spring (the corresponding headwater spring of the East Nueces River) on their way across the upland plains atop the Edwards Plateau, there was no reliable water for about twenty horseback miles until they descended into the South Llano drainage and finally arrived, parched, at Paint Rock Spring.

**The Operation**

About thirty-five Texas Rangers of the Frontier Battalion gathered there secretly on the evening of April 18, 1877. They included twelve men from Lieutenant Dolan's Company F under Sergeant Jones, about twenty men of Captain Coldwell's Company A, three men from Lieutenant Moore's Company D, sent to act as guides and scouts, and Major John B. Jones, commanding.[1] Their task was to systematically scour the drainage basins of the North and South Llano Rivers, arrest every suspicious man who could not satisfactorily explain his presence and occupation, and converge, with their prisoners, on Junction City, the new county seat that was taking shape at the forks of the Llano.

After hearing their assignments from Major Jones, the men spent the rest of the evening around the several campfires, talking with their assigned squad mates, looking to their horses and pack mules, inspecting and readying their gear, cleaning their weapons and ammunition. The sergeants made their night-watch assignments.

They were mostly young, in their early twenties; their leaders were typically only a few years older, except for Major Jones, then aged forty-two. They had enlisted for adventure and because they had useful frontier skills, such as tracking, marksmanship, and horsemanship, and because they wanted to serve Texas. They all knew that tomorrow they would be tested, that there might well be real trouble.

The next morning, Thursday, April 19, 1877, the "Kimble County Roundup"

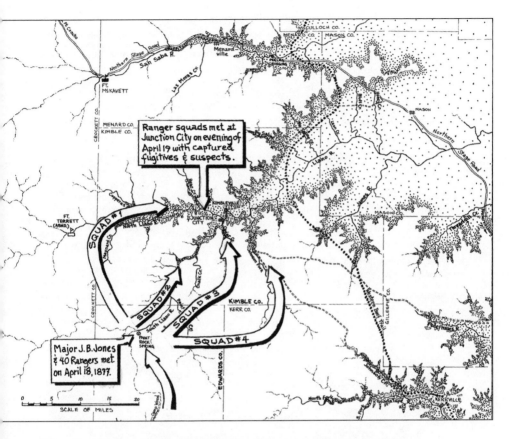

Map 6. Kimble County Roundup. On the first day of the operation, four squads of Texas Rangers swept the north- and east-flowing streams of the Llano watershed and met, with their prisoners, at Junction City. On the second day, Major John B. Jones sent squads to scour the stream valleys on the north side of the Llano (Copperas, Bexar, Gentry, Red, and Big Saline Creeks). Lieutenant Frank Moore brought a detachment of Company D Rangers to Junction City on the second day to serve as guards of the forty-one captured suspects, pending their trials the following week. The stippled area of the map is the outcrop area of the Trinity Formation (sandy soils); the white area is the outcrop area of the Edwards Limestone.

got under way.[2] Jones divided his men into four detachments (see map 6). The first squad rode twenty miles northwest to the head of Maynard Creek, followed it to its confluence with the North Llano, and then traveled eastward down that stream twenty miles to Junction City. The second group headed northeast, directly down the valley of the South Llano, thirty miles to Junction City. The third rode twenty miles northeast to the head of Cedar Creek and then followed it downstream, northwest, ten miles to Junction City. The fourth detachment rode twenty-five miles eastward across the plateau to the headwaters of the Johnson Fork of the Llano, scouted down that stream fifteen miles to its juncture with the main Llano, and then turned back west five miles to Junction City.[3]

All four detachments converged on Junction City, arriving there in the evening of April 19. Suspects were shackled and confined in a "bull pen," to await disposition by Judge Blackburn's district court.[4] Major Jones had achieved a nearly complete surprise—only three persons in the county knew of his coming—and the Rangers' arrival was greeted enthusiastically by large turnouts of citizens, offering any help they could, further affirming the existence of a growing contingent of law-abiding citizens that—for the first time—were willing to openly demonstrate their support.[5]

The next day, in a counterpart operation, five Ranger squads swept the northern and eastern drainages of Kimble County, searching Copperas, Bear, Gentry, Red, and Big Saline Creeks, and returned to Junction City with their captives: every man who could not credibly account for himself.[6] In the meantime, Lieutenant Moore and about fourteen Company D Rangers had arrived in Junction City to look after the accumulating prisoners. The third day, Saturday, April 21, was spent in "mopping-up" operations.

In describing the operation later to Adjutant General Steele, Major Jones gave special praise to his men:

> The work was very fatiguing, much of it having to be done at night. Several parties were caught by surrounding their houses, or finding their camp fires in the woods at night. Sometimes we came in contact with their women and were terribly tongue-lashed by them for searching their houses and arresting the[ir] men . . . no man failed to come cheerfully and promptly up to his duty, or . . . [failed] to give prompt consideration and good treatment to those with whom they came in contact . . . [and] each man seemed to take a personal interest in catching everyone he was ordered to arrest.[7]

## Results

In all, forty-one arrests were made, thirty-seven in Kimble County. The prisoners included men wanted in eighteen different Texas counties.[8] Most remarkably, not a shot had been fired.[9] Among those arrested over the two-week period of the roundup and subsequent district court session were:

Bill Allison, charged with theft in Kimble and Bosque Counties, and accessory to the murder of Jim Williams in Kimble County;[10]

Roll Dublin, charged with theft in Kimble County and accessory to the murder of Jim Williams in Kimble County;

Sheriff J. M. Reynolds, charged with theft in Kimble County, and willfully allowing escape of prisoners in Kimble County;

Frank Potter, charged with theft in Menard County; and

James [K. P.] Potter, charged with theft in Kaufmann County.[11]

But Major Jones was keenly aware that several fugitives, men he particularly wanted, had managed to slip through his net. "Four of the worst men in the county" had committed a murder three days before he arrived, "[and] three of them left the county immediately."[12] On April 27, Adjutant General Steele wrote Captain J. C. Sparks commanding Company E at Lampasas:

Have received telegram from Major Jones at Junction City in which he states that "Dick Dublin, Dell Dublin, Mack Porter [Potter], and Lew [Luke] Cathey, whom I want here, dodged me and have gone to Bailey's, their relatives on Bull Creek, northwestern Travis Co." You will send a detachment to Bailey's neighborhood, and if any of the above parties can be arrested, hold them and notify Maj. Jones.[13]

Even so, the operation had been very successful, and Jones's satisfaction with his Rangers' performance is evident in his April 23 report to Judge Blackburn:

We are cutting out some work for your court next week and I shall remain here to help you make it up. . . . The violaters [sic] of the law are mighty scared up and are "hiding out," while the honest law-abiding citizens are much gratified . . . and are doing all in their power to assist us in ridding the country of lawless characters with which it has been inflicted for some time past. . . . I think one term of your court is all that is lacking now to make Kimble a civil and law-abiding county, safe for good people.[14]

Figure 14. Judge W. A. Blackburn, justice of the 17th Judicial District of Texas, 1876–96. The photograph was taken in the early 1880s. Judge Blackburn presided at the first district court session held in Kimble County and all subsequent sessions for nineteen years. Courtesy of Steve Grimes, San Angelo, Texas. (Image digitally enhanced.)

Major Jones could be forgiven for his optimism. As it would turn out, there was still a great deal of law enforcement work to be done before Kimble County became orderly and law-abiding. The Dublins and the Potters—and their protective, intractable, coercive web of interrelated families—would see to that.

### Holding the First District Court

The next week, Major Jones and a Ranger squad traveled to Fredericksburg, where Judge Blackburn had held district court, and escorted him and District Attorney Frank Wilkes back to Junction City, near where Kimble County's first district court would convene on Monday, April 30, 1877.[15]

Judge Blackburn held the first district court at Kimbleville, the first county seat, about two miles downriver from Junction City, under some large live oak trees on the west bank of the Llano River:

> There was no jail, and prisoners were chained to trees near the center of the proceedings. Boards were nailed from the big[gest] tree to a smaller one nearby, and such was used as a desk by the [J]udge. Using a piece of knotted live-oak branch for a gavel, the court sternly knocked for order, and with a law book and a docket before him, the . . . Judge gravely commanded the Sheriff to announce that the court was in session.[16]

Of course, some of the suspects originally brought in by Ranger squads were not on Major Jones's fugitive list and were released upon examination. Others who were wanted for offenses in other counties were placed in secure jails at Fredericksburg and Menardville, awaiting return for their trials.[17]

A grand jury was promptly convened. After presentation of all evidence, including testimony by courageous law-abiding citizens, twenty-five indictments were returned. Writing from Fort McKavett on May 8, Jones reported:

> The District Judge and District Attorney would not have come to Kimble [County] if I had not sent them an escort. . . . Many of the good citizens have expressed the same opinion and say that they would not have come to court if my force had not been there to protect them against the outlaws and desperadoes. . . . A grand jury of good men was secured who worked industriously and fearlessly. They presented twenty-five bills of indictment and would have found many more but for the absence of witnesses and lack of time to procure evidence. . . . Several indictments were returned against the sheriff . . . and the county judge, but [they] resigned during court.[18]

J. M. Reynolds, sheriff since October 18, 1876, was delivered to jail in Menard County by Corporal Rhodes and two other Company D Rangers, who remained to guard the jail. It is possible that Will Potter, county judge since February 15, 1876, was also taken to jail along with Reynolds, but his resignation during the district court session may have sufficed for him to avoid the disgrace of incarceration.[19]

Members of the grand jury appointed J. B. Gorman as the new sheriff, N. Q. Patterson as the new County Judge, and George Perryman as the new County Attorney, relieving Henry W. Shannon, whose 1876 appointment Judge Blackburn revoked. Apparently, J. A. "Black" Burt was also soon relieved of his job as county hide inspector, as William B. Meeks was appointed to the vacant post at the next term of district court in November 1877.[20]

Unfortunately, the pool of solid citizens used in constituting the grand jury had so depleted the law-abiding population of the infant county that not enough candidates were left over to form a twelve-man jury to hear the cases. As a consequence, all the indictments were carried over to the next term of court, and the indicted felons were placed in jails in adjoining counties.[21] Most who were not accused of capital crimes, of course, made their bonds and were bailed out, pending their trials. Many of these men left the country and never returned.

The Kimble County Roundup was over, and the entrenched outlaw confederation had been dealt a substantial blow. After earlier forming a secret resistance organization against the outlaws, some citizens had now publicly stood up in support of civic order and law, by standing with the Rangers during the roundup, and by forming a grand jury that returned indictments against many members of the confederation. Although they were outnumbered by the outlaws, the order and law contingent had set an essential precedent, and other examples of courageous actions by individual citizens would follow over the next few years.

To reinforce the advent of law and order in Kimble County, Major Jones decided to keep Lieutenant Moore and his twenty Rangers at their encampment at the mouth of Bear Creek in the North Llano valley just six miles west of Junction City.[22] As it turned out, the Bear Creek site would be the frequent headquarters of a Ranger company for another five years before Kimble County was finally capable of maintaining its own order.

The Kimble County confederation proved to be resilient, however—prisoners escaped frequently from rickety jails; friendly or intimidated juries routinely acquitted their fellow citizens; and wanted men from the eastern counties continued to migrate into Kimble County, fleeing the clutches of the law. The work of the Rangers—and the law-abiding citizens—was just beginning.

# 8 :: Ranger Law

The forks of the Llano was a rough place, even by 1877 standards. An objective measure of just how unsettled and violent it was can be gained simply by reading the Ranger accounts of their patrols and arrests in Kimble and adjoining counties for the eighteen-month period from May 1877 to October 1878. Names of the Kimble County confederation are conspicuous by their frequency in the Ranger records, involved in a variety of offences. Cross-border raids by Indians from Mexico were also more frequent in and around Kimble County during 1878 than in previous years.

Following the Kimble County Roundup, Company D operated out of its Bear Creek headquarters for the next four months. Lieutenant Frank Moore's Rangers kept up a continuous series of ever-widening patrols, with occasional arrests of wanted men in addition to routine apprehension of horse thieves and cattle rustlers. Moore's men maintained a steady lookout for the Dublin boys and their associates, aware of Major Jones's frustration that they had escaped his net during the roundup.

On May 20, Moore and nine Rangers sighted two of the Dublins (wanted for the April 16 murder of their neighbor, Jim Williams) near their home but lost them in adjacent dense cedar brakes. The Rangers remained camped nearby for three days without again sighting their quarry.[1]

On May 28, Corporal Merrill's seven-man detachment stumbled onto J. A. "Black" Burt, the notorious cattle thief, at the head of Bear Creek, and took him to the Menardville jail, from which he promptly escaped and was again at large.[2]

On July 10, Sergeant Lane and seven Rangers went to Dublin's ranch on the South Llano, attempting to capture one or more of the Dublin boys: "[We] remained encamped nearby for four days, keeping a close lookout for lawless parties that have been in the habit of stopping at this place (especially his two [three] sons) when in the country." The Rangers returned to their Bear Creek camp on July 15 without encountering the fugitives.[3]

On August 10, Sheriff Gorman asked for a Ranger squad to help him corral "a party of ruffians [who] came into Junction City, got on a drunk, and set the Sheriff at defiance." Corporal Merrill and seven men arrested "Black" Burt and delivered him to the sheriff; Burt paid his fine and was released.[4]

Figure 15. Lieutenant Nelson O. Reynolds, commander, Company E, Frontier Battalion, Texas Rangers, about 1875. Courtesy of Western History Collections, University of Oklahoma.

### Reynolds Arrives

Lieutenant Frank Moore resigned his commission on August 31, 1877, and Company D was sent to South Texas to address unrest along the border involving Mexican raiders.[5] But before the end of November, newly reorganized Company E reoccupied Moore's previous camp at the mouth of Bear Creek on the North Llano. Commanding Company E was the newly promoted but already legendary Lieutenant Nelson O. Reynolds, recognized by his peers and subordinates alike as "Reynolds, the Intrepid."[6] Under his relentless leadership, the Kimble County confederation would be dealt a further series of heavy blows over the next seven months.

Departing Austin on October 23, 1877, Lieutenant Reynolds and Company E escorted Bill Allison and Wes Johnson to Junction City for their trials, continued from the May 1877 district court.[7] This time Judge Blackburn convened the court in a blacksmith shop in Junction City. As reported on November 5, 1877, by a correspondent for the Mason, Texas, *News-Item,*

> there were twenty-five cases on the criminal docket, to wit: three for murder, one for theft of a wagon, nine for theft of cattle, one for threat to take life, one for permitting prisoners to escape, two for horse stealing, and eight [for which] no arrests had been made.

> Only one case [was tried], the State vs. Wm. Allison, who was charged with a little killing scrape [accessory to the murder of Jim Williams], and the defendant acquitted. Four cases were dismissed and the balance continued.

On Friday night the Indians paid us a visit and confiscated fourteen
horses belonging to natives of the county seat, besides Amos Coyote
Grey, a gallant steed belonging to Judge Cooley of Fredericksburg.[8]


After district court adjourned, Company E took station at the old Ranger headquarters on Bear Creek, vacant since Moore's departure in early September. Then
Lieutenant Reynolds began sending Company E Rangers on intensive scouts for
fugitives and livestock thieves.

On November 21, Reynolds and ten men went in pursuit of the Dublin brothers, both wanted for murder.[9] They captured Dell Dublin working unarmed in a
corral at Luke Stone's ranch, about four miles from Junction City. Dublin, angered
by his inability to escape, tore open the front of his shirt and dared the Rangers to
shoot. While he was being arrested, his older brother Dick appeared, approaching
within gunshot range of the Rangers. Alerted by his brother's shouted warning,
Dick Dublin wheeled his horse back into the brush and escaped in a volley of
misdirected gunfire.[10]

Two days later, Corporal Gillett and five men conveyed Dell Dublin to Llano
for his habeas corpus trial, the results of which are not known.[11] Dublin either
escaped from the Llano jail or was released, possibly on bond—which seems unlikely, as he was charged with murder—or, more likely, because of some legal
technicality, such as absence of key witnesses. Either way, Dell Dublin was again
at liberty by the end of November 1877.

Squads from Company E continued their frequent patrols throughout December, focusing especially on fugitives Dick Dublin and Stark Reynolds, but neither
man was found. During the eight months following the Kimble County Roundup, there had been no stage robberies in the region. But on December 15 and again
on December 25, the San Antonio–Fort McKavett stagecoach was robbed again,
near Pegleg Crossing.[12] As before, the robbers remained unidentified.

On December 27, 1877, Private Anglin and six men assisted Sheriff Gorman
in arresting J. A. "Black" Burt, James K. P. Potter, and E. T. Denson for theft of
hogs, and placed them in his custody.[13] The trio was apprehended with four head-
less hogs in their possession, decapitation having removed the evidence of ear
markings that would have identified their true owners. Burt was also wanted for
previously breaking jail in Menard County.[14] The prisoners were escorted to the
Burnet jail early in January 1878.[15]

Lieutenant Reynolds continued the pressure into the new year. Company E's
Monthly Return reported that Reynolds sent Sergeant Nevill and four men on
January 12 to assist the sheriff of Tom Green County, who was following a trail

of stolen cattle.[16] The trail led over to the South Llano, where the cattle were soon located late in the afternoon.

As Nevill was scouting around the herd, he spied a lone horseman riding toward them in the dusk. The newcomer almost rode over them, whereupon the concealed Rangers stood up, presented their guns, announced themselves, and ordered him to surrender. "Yes, like hell!" he responded, and spurred his horse into a thick cedar brake, followed by another ineffective volley from the Rangers. The notorious Dick Dublin had escaped again.

As related by Ranger Corporal J. B. Gillett, with more than a touch of humor:

> Sergeant Nevill returned to camp with about fifty head of cattle on which the brand had been defaced with a hot iron, but he had let the most notorious criminal in the county escape. Lieutenant Reynolds was disappointed at this, and said he did not understand how four crack rangers could let a man ride right over them and then get away. He declared his . . . cook could have killed Dublin had he been in their place [which] mortified the boys a great deal.[17]

### The End of Dick Dublin

Declaring that Dick Dublin seemed "a regular Jonah to this company," a frustrated Lieutenant Reynolds promised to keep a scout constantly in the field after the notorious outlaw: if he could not capture him, he was determined to make his life miserable. On January 16, Reynolds sent Corporal Jim Gillett and five men on another patrol, searching for the elusive outlaw, and admonishing Gillett not to let Dublin escape if he encountered the fugitive.[18]

Avoiding spying eyes in the vicinity of Junction City, Corporal Gillett led his squad south from the mouth of Bear Creek into the broken country west of the South Llano river valley. They rode to the head of Packsaddle Creek (now known as Cajac or Kyak Creek), turned down the canyon to Tom Potter's ranch, where "Old Man" Potter lived with his sons and where Dick Dublin was known to frequent.[19]

Finding no one home, the Rangers then headed south across country to the headwaters of the South Llano River, where Gillett thought Dublin might be hanging out near a brush stock pen, which cow hunters had built to contain captured range cattle. But the place was deserted.

Gillett's squad continued their patrol of the upper South Llano country for a third day and then returned to the Tom Potter ranch at dusk on the fourth day, January 19. Two Rangers stayed with the horses while the other four went to watch the Potter headquarters. Gillett spied a horseman riding down the opposite hillside toward the one-room Potter cabin. The four Rangers then slipped along the creek bed to within about fifty yards of the cabin, near where Tom Potter and two sons were unloading some hogs from a wagon into a pen. Now they could see the horse tied outside the cabin's single door.

The four Rangers rose from the creek bed already at a full sprint, intent on capturing the horseman who had ridden up to Potter's camp. Tom Potter saw them coming and called, "Run, Dick, run! Here come the Rangers!" whereupon they knew they had their man.[20]

With no time to mount his horse, Dick Dublin headed for the brush, "running as fast as a big man could." Gillett ordered him to stop, but Dublin kept running, whereupon the Ranger corporal snapped off a shot with his Winchester, without effect. Dublin disappeared momentarily and then Gillett spied him running up a little north-reaching ravine east of the Potter premises, stopped,

> drew a bead on him, and again ordered him to halt. As he ran, Dublin threw his hand back under his coat as though he were attempting to draw a pistol. I fired. My bullet struck the fugitive in the small of the back just over the right hip bone and passed out near his left collar bone. It killed him instantly. He was bending over as he ran, and this caused the unusual course of my ball. . . . I examined the body to make sure it was Dublin, for I knew him intimately, as I had cow-hunted with him before I became a ranger. We found him unarmed, but he had a belt of cartridges around his waist. . . . Dublin's brothers, Roll and Dell, swore vengeance against me . . . but nothing ever came of the oath.[21]

### Rumored Indian Connections

The death of Dick Dublin drew national attention. On March 17, the *New York Times* reprinted an earlier undated report from the *Austin Gazette* celebrating the end of the Dublin gang, which alluded to the Dublins' possible Indian connections:

> In the wilds of Kimble and Menard Counties . . . for years have dwelt a gang of white men as savage as the Indians, after whom they model in

their modes of living. This gang for 9 or 10 years [4 or 5 years] acknowledged Dick and Dell Dublin as leaders. They halted at no crime, they feared no law. After they passed beyond the Pecos [they would] return as painted Indians, to rob, murder, and ravish on the credit of the red man. . . . Dick Dublin is dead, killed by the rangers in resisting arrest. Dell Dublin is in jail. Others of the renegade band are killed, and the rest are scattered into Mexico. Kimble and Menard Counties are quiet now."[22]

This possible Indian connection of the Dublins echoed a report from the *Galveston Daily News* from the previous month that described Dick Dublin as a "daring cut-throat and renegade who has headed Indian raids into Kimble and Menard Counties for the past seven [five] years."[23]

Regarding their claims that the Dublin gang masqueraded as Indians in their raids among frontier settlements, it is difficult to assess the trustworthiness of these two newspaper reports, as they are without attribution. Nevertheless such allegations should not be dismissed out of hand, as they may indeed rest upon unofficial rumors and official suspicions, gleaned directly or indirectly from local lawmen, U.S. military personnel, Texas Ranger officers and men, or local settlers. Certainly, the strategy of conducting horse-stealing raids disguised as Mexican Indians would have been an ingenious way to deflect suspicion from white renegades operating in Texas to a widely feared and despised nemesis coming from Mexico.

Other incidents also seemed to indicate that some of the "Indian" horse-stealing raids in Kimble County, particularly on the South Llano, may have been carried out by white men masquerading as Indians, such as the reported Indian raid of May 9, 1878, that resulted in a Mr. Leonard's loss of two fine horses, which he later recovered from a San Antonio auctioneer who was unable to provide the name of the person from whom the horses were acquired.[24] In another horse-stealing raid on the South Llano on January 30, 1879, first ascribed to Indians, Captain Roberts concluded that it was probably the work of white men.[25]

Moreover, from 1876 through 1880, the South Llano valley seemed to be a preferred place for horse thievery to originate in, or for fleeing horse thieves—Indian or Anglo-Saxon—to move through. Perhaps it was coincidental that it also just happened to be the neighborhood of the Dublins and Potters, and many of their confederates.[26] Most coincidental, of course, was the fact that the sons of Tom Potter were of Indian descent—the Indian cousins.

Finally, there was the peculiar attitude prevailing among the local citizenry, with regard to informing the Rangers about Indian raids, as described by Captain Dan Roberts in June 1878:

> The people here seem to be contrary about bringing any information to me about Indians. I think they will get over their pouts after awhile— when they find out it will not profit them. My men obtained news about Indians being in [i.e., in the Llano valleys] by accident, and was [sic] not certain that the report was true—even when they went to hunt for the trail. They [the Indians] stole about 20 head of horses.[27]

### Kimble County Reactions

Predictably, Dick Dublin's death generated diametrically opposed responses from the local community. In reporting the details of Dublin's death, Lieutenant Reynolds indicated that some threats had been made by Dublin's friends, but he expected things to settle down in a few days. He assured Major Jones that the Company E Rangers had the support of the law-abiding citizens and claimed that his Rangers presently oversaw the quietest sector of the frontier.[28]

On March 27, 1878, Reynolds alerted Major Jones to the continuing unsettled state of affairs in Kimble County. Soliciting Major Jones's presence at the approaching term of district court, and seeking his commander's counsel if Corporal Gillett and his squad were to be indicted for killing Dick Dublin, Reynolds closed with the laconic observation that "some of the citizens say that Company 'E' cannot keep order here during Court, but I am of the opinion that we can without much trouble."[29]

Jones responded on April 8. After cautioning Reynolds that reports had reached him that his Company E men had made enemies in Kimble County, and to take pains that, in future, his men should maintain a strictly neutral posture with regard to personal feelings in the discharge of their official duties, Jones advised that,

> if Corporal Gillett and his squad are indicted for killing Dublin they must give bond for their appearance and stand their trial. I will engage a lawyer to defend them and will probably have the case moved to Menard County for trial. I do not think there is any danger of their being indicted, however, and they need not be uneasy about it, but keep quiet and attend to their duties properly, and they will come out all right in the end. It will be impossible for me to be at Court, as I will not be able to get off from here before the first of May.[30]

Reynolds wrote back two days later, stoutly defending his men:

> I do not believe that any of them have ever done any thing or said any thing that would be considered out of our regular [d]uty. . . . On the other hand I have received many [very] insulting messages from different parties but have never given them any notice. . . . I am of the opinion that your information comes from [p]arties that are very much predisposed or from some [p]ersonal [e]nemy. . . . I would like for you to investigate this [m]atter thoroughly since it has commenced.

Reynolds concluded by assuring his commander that he had the full and vocal support of the law-abiding citizens, who were perfectly satisfied with Company E's operations in the area.[31] Responding to a personal friend on April 8, Corporal Gillett wrote that things were going pretty much as usual, and that the Dublins had made some pretty big threats.[32]

On April 16, about two weeks before the district court was scheduled to convene for the spring term, Reynolds advised Major Jones that Margaret G. Williams had written him from Fort Concho, where she and her three-year-old daughter

Figure 16. Reuben H. "Rube" Boyce (*far left*), with his brothers, about 1879. An accomplice of the Dublins and Potters, Boyce was arrested, charged with U.S. mail robbery, and confined in the Austin jail, from which he made a spectacular escape on January 4, 1880, aided by his wife, Adeline. Image courtesy of Frederica B. Wyatt.

lived with her sister's family, stating her fears that "she would be assassinated if she could not get an escort from her place to Kimble County for the next term of district court and that she could not attend court unless conveyance could be promised her."[33] This was the widow of Jim Williams, who had been murdered the preceding April 16 at his ranch on the South Llano by Dell Dublin, Lew Cathey, and other members of the confederation. It appears that she had received threats of mortal retaliation if she came to Kimble County to testify against her late husband's murderers and was seeking protection from the Rangers as a witness for the state. The confederation, even though badly wounded, was still capable of intimidating key witnesses against its brotherhood.

### Maintaining the Pressure

Lieutenant Reynolds and his Company E Rangers did not relax their pressure on the Kimble County confederation after Dick Dublin was killed. In the course of maintaining their frequent patrols and arresting various men for livestock theft and other assorted offences, they arrested Reuben H. Boyce for the 1876 murder of his brother-in-law, Justice of the Peace Robert F. Anderson, in Kimble County, and delivered him to the Kimble County sheriff in late January.[34]

On February 21 Reynolds and seven men left for Austin, carrying five prisoners, including Rube Boyce and probably the recaptured Dell Dublin, shackled in a mule-drawn wagon.[35] About ten miles east of Junction City, they passed the ranch of Stark Reynolds, a frequently sought-for fugitive wanted for murder and horse theft, who had evaded the Rangers for months.[36] By chance, they happened to encounter the wanted man, who immediately spurred his horse for the Llano bottoms, where he hoped to escape in the heavy vegetation along the river. A wild horse race ensued, punctuated by more than twenty shots, before Stark Reynolds surrendered and was brought, disarmed and handcuffed, to join the five prisoners in the wagon.[37] On the way to Austin, the six prisoners attempted to escape, using secreted fragments of hacksaw blades to cut through their shackles, but were detected and delivered safely to the Travis County jail.[38]

On March 22 Sergeant McGhee was sent in pursuit of cattle stolen in Menard County, now supposed to be in the vicinity of the Dublin and Allison ranches on South Llano. The Rangers found thirteen head of cattle, arrested Mack Potter for cattle theft, and returned to camp. Two days later they escorted him to Menard County, where they turned him over to the sheriff.[39]

### A Troubled Community

Reynolds' Rangers were not involved in the deadly gunfight that erupted in Junction City on March 4, 1878, leaving four men dead. At issue was a yoke of oxen;

the dispute was to be tried that day in a local justice of the peace court. The disputants had met on their way to the court, and Deputy Sheriff Sam Gorman, brother of Sheriff J. B. Gorman, tried to head off a fight. When the smoke cleared, all three litigants—cousins Button and Pete Brashear and their opponent, Major Wright—as well as Deputy Gorman, lay dead in the street.

Deputy Gorman, frustrated in his unsuccessful attempt to disarm the cousins, drew his pistol and shot Pete Brashear, who returned fire and killed the deputy before himself succumbing. Button Brashear then shot Major Wright several times, killing him. The fight was brought to a close when Sheriff J. B. Gorman shot and killed Button Brashear with a Winchester rifle from some distance away. The entire episode lasted no more than one minute. A total of twenty-four shots were fired; eighteen took effect and sixteen were judged later to be "dead shots."[40]

Kimble County politics were also turbulent, probably reflecting pressure and intimidation by the criminal element, now raised to a fever pitch by the killing of Dick Dublin by the Rangers. All county officers remembered that Justice of the Peace Robert F. Anderson, a Scottish immigrant, had been killed the previous year by outlaw Rube Boyce. N. Q. Patterson, who had been appointed as county judge on May 3, 1877, in place of the ousted Will Potter, himself resigned less than a year later, on March 11, 1878. So did County Treasurer John C. Kountz. J. J. Ramsey, a thirty-three-year-old family man originally from Iowa, was appointed county judge in Patterson's place but remained in office only three months before stepping down on June 11 and leaving the country, presumably in fear of his life. The county commissioners then appointed George E. Stewart, age thirty-two, a family man from New York, to succeed Ramsey, and Stewart served as head of county government for nearly two and a half years.[41]

Figure 17. John B. Gorman, sheriff of Kimble County, 1877–80 and 1882–84. Gorman was appointed when J. M. Reynolds was forced to resign by Major John B. Jones and District Judge W. A. Blackburn. Photo taken about 1880. Courtesy of Kimble County Historical Commission. (Image digitally enhanced, with permission.)

## Guarding an Intimidated Court

In addition to Company E's continuing routine patrols, most of April 1878 was taken up by duties related to the spring term of district court—its third meeting—in Junction City. Sergeant Nevill and four men went to Austin and returned to Junction City with Dell Dublin for his murder trial. Corporal Warren and two men escorted Judge Blackburn from Fredericksburg to Junction City, returning on April 28, and Corporal Gillett and two men escorted state witnesses (who had been intimidated by the Dublin party) to Junction City on April 27 for the Dublin trial. Lieutenant Reynolds moved his entire company to Junction City on April 28 "to assist Sheriff Gorman in guarding the prisoners and keeping order."[42] For the first time, the district court convened indoors, in Kimble County's brand new two-story frame courthouse.[43]

Before the court convened, Company E Rangers assisted Sheriff Gorman in guarding prisoners, including J. A. Burt, James K. P. Potter, Dell Dublin, and Lou Walton. Then, on May 5, Lieutenant Reynolds led Company E back to its regular location at the mouth of Bear Creek. Walton, Burt, and three others were apparently convicted and sent to jail in Austin. Ranger records are silent as to the results of the trials of Dell Dublin and Jimmy Potter, but they were not escorted by the Rangers eastward to secure prisons or jails, thus "not-guilty" verdicts from friendly—or intimidated—Kimble County juries may reasonably be inferred.[44]

We do not know if Margaret Williams, widow of Jim Williams, was one of the witnesses escorted by the Rangers to Junction City, or if she was able to summon up the courage to testify against her husband's murderer, Dell Dublin. The question is moot—apparently, Dublin was not convicted of the crime. Once again, the confederation had protected its own. But its power in the community was gradually waning—the threats to indict Corporal Jim Gillett and his five-man patrol for the shooting death of fugitive Dick Dublin failed to materialize at the spring term of district court, and no more was heard about retribution—legal or otherwise—from the Dublin-Potter faction.

Whether sobered into honest work by their narrow escapes from conviction, busy conducting their livestock operations elsewhere, or just operating more circumspectly in Kimble County, the names of Dell and Roll Dublin, Mack and Jim Potter, and Rube Boyce do not appear as sought-for fugitives in the Ranger records for almost a year after district court adjourned in early May 1878.[45]

Perhaps in response to political pressure from ambivalent citizens of Kimble County, or confederation allies themselves, Major Jones ordered Reynolds and Company E to move to Burnet County on May 7; three weeks later they were sent to keep order in turbulent San Saba County.[46] Although he may have alienated some Kimble County citizens (who may have been affiliated with, or sympathetic to, the confederation), Reynolds received high praise from Dr. E. G.

Figure 18. Captain Dan W. Roberts, commander, Company D, Frontier Battalion, Texas Rangers, May 1880. Courtesy of Institute of Texan Cultures, University of Texas at San Antonio.

Nicholson, surgeon of the Frontier Battalion and a close friend of Major John B. Jones. Writing to Adjutant General William Steele on May 24, Nicholson indicated that Reynolds's transfer to Burnet would give him new "opportunities . . . to display his efficiency." Nicholson observed that army officers at Fort McKavett praised him as "the dashing young [Ranger] Lieutenant." He went on to say that Reynolds's management of law-enforcement affairs in Kimble County had been "admirable, he stood pat and went for all alike; he was respected but not popular, which was the highest compliment," coming from the likes of the class of people such as lived in Kimble County.[47]

### Dan Roberts Returns

Even though he may have been sensitive to political pressure, Major Jones intended to keep the Kimble County confederation under his scrutiny. He ordered Reynolds and Company E to remain at the Bear Creek camp until Dan Roberts, recently returned to the Frontier Battalion as a captain, had arrived from south Texas with his old command, Company D.[48] Roberts arrived on May 10, ready to pick up Reynolds's torch; the two old comrades spent a day or so acquainting and updating Roberts and his sergeants and corporals with background information and insights about the Kimble County confederation. Then Company E, with Lieutenant Reynolds at its head, pulled out for Burnet County.

Dan Roberts was an old Indian fighter, and from his arrival at Bear Creek on May 10, 1878, he focused on the increasing reports of Indian raiders entering the Llanos on horse-stealing expeditions. These marauders were Indians from Mexico or white renegades masquerading as Indians, or both. Whereas most of Roberts's reports record some encounters with, and arrests of, outlaws—primarily horse thieves and cattle rustlers, many of them the familiar culprits that had been showing up in the Monthly Returns off and on since 1876—the majority of Company D's energies for almost a year were devoted to intercepting and tracking "Indian" raiding parties, primarily in the Llano valleys.[49]

An exception was in late May 1878, when Corporal Weed and four privates arrested Bill Allison on the South Llano. Allison was the brother-in-law of the Dublin boys. Wanted on several charges of cattle theft, he was taken to Austin for safekeeping in early June. His bail was set high enough that he remained in jail there for more than a year, increasingly frustrated and bitter that his Dublin relatives did not bail him out and secure his freedom.[50] Cracks were beginning to appear in the confederation's external walls.

The focus of Captain Dan Roberts on the detection and apprehension of Indian raiders may indicate that Major Jones thought, like Reynolds, that the back of the Kimble County confederation had been broken and that the Rangers could now bring Indian raids into the region under control.[51] It may also indicate that the Kimble County outlaw confederation had indeed been cowed by Reynolds and his Company E Rangers. Certainly, lawlessness in the Llano valleys was relatively muted from May 1878 through March 1879—just as it had been in the months following the Kimble County Roundup of the preceding year.[52]

The fall term of district court for Kimble County was held in Junction City the week of October 29, 1878, and for Menard County at Menardville the following week.[53] Roll and Dell Dublin showed up on November 7 at the Menard County courthouse, where they testified on behalf of Jordan A. "Black" Burt, charged with three counts of cattle theft. Burt was acquitted. Mack Potter's trial for the same offense was continued until the March 1879 term of district court, but the Dublin brothers gave bond that they would also appear at Potter's trial and testify as witnesses for the defense. By the time March rolled around, Mack Potter had obtained yet another continuance and remained at large.[54]

A bitter race for sheriff of Kimble County took place in the fall of 1878, pitting the incumbent, John B. Gorman, against his challenger, H. J. Garland. Having worked with Kimble County officers for about six months, Captain Dan Roberts provided Major Jones with an informed but pessimistic assessment of the state of the county as well as the performance of Sheriff Gorman:

I don't know how to conjecture the future of things in this County. I've lost confidence in Gorman as a sheriff, and the man who is now contesting his election [H. J. Garland] is talked about in a manner that would make an honest man blush, but of my *own* knowledge I can say nothing of him. The contesting suit will come up at Mason on January 20 before Judge Blackburn. A good deal of rough talk has been indulged in by both parties.[55]

## A Woman's Perspective

Captain Dan Roberts had married Miss Luvenia (Lou) Conway in Columbus, Texas, in 1875, and she lived thereafter with Roberts in the various Company D camps. Her description of her experiences in the Junction City community during the summer of 1878 is revealing.

Having been warned that Kimble County was "a bad man's country," she went to Junction City with a squad of Rangers to leave her laundry to be done. On the way back, several of her escort informed her that the women of the town washed on the riverbanks, and that they had had several fights there. A few days later, when the apprehensive young woman came back to reclaim her laundry, she was greeted by three belligerent washerwomen, who returned the finished laundry but told her that they would never wash for her again. They conveyed their bad opinion of "people who thought themselves better than others," and told Mrs. Roberts that "they had been well-raised . . . always kept the best company, and . . . pour[ed] forth a tirade of abuse, mixed with swear words, about stuck-up people. 'Money,' they said, 'doesn't make anyone better.'"

Lou Roberts retorted, "Surely, you are not mistaking us for rich people. Rangers are all poor." Immediately they became friendly, and one of the laundresses offered Mrs. Roberts "a chaw" of tobacco. Seeing her Ranger escort ride up, she diplomatically declined. Later Lou Roberts learned that she had offended the townswomen on her first visit by not inviting them to visit her at her quarters at the Ranger camp.[56]

## Citizen John Temple Takes Action

Tom Doran was a member of the Kimble County confederation, named by Ranger H. B. Waddill in his February 27, 1877, report to Major Jones. His name was also on the "hit list" compiled by Menard County Deputy Sheriff W. W. Elliott, from his interrogation of incarcerated gang member Ben Anderson, which was delivered to Major Jones by Lieutenant Frank Moore of Company D prior to the Kimble County Roundup.[57] Doran was known as a dangerous gunman who already had killed another Kimble County rustler, Jim Deaton, on September 12, 1878, and had been tried and acquitted at the fourth session of district court, on the basis of self-defense.[58]

John E. Temple's eldest son, Lewis Temple, then in his late twenties, was a deputy serving under Sheriff John B. Gorman. For several months there had been bad blood between the younger Temple and Doran, which culminated in a shootout in the Double-O saloon in Junction City on December 21, 1878. Lewis Temple wounded Doran in the right chest, and Doran killed Temple with a shot to the head. When the wounded Doran left the saloon, he ran into gray-bearded John Temple, who was waiting outside, presumably in support of his son. In the ensuing fight, Doran and the elder Temple struggled back into the saloon, where Doran lost his revolver. Temple picked up the pistol, shot Doran through the hips as he again fled out the saloon door, and then followed Doran out into the street, where, in a frenzied rage he slashed the wounded outlaw "thirteen times with a knife, killing him on the spot." Afterward, Temple returned to the saloon, and announced, "[Doran] killed [my son], but he won't ever kill another."[59]

John Temple, then Kimble County treasurer, was never charged in the affair, and the Temple-Doran fight represents the first example of a Kimble County citizen personally taking on a member of the confederation and prevailing, though at terrible cost. Other confrontations would follow, though they would be better organized and less dramatic, as the community faction favoring order and law gradually gained numbers, strength, and confidence.

### A Work in Progress

Although the actions of the Frontier Battalion—primarily those led by Lieutenant N. O. Reynolds and Company E—had reduced lawlessness and violence in Kerr, Kimble, and Menard Counties during 1878, frontier criminals had by no means been eliminated. The Rangers were still routinely searching for and arresting cattle rustlers and horse thieves, and on July 6, 1878, the San Antonio–Fort McKavett stagecoach was robbed once again near Pegleg Crossing.[60]

Moreover, the original charge of the Frontier Battalion—to guard the frontier against marauding Indians—was still occupying a substantial part of the Rangers' time and resources.

### 1878 Indian Encounters and Patrols

Despite increased U.S. military presence along the Rio Grande, the repeated cross-border raids of Colonel Shafter and Lieutenant Bullis, and the frequent westward scouts of Texas Ranger Companies D, E, and F, raiding into Texas by Mexican Indians did not diminish in 1878 and indeed may have actually intensified.

The worst raid took place during April 14–19, 1878, when about forty raiders, reported as Kickapoo, Lipan, and Seminole Indians, Mexicans, and at least one white man, crossed the Rio Grande on foot about fifty miles southeast of Eagle Pass. They stole enough horses for all to be mounted and then moved rapidly as a body—which repeatedly dispersed and then reassembled—in an eastward rampage across Webb, LaSalle, McMullen, Duval, and Nueces Counties, after which they turned back westward, returned to Webb County, and recrossed the Rio Grande about twenty-five miles south of Laredo on their way back to the Santa Rosa Mountains. For reasons still unexplained, U.S. troops, stationed at several military posts in the area, were unable to mount any significant response or pursuit. A small party of citizens, led by rancher Frank Gravis, attacked the marauding Indians near the Rio Grande toward the end of the raid, but was readily driven off. During this foray the raiders killed at least eighteen Texas settlers, men, women, and children; sacked numerous ranches; and made off with 150 to 250 horses.[61] The raid received widespread publicity, stimulated a statewide outcry, and almost certainly gave strong justification to the official government policy endorsing cross-border raids into Mexico by U.S. troops pursuing Mexican Indian raiders.[62]

The April 14–19 raid stimulated a strong response by Mackenzie, Shafter, and Bullis, who carried out an extended retaliatory raid in late May. Mackenzie and Bullis crossed the Rio Grande with about three hundred men and scoured the Serranía del Burro for several weeks, while Shafter, with about seven hundred men, waited for several weeks opposite Piedras Negras, planning to travel about ninety miles westward to the Santa Rosa Mountains, where he would set up a supply base for future operations. Shafter, Mackenzie, and Bullis encountered threatening Mexican military forces, however, and returned across the Rio Grande on June 22, 1878, to avoid an international incident.[63]

Two other engagements with Mexican Indians were reported by the U.S. Army in Texas during 1878.[64] But the Rangers had a much larger share of Indian work. During the first nine months of 1878, more than a dozen Indian raids took place around the margins of the Edwards Plateau. Texas Ranger Companies D, E, and F mounted more than fifteen extensive scouts for reported Indian raiders and engaged them twice. Most of these raids took place after the devastating April raid in south Texas. The Mexican Indians, possibly anticipating heightened military patrols to the south, apparently shifted their forays northward, into Edwards, Kerr, Kimble, and Menard Counties. Many of the raids after April 1878 took place in the watershed of the Llano River.[65]

On October 3 Captain Roberts, camped on the North Llano at the mouth of Bear Creek, west of Junction City, heard rumors of possible incoming Indian raiders and mounted a westward scout by Company D Rangers, without encountering them.[66] The next day, he received reports that Indians had stolen horses on the

South Llano, twelve miles above (southwest of) Junction City. The Indians had come in down the South Llano valley and went out the same way.[67]

On the morning of October 5, a party of Indians was sighted in eastern Kimble County, near the head of the James River. Settlers alerted local families, who gathered for safety near Noxville. The Indians, reported to number twenty-five to thirty, were headed southwest across the divide in the direction of Johnson Creek, a tributary of the Guadalupe River.[68]

These October raids represented an unusually large concentration of Mexican Indian raiders, and they coincided with the arrival of the James Dowdy family at their new homestead in northwestern Kerr County, at the headwaters of Johnson Creek, in a narrow bluff-bound valley cut into the mass of the Edwards Plateau.[69] Unfortunately, the new Dowdy headquarters was situated at a strategic crossing site, used for years by Indian renegades in returning westward from their raids on the settlements around the margins of the Edwards Plateau to their homes in northern Mexico.

Unknowingly, the Dowdys had come to the wrong place at precisely the wrong time.

# 9 :: The Dowdy Raid

## A Southern Family

For the first twenty-five years of their married life, James Elias and Susan Cassell Dowdy lived a settled farming life on the lush rolling prairies and moist fertile bottomlands of the Texas Gulf coastal plain. They had married in 1852 in the old town of Goliad; James was thirty-four and Susan twenty-two.[1]

Goliad County was a relatively benign area, for pre–Civil War Texas. The violence of the Texas Revolution was sixteen years in the past, and the Karankawa Indians had been killed off.[2] It was too far east for Mexican raiders, and too far south for Comanche and Kiowa war parties. Furthermore, the country was rapidly filling up with new settlers from the east, which promised even more security against raids by Indians and banditti.

The luxurious grasslands of the lower coastal plain nurtured the infant range-cattle industry of Texas. After the Civil War, legendary cattlemen such as Dillard Fant, Buck Pettus, and Shanghai Pierce began gathering wild longhorn cattle and driving them north to Kansas railheads.[3] James Dowdy and his younger brother John G. (Gib) were farmers;[4] even so, they also owned cattle that grazed the open prairies of the lower Gulf plain—Goliad County's registry of cattle brands and earmarks contains those registered under the Dowdy name.[5]

The Dowdys farmed in the far south corner of Goliad County, in rich alluvial soil where Blanco Creek, the southwestern boundary of Goliad County with neighboring Bee County, joins its tributary, Mucorrera Creek. Goliad town lay about twenty miles north.[6]

James and Susan Dowdy raised a stair-stepped family of eight: Tom (born in 1854), Dick (1856), Mary (1857), Alice (1860), Martha (1862), Susan (1864), James (1868), and George (1871).[7] In 1870 the four eldest children attended school. Nearby lived James's brother John G. (Gib) Dowdy, his first wife Juduth, and their seven children.[8] After Juduth's death, Gib Dowdy remarried and moved his family just over the line into Bee County.[9]

Like most of their neighbors, they were southerners—James and Gib from Georgia, Susan and Juduth from Mississippi. Both Dowdy brothers were reasonably prosperous, compared with their neighbors. In 1860 each showed real estate valued at $1,000 and personal property worth $2,000. Ten years later, with Texas

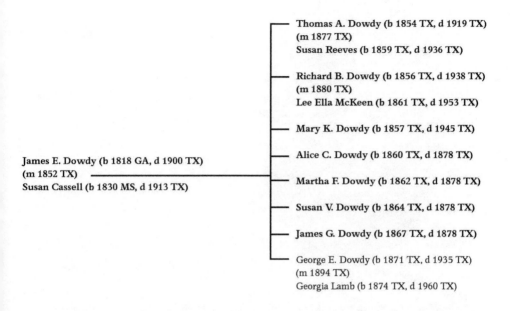

James E. Dowdy (b 1818 GA, d 1900 TX)
(m 1852 TX)
Susan Cassell (b 1830 MS, d 1913 TX)

Thomas A. Dowdy (b 1854 TX, d 1919 TX)
(m 1877 TX)
Susan Reeves (b 1859 TX, d 1936 TX)

Richard B. Dowdy (b 1856 TX, d 1938 TX)
(m 1880 TX)
Lee Ella McKeen (b 1861 TX, d 1953 TX)

Mary K. Dowdy (b 1857 TX, d 1945 TX)

Alice C. Dowdy (b 1860 TX, d 1878 TX)

Martha F. Dowdy (b 1862 TX, d 1878 TX)

Susan V. Dowdy (b 1864 TX, d 1878 TX)

James G. Dowdy (b 1867 TX, d 1878 TX)

George E. Dowdy (b 1871 TX, d 1935 TX)
(m 1894 TX)
Georgia Lamb (b 1874 TX, d 1960 TX)

Figure 19: The James E. Dowdy family in Texas. Bold font signifies characters who were prominent in the events related herein.

beginning to recover from the Civil War, Gib Dowdy owned real estate worth $1,000 and personal property valued at $1,400. James Dowdy had fared less well, with real estate worth $550 and personal property worth $1,500. Even so, they were better off than most of their neighbors.[10]

Then the Dowdys lost their land.

In July 1876 they found themselves in a dispute over 603 acres of land in far southern Goliad County with one H. C. Withers of Austin.[11] Withers may have filed officially on the tract even though the Dowdys had been living there for some time without holding legal title. Or perhaps Withers discovered a flaw in the Dowdys' title and filed upon the land. His complaint indicates that on July 11, 1876, "John G. and James Dowdy with force and arms entered upon the lands aforesaid and ousted your petitioner therefrom, since which time [they] have continually possessed and occupied said land."[12] One may speculate that perhaps the Dowdys ejected Withers from the disputed tract when Withers came to notify them of his title claim, or to complain about their occupancy. In any case Withers brought suit against John G. and James A. [E.] Dowdy on February 1, 1877, in

Figure 20. James Elias Dowdy, early 1870s. Courtesy of W. C. Dowdy.

Goliad. Adding insult to injury, Withers also claimed damages of one thousand dollars for removal of one thousand post oak trees, valued at one dollar each, as well as unpaid rents of three hundred dollars. Final judgment in favor of H. C. Withers was handed down sometime early in 1878. The Dowdys also probably lost the value of their improvements. This reversal in family fortunes may well have contributed to a decline in James Dowdy's health at about this time.[13]

In 1877 James Dowdy's eldest son, Thomas A., married Susan Reeves in Goliad. She came from an old Texas ranching family that was prominent in the area. The newlyweds left the hearths of their respective families and set up housekeeping on their own in Goliad County.[14]

Family tradition maintains that the eldest Dowdy daughter, Mary, became engaged to a young man at about the same time. She and her family had gathered a fine trousseau. Unfortunately, the bridegroom failed to show up for the wedding.[15] One can sympathize with the humiliation Mary Dowdy and her parents may have felt, especially so soon after the wedding of her older brother, Tom. Whether the Dowdys' impending loss of land may have figured in the aborted marriage is not known.

Dowdy family tradition also maintains that the next two daughters, Alice and Martha, then seventeen and fifteen, respectively, were the objects of ardent attention by young men of whom the Dowdy parents disapproved.[16] If so, this certainly could have further humiliated their spurned elder sister, Mary.

Figure 21. Original Dowdy home site at the head of Johnson Creek, northwestern Kerr County, Texas, looking north. Johnson Creek lies fifty yards to the right (east). This is the location where James E. and Susan C. Dowdy first brought their family to Kerr County in early October 1878. The massacre took place about one-half mile to the left (west) of this site, up on the easterly slopes of the Edwards Plateau. The original cabin and tent were located about halfway between the windmill and the large tree to the right. Photo by the author, 2008.

## Starting Over

Faced with this series of major changes and setbacks, James and Susan Dowdy decided to pick up stakes and make a new start. They probably expected to homestead newly issued railroad or Texas school land in sparsely settled Kerr County, or purchase recently patented land. Earlier, James's brother Gib had acquired a 640-acre section of land in northwestern Kerr County, on Henderson Branch, two miles north of the junction of the Guadalupe River with its south-flowing tributary, Johnson Creek, near present Ingram, Texas.[17]

So after twenty-five years, James and Susan Dowdy left their settled southern life on the lush, peaceful prairies of Goliad County and moved their family 160 miles to the northwest, to a rough, semiarid, canyon-laced frontier land in northwestern Kerr County. They selected a home site near the headwater spring of Johnson Creek, nearly ten miles upstream from Gib Dowdy's section.[18] They probably made some kind of arrangement with Charles Schreiner, Kerr County's prominent merchant and land speculator, to occupy a 640-acre tract that he owned there, with provision toward a future purchase.[19]

Their new home site lay in a tight valley cut into the Edwards Plateau, whose

vast expanse stretched away, rising westward from their front doorway, unin-
terrupted and unpopulated, for 150 miles, clear to the Rio Grande and beyond,
into northern Coahuila, Mexico. Kerrville was twenty miles southeast. The northern boundary of Kerr County with adjacent Kimble County lay just seven miles
north. Junction City was forty miles northwest; the road thereto, such as it was,
ran just west of the Dowdys' new homestead. And the outlaw community along
the South Llano River lay just thirty miles northwest as the crow flies.

James and Susan Dowdy, together with three sons and four daughters, arrived
in Kerr County toward the end of September 1878.[20] By the first of October they
were at their new home site, accompanied by a half-dozen horses and several
thousand sheep, which they immediately put to pasture on the virgin grasslands
of the plateau's easterly slopes, declining into the valley of spring-fed Johnson
Creek.[21] A cabin had already been built on the property, on a gently sloping terrace along the west side of the creek, but for additional shelter they also set up
a tent nearby.[22] It was a scenic location, under stratified bluffs of gray limestone
immediately east of the creek, with majestic elm and pecan trees scattered along
the west bank, and the limpid waters of Johnson Creek murmuring in between.
The newcomers began to unpack their goods and set about making their new
home site livable.[23]

Kerr County had existed as an organized community for almost as long as
James and Susan Dowdy had been married. They apparently assumed that it was
orderly and law abiding, that their new location was as safe as Goliad County.
They were mistaken—their Johnson Creek home site was immediately adjacent
to the uninhabited and lawless Edwards Plateau. Their new home lay astride an
often-used raiding trail, at a strategically located watering place. Outbound Indian
raiders often stopped there before heading west across the flat divide of the Edwards Plateau, toward Mexico and safe haven.

Unknowingly, the Dowdys were now vulnerable, surrounded by the vacant
wilderness of the Edwards Plateau and its continuing silent menace of sudden
violence.[24]

### A Scene of Unparalleled Horror

On Saturday morning, October 5, after a norther on the previous day brought a
heavy rain, James Dowdy's second eldest son, Dick, went out on foot to verify the
whereabouts of the Dowdy livestock, the Dowdys' young Mexican sheepherder
apparently being ill and unable to look after the flocks.[25] About half a dozen horses grazed with the sheep.[26]

Mr. Dowdy had contracted for his winter supply of corn. Despite Friday's
hard rain, the first load of grain arrived on Saturday morning around ten o'clock,

Figure 22. Portraits of the four murdered Dowdy young people, about 1877. *Clockwise from upper left*, Alice (then about seventeen), Martha (fifteen), James (nine), and Susan (thirteen). Courtesy of W. C. Dowdy. (Images digitally enhanced, with permission.)

and Dick Dowdy returned to the ranch headquarters to receive and measure the grain.[27] Three of the Dowdy sisters—Alice, Martha, and Susan—and their younger brother James walked up through the muddy pasture to take Dick's place, looking after the livestock. They were on a rising slope about half a mile west of the Dowdy headquarters.[28]

Before returning to the livestock, Dick Dowdy and another unnamed young man, said to be Alice's fiancé, and probably visiting from Goliad County, took an early dinner.[29] Then, about noon, Dick walked back out in the pasture to relieve his sisters and brother.

In less than an hour, he reported back stunned and dismayed—he had found the bodies of two of his younger sisters and his brother James, mangled and bloody, pierced by arrows, in the pasture less than a half mile west of the new Dowdy homestead. The sheep were scattered and the horses were gone. His mother sent him to warn the neighbors while she immediately rushed to the murder scene.[30]

Susan Dowdy set out in search of her children. She found Alice "where she had fallen, about 300 yards from the house, pierced by arrows and wounded in the side by the thrust of a spear, and through the neck by a rifle shot. Alice lived long enough to recognize her mother, spoke the dear name of 'Mama,' and expired."[31]

Another source indicated that Alice lived long enough to whisper to her mother "the name of a white man who had been with the raiders" before she died.[32]

The bodies of the other three Dowdy youngsters were found scattered over an area of several hundred yards. Martha, who had apparently been reading under a tree, had been shot where she sat, about fifty yards from Alice's body.[33] James's body lay about two hundred yards away.[34] Their footprints on the wet ground indicated that Alice, Susan, and James had run as many as several hundred yards in trying to escape their assailants, who were on horseback. Susan's body was not found for several hours, leading to fears that she had been taken hostage.[35] Finally Susan's body was found where she "had run nearly 400 yards before she was overtaken and shot full of arrows." In her terror, she had run west, directly away from the safety of her new home.[36]

All four of the bodies "were in a horrible condition from bullet, lance, and arrow wounds, but none were scalped."[37] According to an account by Ben F. Pepper, a citizen of adjacent Kimble County, "examination of the bodies of the three girls disclosed the appalling fact that their persons had been brutally outraged and then murdered. Each of the mouths of the three girls had been split open with a knife from ear to ear, while the boy's mouth was not. Evidently this was done to silence the voices and screams which would have brought them assistance, perhaps, while [the Indians] consummated their dark, damnable crime. . . . There could have been no other motive for the murder[s] but the one indicated by the circumstances of the killing[s] as described."[38]

Other accounts, subsequent and more distant, provide differing details of the murders. General John S. Mason, U.S. Army, reported in the *Washington Post* that the Dowdy girls "were first outraged and then had their scalps removed and were left with their skulls bare and bleeding [after which] the human devils butchered the three innocents in a most horrible manner . . . [and] that the little boy's scalp was sheared."[39] Additional particulars provided by a Major Bates in the *Denison Daily News* on October 12 reported that the bodies had been "somewhat mutilated," and that "the outer garments of the girls and the pants of the boy had been taken," but that the girls had not been raped, and there had been no scalping."[40] In Major John B. Jones's December 17 report to Texas Adjutant General William Steele on the Dowdy murders, "the killing was done with firearms and a lance or narrow-bladed knife . . . and [the bodies] bore no marks of violence save those inflicted in the killing."[41] However, Jones did not visit the crime scene until about two weeks after the murders, and it is easy to understand that, by then, the Dowdy family might have chosen to forget—or decided not to mention—the disagreeable fact that their daughters had been sexually assaulted.

Dick Dowdy ran to the home of the nearest neighbor, Louis Nelson, to report

Figure 23. Dowdy gravesites, Sunset Cemetery, near Mountain Home, Kerr County, Texas. The four murdered Dowdy young people are buried two to a grave in the center of the photo. The graves of the two infant sons of Tom and Susan (Reeves) Dowdy are in the foreground; the tall gravestones in the background are those of James E. and Susan (Cassell) Dowdy, parents of the murdered young people. The graves of the Dowdy children are embedded with clam shells brought from the Gulf Coast. Photo by the author, 2008.

the murders, and to pass the word to settlers in the Johnson Creek valley of the presence of Indian marauders.[42] Then he returned to help his mother. Nelson, together with neighbors Samuel Fessenden and Freeman Smith, brought along a wagon and team to collect the bodies of the victims and bring them home.[43]

Kerrville resident William V. Gregory "left town on Saturday [October] 5th on a visit to the [Dowdy] family, and on reaching Captain Louis Nelson's, two miles this side of the Dowdy ranch, he first heard of the Indian raid. He pressed forward and, arriving at his destination, a scene of unparalleled horror met his gaze. The dead bodies of the three girls and their young brother had just been borne in and lay before him in their warm blood, mangled fearfully. The survivors of the family were there, dumb, under God alone knows what feeling, peering dazedly at each dead form."[44]

Mrs. Samuel (Elizabeth) Fessenden and Mrs. Wash Floyd went to the Dowdy home that afternoon and "helped to wash and dress the girls and comb out their hair, and then sat up all night with them."[45] Mrs. Floyd's daughter, who was a young girl at the time of the murders, related, "I remember Mama telling me

[that] Mrs. Dowdy said to her [when the bodies were being prepared for burial], 'I can't bear to see you pull out those arrows because I know it will hurt.' Mama told me they were buried with the arrows still in their bodies."[46]

All four of the murdered young people were buried the next day, Sunday, October 6, 1878, the first to be buried in what would become the Sunset Cemetery, overlooking Johnson Creek valley, two miles south of the Dowdy home site. They were buried side by side, two to a grave, James and Martha in one, and Susan and Alice in the other.[47]

It must have been a grim and somber congregation of neighbors and friends who stood on that stark new burial ground, mourning with the surviving members of the Dowdy family.

### Indians, Mexicans, or White Men?

From evidence found on a nearby vantage point, a bluff on the east side of Johnson Creek, it appeared that "the sheep and their herders had been under observation by the redskins for some time; on seeing the only man leave, they descended upon the defenseless girls and boy and killed them."[48]

Numerous arrows still littered the murder site, and many footprints gave mute testimony to the desperate flights of the Dowdy youngsters from their pursuers. Some of the footprints were made by moccasins whereas others were made by boots, and the usual questions as to the identity of the raiders—Indians, Mexicans, or white renegades—began to appear in newspaper accounts.[49] Major John B. Jones, relying later on the experienced opinion of frontiersman Captain Louis Nelson, who was at the crime scene only a few hours after the murders were committed, concluded that the perpetrators were Mexicans. Two or three hours after the murders, the raiders were seen about ten miles west of the murder site by a reliable Kerr County citizen—momentarily, and at a distance of less than half a mile—who thought they were Mexicans.[50]

Mary Davis Knox, then eight years old, together with her brother and mother, were gathering wild dewberries on the banks of Jim Little Creek, in the Noxville area, on the morning of the murders, when they heard horsemen approaching and hid themselves. She reported that the riders were definitely Indians.[51] The same morning, a band of thirty-five or forty mounted Indians was sighted by James H. Parker and Creed Taylor near the head of James River, headed in the direction of the Dowdy home site at the head of Johnson Creek.[52] Texas Ranger Jim Gillett, who later was stationed for several months near the Dowdy murder site, believed the raiders "were probably Kickapoos and Lipans from the Santa Rosa mountains of Mexico."[53]

Whoever they were, the raiders departed westward, across the high divide of the Edwards Plateau, with a large herd of stolen horses, toward Mexico.[54] A party of local citizens followed their tracks westward for nearly one hundred miles, until they "ran out of the section of recent rains" and lost the trail in the rough Devils River country.[55]

Word of the Dowdy massacre went out immediately to U.S. Army posts throughout the area. General Thomas M. Vincent, Adjutant General of the Department of Texas, reported that he had received word from each of the posts on the "supposed line of retreat of the raiders, that an active lookout [was] being kept for the [raiding] party and it [was] hoped that they [would] be captured and summarily dealt with."[56]

Major John B. Jones inspected the crime scene about two weeks after the murders, in company with Captain Louis Nelson. He reported that the trail of the murderers

> was still very plain when I visited the locality [and] led northwest in the direction of the South Llano, on which stream some of the horses taken from the Dowdy family were dropped, and three or four others taken. Thence, the trail led off south, [and] a little west, across the plains in the direction of San Felipe, on the Rio Grande. So great a time had elapsed that it could not be followed further than the rocky divide between the Llano and head of Nueces River.[57]

### Captain Roberts's Scout

Texas Ranger Company D, commanded by Captain Dan Roberts, was stationed at the mouth of Bear Creek in western Kimble County about forty miles northwest of the site of the Dowdy murders. Warned on October 3 that Indian raiders had stolen horses at Fort McKavett the day before, Roberts and an eleven-man Ranger squad mounted a scout for the raiders in Kimble County the next day, heading for the "last water west" in the North Llano drainage, anticipating that they would find the trail of the fleeing renegades and follow it.[58] But a courier reached him on the night of the fourth, bringing word that on the previous night Indians had stolen horses twelve miles out the South Llano valley (the Potter-Dublin neighborhood), cleaning out the settlement of saddle stock.

Believing that the Indians would now be heading back to Mexico, Roberts then changed his plans, and started the next morning—October 5, the day of the Dowdy raid—across the Edwards Plateau for Beaver Lake, the headwater spring of the Devils River, about eighty miles away. Roberts's squad reached Beaver Lake thirty-six hours later. Hearing no reports from passing wagon trains as to any sightings of Indians with horse herds, Roberts then took his squad down the Devils River fifteen miles to Pecan Springs, where he camped and kept watch the night of October 6.

The next morning, Roberts and his Rangers continued south, down the Devils River canyon to abandoned Camp Hudson, where he encountered a squad of U.S. Army buffalo soldiers escorting a surveying party. The soldiers had neither seen any Indians nor observed any trail of a passing horse herd but volunteered to send word if they encountered either. So Roberts returned to Beaver Lake for a few hours and then headed for an isolated waterhole on Dolan Creek, about twenty-five miles east, where the Rangers camped on the night of October 7.

Finding no sign of the raiders and their horse herd the next morning, Roberts then led his squad fifty waterless miles northeast, back across the plateau, arriving late the evening of October 8 at the Eight-mile Waterhole on the North Llano drainage, where he found another squad of buffalo soldiers of the 10th Infantry Division from Fort McKavett, who were keeping watch for the fugitive Indians.

### Sergeant Sieker's Scout

While Dan Roberts and his squad were fruitlessly scouring the plateau west of Kimble County, on October 4 Company D's Sergeant Lam Sieker took the rest of the Rangers out the South Llano valley, cutting for Indian sign.[59] By the afternoon of October 5, Sieker concluded that the raiders had scattered, so he led his squad south across the plateau to the upper drainage of the East Nueces River, hoping to cross their trail. Thwarted in his search, Sieker broke camp early the next morning, riding northeast back across the plateau, to the upper reaches of the Paint Creek watershed—where he was within twelve miles of the site of the Dowdy massacre—and followed it northward to its confluence with the South Llano River.

During the evening of October 6, Sieker's squad unknowingly crossed the trail of the departing Indians a few miles south of the mouth of Paint Creek. The raiders had passed by earlier, fleeing from where they had murdered the Dowdy youngsters. A weary and frustrated squad of Rangers finally made a late camp on the South Llano River, at the mouth of Paint Creek, thirty-six hours after the Dowdy youngsters had been murdered.

The next morning, October 7, a local settler found the trail of the departing Indian raiders and notified Sergeant Sieker. Because the Indians' outbound trail was bearing toward the North Llano, Sieker returned to Company D's camp, thinking that additional news might indicate where next he should lead his squad.

### Roberts's Report

On his return to the Ranger camp on Bear Creek on October 10, Roberts learned that the Indians had been seen on October 7 at Wilson's ranch on the North Llano

River, only a few miles east of the Eight-mile Waterhole (where Roberts had arrived twenty-four hours later). Roberts then sent his two best trackers to ascertain where the Indians went next. They found the trail and reported that the Indians had followed Maynard Creek southward from the North Llano River onto the plateau. They believed that there were about ten Indians in the raiding party.

Seven days after returning from the fruitless searches for the Dowdy raiders, Dan Roberts wrote to his commanding officer, Major John B. Jones. He described Company D's extensive but unsuccessful efforts to intercept the Indian marauders as well as his frustration at their elusive behavior in dodging his patrols.

Roberts reported that Indians had murdered four people on Johnson Creek—the Dowdy youngsters—but could not be sure they were the same Indian raiders that he had been trying to apprehend, since two separate Indian raiding parties had been seen on October 6 near Johnson Creek. Roberts concluded his report with a passage that reveals his frustration at not intercepting the Dowdy murderers:

> I feel completely baffled, and a good portion of conceit has left me in regard to catching them every time they come in [to the settlements]. I should feel humiliated if my conscience didn't acquit me of having done all I could. I will never start after them again until I get the trail for certain, and keep it. I rode 250 miles over a miserable dry country and accomplished nothing, when if I'd been on their trail in that distance I could probably have caught them. They acted very strangely this time. Most of the horses they stole came back to their respective ranges and owners [after] they probably picked [and kept] the best ones. I am very truly your obedient servant, D. W. Roberts, Captain, Company "D."[60]

### Impact on the Public

Texas newspapers spread stories of the Dowdy raid like wildfire, sending shock waves throughout the state. Newspaper reports even reached the nation's capital via the front page of the *Washington Post*. Political discussions as recent as the fall of 1878 had included further reductions in the Texas Ranger forces because of the perception that the Indian threat was essentially past.[61] Similar sentiments were being heard in Washington with regard to U.S. Army troops assigned to frontier defense against Indian raiders. Citizens on the Texas frontier worried that state and national protection might be significantly reduced, and editorials in newspapers such as the *San Antonio Daily Express* articulated such concerns only a week after news of the massacre became known:

**A Bloody Arrow**—The Express has received through the mails an arrow taken from the body of one of the young ladies of the Dowdy family, killed by raiders in Kerr Co. on the 5th instant. It is an ordinary Indian arrow made of ash, about 2 feet in length, with a triple feather neatly lashed on with sinew, being painted blue over the sinew and finished with the usual little parallel grooves from the head to the feather. The arrowhead is missing and the arrow is broken at about 1/3 its length from the head, and is stained with blood for that distance, presenting the appearance of having been broken by the struggles and writhings of the poor prostrate victim, after the deadly missile had been buried in her vitals. Around the arrow was wrapped a strip of paper upon which was written, by one who was probably a witness of the scene of the massacre, the following words:

"This is from the dead body of one of the victims of the late Kerrville massacre. The innocent blood here visible cries aloud for revenge. October 5, 1878."

Such bloody testimony to the wrongs endured by our frontier is not rare in the border counties, but those [eastern Texans] who are happily secure from the scalping knife [do not often] see for themselves these evidences of the barbarities to which our kindred and friends in the western countries are subjected.[62]

### The Rangers Arrive

Major John B. Jones returned to Austin from the Kerr County frontier on October 29, 1878. Meanwhile, cognizant of the alarming impact of the Dowdy raid on frontier citizens, he had already decided to move Company E of the Frontier Battalion, under the command of Lieutenant N. O. Reynolds, from its camp in San Saba County to the general area of northwestern Kerr County, in the vicinity of the Dowdy murders. On October 24, he directed Reynolds to prepare to relocate his camp, and instructed him "to look out for Indians and . . . use all means in your power to prevent a repetition of the outrages recently perpetrated by them in this section of country." Jones ordered Reynolds to "send out scouts and notify all the settlers on the upper waters of the Guadalupe and also the south tributaries of the Llano, where your camp is, and request them to send you information promptly if any Indians come into the country, or of depredations by white thieves." In the same letter, he informed Reynolds that he intended to move Captain Dan Roberts's Company D northward to the upper reaches of Bear Creek in Kimble County, and instructed Reynolds to coordinate his patrolling activities with those of Roberts's Company D Rangers.[63] Subsequent exchanges of letters between Jones and Reynolds resulted in the establishment of Company E's camp on Contrary Creek, within a mile of the Dowdy home site, by November 1, 1878.[64]

Jones now had his Ranger Companies—D, E, and F—positioned so as to focus on the deadly area of the Edwards Plateau through which Indian raiding parties from Mexico entered and escaped. Dan Roberts was located on the north, on Bear Creek in northwestern Kimble County. N. O. Reynolds was now positioned on the east, in northwestern Kerr County. And Pat Dolan was stationed to the southwest, at Camp Wood.[65] Regular patrolling began and continued for more than six months.

Reynolds's Company E men mounted frequent westward sorties from their camp on Contrary Creek. Their most common route scoured the broad, high divide area between the upper watershed of the South Llano River on the north— Paint Creek and Paint Rock Spring on the South Llano headwaters—and the upper reaches of the Guadalupe and East Nueces Rivers on the south. Sometimes their patrols rode as far west as the upper slopes of the Devils River drainage, or as far southwest as the divide between the south fork of the Guadalupe and the Medina, Sabinal, or Frio Rivers.

Dan Roberts was doing likewise in his area of responsibility in the North Llano and San Saba watersheds. Pat Dolan's Company F Rangers continued their previous frequent scouts in the southern breaks of the Edwards Plateau, all the way to the Rio Grande.[66]

Reynolds's Company E Rangers, stationed at Camp Contrary beginning November 1, 1878, pastured their horses in the area where the Dowdy youngsters were killed.[67] In their memoirs, two of Reynolds's Rangers, John Banister and Jim Gillett, reported seeing the heart-rending sight of the still-present tracks of the murdered Dowdy youngsters, fleeing from their mounted pursuers. John Banister recalled that

> the Indians came from the brush like wolves into a flock of lambs. A recent rain had saturated the ground, and the helpless children and their terrible attackers left the plain story of each separate atrocity in the soft mud, each victim running as far as she could and then being tortured to death. . . . One of the girls had run a long way farther than the rest, and several Indians had ridden along beside her and shot her to death with

arrows. The Rangers retraced this trail more than once; they were all experienced trackers and the story was as plain to them as if they had seen the girl falling, rising to run again, until she could run no more. They did the only thing within their power, they built a monument of cairn stones to mark the tragic spot [where each victim fell].[68]

For the remaining months of 1878, no sign of Indian raiders was found. Only after January 1, 1879, did a few Indian raids—horse-stealing forays into the Llano valleys from the west—begin to be reported.[69]

For the Rangers, attempting to intercept the secretive, highly mobile Indian raiders in the empty vastness of the plateau was like trying to catch the wind.

**The Dowdy Family Responds**

As soon as he learned of the brutal murders of his sisters and brother, Tom Dowdy began to wind up his Goliad County affairs, preparing to join his parents and surviving siblings in Kerr County. Together with his wife Susan and baby son, Thomas (born the previous February), he traveled to the Dowdy home site at the headwaters of Johnson Creek.[70] Lieutenant Reynolds's Company E Rangers had already arrived and were busy patrolling to the west.

More tragedy was in store: Tom and Susan Dowdy's infant son contracted pneumonia during their journey from Goliad to Kerr County and died on December 1, 1878. A second son, William, was born on September 15, 1879, but died five months later.[71] Nevertheless, Tom Dowdy and his family stayed in Kerr County. They built a home and store on the original James Dowdy home site, where they soon opened the first post office in the new Mountain Home community.[72]

Gib Dowdy also came to the aid of his brother. He moved with his family to Kerr County only a few months after the Dowdy massacre and occupied his previously acquired 640-acre section on Henderson Branch, a tributary of Johnson Creek. James and Susan Dowdy moved with their three surviving children (Dick, age twenty-two; Mary, twenty-one; and George, seven) to a vacant section close by, on an alluvial terrace along the western side of Johnson Creek. Apparently they made this move in early 1879, after Tom Dowdy had arrived and taken up residence at their former homestead. The bereaved parents built a single-story dog-run house at the edge of a live-oak grove about a mile from Gib's home. James, Susan, and Mary Dowdy lived there for the rest of their lives.[73]

The unnamed young man who was said to be Alice Dowdy's fiancé returned, broken-hearted, to his home "down the country."[74]

## Rumors of Guilt

Shortly after the Dowdy massacre, questions began to be asked and rumors began to circulate about the identity of the man whose name the dying Alice Dowdy was said to have whispered to her mother. Once the rumored man's name was shared among the Dowdy family, another connection was identified: Tom Dowdy's wife, Susan, claimed to remember the man as having stolen some horses from her family earlier in Goliad County.[75]

The rumored suspect's name circulated among knowledgeable local settlers and the Texas Rangers of Company E. Additional suspicions began to arise. The suspect was a young man who lived with his father and five brothers in adjoining Kimble County, near his uncle and cousins, in the South Llano River valley, only about thirty miles northwest of the Dowdy home site. That location was notorious for the frequency of reported horse-stealing raids as well as for the outlaws who congregated there. The Company E Rangers knew him from recent experience—several members of his extended family, together with men from several other South Llano families, were part of a tightly knit clan of desperados who were individually and collectively wanted for various crimes, including theft of horses and cattle, robbery of the U.S. mails, and murder.[76] The Rangers may have suspected that the young man was not only involved in the Dowdy massacre but also represented a possible operating connection between the Kimble County outlaws and Mexican Indian livestock markets in Mexico. And he and his five brothers were Indians.

The general perception of the Dowdys' Mountain Home neighbors about all this, correctly or incorrectly, may perhaps be represented by the following opinion, expressed years later to her granddaughter by Ann Morriss, a local school-teacher and "pillar of the community":

> Many people believed [the Indians who murdered the Dowdy young-sters] were a wandering band of braves who had fallen in with, and been influenced by, a discontented halfbreed who lived in an adjacent county, who had often run afoul of the law, and who hated white men and raised his hand against them whenever he could, with no provocation other than that his victims were white.[77]

The subject of these rumors and suspicions was a young man named John Potter.

# 10 :: The Pegleg Robbers

### Changes

William Steele, adjutant general since 1874, resigned his post in January 1879. John B. Jones succeeded him two weeks later, but did not relinquish control of the Frontier Battalion.[1] Lieutenant N. O. Reynolds, whose health was suffering from nearly five years in the saddle, resigned his command of Company E effective March 1, 1879.[2] He was succeeded by Charles Nevill, under whom Company E left its six-month station near the site of the Dowdy murders and moved to Austin, where on May 15, 1879, it became the "home" Ranger company at the service of new Adjutant General Jones.[3]

In early 1879 citizens and leaders of the frontier counties were aware of increasing political pressure in the eastern counties to eliminate or reduce the Frontier Battalion.[4] They wrote many petitions to their representatives and senators as well as to the adjutant general himself, praising the Rangers' work, pleading for the existing companies to remain at their present stations, and forecasting the return of widespread lawlessness if they were removed.

Such a petition was prepared and signed by all nine elected officials and fifty-eight citizens of Kimble County and submitted to the Texas Legislature on February 17. The law-abiding party of Kimble County was openly and firmly declaring that it stood for the continuation of police pressure against the confederation of Kimble County criminals. One of the citizens who signed it was Will Potter; missing are the signatures of James Dublin, Tom Potter, and James K. P. Potter.[5]

Nevertheless, the Texas Legislature reduced the appropriation for the Frontier Battalion once more, necessitating further reductions among the Ranger force in the field. The first casualty was Captain Pat Dolan's Company F, stationed at Camp Wood. Company F was disbanded in May 1879.[6] However, Dan Roberts's Company D remained in place in northwestern Kimble County. Major Jones recognized that the forks of the Llano was still a troublesome area.

After the Dowdy murders, the western Hill Country region would have a six-month respite before the Rangers began their concluding campaign against the Kimble County confederation. Toward the end of that period of grace—and as a harbinger of things to come—Mack Potter was arrested by Corporal D. W. Gourley and three other Rangers on April 5, 1879, charged with cattle theft in Kimble County. He was probably carried to jail in Menardville for safekeeping.[7]

And long-imprisoned Bill Allison, embittered that his Dublin kinfolk had allowed him to languish for almost a year in the Travis County jail, signaled that, at last, he was ready to talk about the repeated stage robberies at Pegleg Station.

## Pegleg Station

Pegleg Station was a stage stop on the south bank of the San Saba River about twelve miles east of Menardville, on the road between Fort Mason and Fort Mc-Kavett. About a mile west of the station the road squeezed between the river and two high, rounded, cedar-choked hills separated by a steep draw. The eastern hill came to be called "Robbers' Roost" because hidden lookouts were sometimes posted there to alert their outlaw accomplices to the approach of the westbound stagecoach, and to the presence or absence of accompanying armed guards. On either the westbound or eastbound routes, stagecoaches were easy prey for lurking road agents where the mules slowed on the steep upgrade coming out of the draw.[8]

The station was named by the first occupant of the place, one Wilhelm Harlen, in honor of Thomas W. "Pegleg Willie" Ward, a hero of the Texas Revolution who lost his leg during the storming of Bexar in 1835, and thereafter wore a wooden leg. Ward was Texas land commissioner when Harlen obtained his title to the land in 1848.[9]

## Repeated Robberies

By April 1879 the Mason–Fort McKavett stagecoach near Pegleg Station had been robbed at least five times within about three years.[10] All the robberies remained unsolved. Scouts of the site after each of the several robberies, dating back to 1876, had all proved unfruitful because the trail of the departing highwaymen was quickly lost in the rocky and brushy terrain. A recurring and puzzling clue was the presence of particularly small footprints at the robbery sites—so small that some rangers and lawmen suspected that a woman might be operating with the road agents. Circumstantial evidence and the process of elimination directed strong suspicion toward the Dublin-Potter parties but proof remained elusive.[11]

Various schemes were floated by the Rangers as well as by local lawmen for trapping the robbers. Through an informant with connections to the Dublins, Captain Dan Roberts, in October 1878, planted false information that an affluent cattle buyer carrying a large bankroll would be on a particular stage, with the hope of secreting a Ranger as an armed guard on the roof of the stagecoach, and capturing the robbers, but they apparently detected his presence, and let the stagecoach pass unhindered.[12] On December 18 Menard County Sheriff Comstock proposed to Major Jones that some marked counterfeit bank notes be placed in the mails on board the stage, which money could later be traced back to whoever spent the money.[13] On December 30, responding to an earlier letter from Lieutenant N. O. Reynolds, Major Jones approved the policy of making deals with criminal informants in exchange for their testimony against their accomplices.[14] On January 16, 1879, Captain Roberts sent Sergeant Lam Sieker and a four-man squad to the Menardville vicinity to watch for stage robbers, responding to a message from the military paymaster at Fort McKavett that considerable money would be sent by coaches during the next six days. No robberies were attempted during that period.[15]

### A Break in the Case

Bill Allison, the brother-in-law of the surviving Dublin brothers and their criminal accomplice, had remained in the Austin jail since mid-June 1878, unable to make bond.[16] He was charged with several counts of cattle theft. Allison believed that his brothers-in-law were not assisting him in making bond, thus keeping him imprisoned. Bitter and resentful, he decided to turn state's evidence, exposing their involvement in the Pegleg robberies. As Ranger Sergeant J. B. Gillett related,

> in the spring of 1879, Dick Ware and I took some prisoners to the Austin jail. Allison saw us and called to me. He and I had been cowboys together long before I became a ranger. "Jim," said Allison, "you know that I have been cooped up here in this jail for nearly a year. People who ought to be my friends have evidently abandoned me and I am not going to stand it any longer. I can put the Pegleg stage robbers behind the bars, and I am going to do it."
>
> Ware . . . said, "Hold on, Bill. If you have anything to confess we will get an order from the sheriff to take you to see General Jones so you can talk to him."[17]

Alerted to the possibility of a break in the Pegleg case, Adjutant General Jones immediately wrote a note to the sheriff of Travis County, requesting that Allison be released to the custody of Rangers Gillett and Ware. The sheriff complied promptly. Gillett and Ware then conveyed Allison to the adjutant general's office, where he was soon involved in an extended private conversation with John B. Jones, after which Gillett and Ware returned him to his Austin jail cell.[18]

Shortly thereafter, Jones sent orders to Captain Dan Roberts to send Ranger patrols into Kimble County, seeking the capture and arrest of the Dublins, Mack Potter, and Rube Boyce.

Of course, Jones recognized that robbery of the U.S. mail was a federal offense, which required trial in federal court in Austin, with a much larger pool of better educated and more impartial jurors. Finally, he had an opportunity to break the cycle of arrest-indictment-acquittal which had already resulted in the repeated release of members of the confederation by friendly or intimidated Kimble County juries in district courts. Here was Jones's chance to put the Dublins and their accomplices away for a long time. He had warrants issued for Roll and Dell Dublin, Mack Potter, and Rube Boyce; later there would be more warrants issued for the arrest of other suspected accomplices.[19]

Mack Potter, who had been captured by the Rangers in Kimble County in early April, charged with horse theft and jailed in Menardville, was soon bailed out and back on the South Llano again. In mid-July 1879, presumably after local informants had begun to provide information as to the whereabouts of the Pegleg suspects, Company D and Company E began to focus on the rest of the South Llano confederation.

### Rounding Up the Pegleg Robbers

On July 14, operating from their Austin camp, Sergeant Nevill led five Company E Rangers in search of Matthew Wilkins, wanted in connection with attempts to rob the U.S. mail. They arrested him in the town of Llano, and brought him back to Austin five days later.[20] Wilkins was Rube Boyce's uncle by marriage.[21]

On July 15 Sergeant L. P. Sieker and six other Company D Rangers went on a scout of the South Llano valley, where they arrested Roll Dublin and Bill Potter, Mack Potter's younger brother. On the same day, Sergeant E. A. Sieker and a five-man squad arrested J. A. "Black" Burt and Rube Boyce near Junction City.[22]

The next day, Corporal Ashburn and four Company D rangers arrested John Boyce, James Cravens, John Pearl and Henry Pearl on Big Saline Creek, charged with robbing the U.S. mails; the arrested men were relatives and neighbors of Rube Boyce.[23] On July 17 Corporal Gourley led an unsuccessful scout up the South Llano valley in search of Dell Dublin, Mack Potter, and Luke Cathey.[24]

On July 18 Sergeant E. A. Sieker and a five-man squad of Company D rangers left their Kimble County headquarters for Austin, with prisoners Rube Boyce, Bill Potter, James Cravens, Roll Dublin, and J. A. Burt, to deliver them to the Sheriff of Travis County.[25]

Following several unsuccessful scouts of the South Llano valley during late July, searching for Dell Dublin and Mack Potter, Corporal Ashburn and three Company D Rangers returned to the area on July 31 and finally ran into the two outlaws near the Dublin home in the South Llano valley. Ashburn and his squad fired about ten shots; killed Dublin's horse; collected his saddle, bridle, and gun; and found some blood on the trail. When the shooting was over, the Dublin women stormed out of the house, demanding to know what had become of "the boys." When Ashburn's Rangers replied that they did not know, the Dublin women "poured execrations into them by the broadside, called them liars, and accused them of having killed the fugitives."[26]

The next morning, August 1, Captain Roberts went to Junction City to find out what his sources could tell him about the previous day's gun battle. Roberts learned from Junction City physician William M. Donnan that the good doctor had been called away at 2 a.m. to attend Dell Dublin, who explained that the nasty bullet wound in his hip was the result of an accidental, self-inflicted shooting, in which the bullet had struck a pocket knife in the back pocket of his pants and "shivered" into him, split into three pieces, which Dr. Donnan reported having cut out.[27] Based on Donnan's report, Roberts anticipated capturing the wounded Dell Dublin.[28]

Roberts also reported that the horse Dublin had been riding, which Corporal Ashburn and his men had shot out from under him, had been stolen the day before the gunfight, its legal brand picked and changed. The owner of the dead horse had accompanied Roberts to Junction City.

Roberts sent Sergeant L. P. Sieker and five other rangers back out the next day to scour the area, with no success, and advised Major Jones that he was satisfied that "Dell Dublin [had] been moved out of the neighborhood where he was shot. I think he was hauled off in a wagon . . . [and] Mac[k] Potter may have gone to the same place."[29]

Over the next week, Roberts expanded his search without success. On August 10, however, Dell Dublin and Mack Potter were captured by new sheriff John Garland and a posse of Kimble County citizens. Having no warrants, Garland immediately turned the two men over to Captain Roberts. They were served with papers from the U.S. marshal's office for robbing the U.S. mail and held in custody by the Rangers.[30]

The courageous initiative by Kimble County citizens, with their new sheriff, in capturing Dell Dublin and Mack Potter and conveying them to Captain Roberts, marks an important milestone in the gradual emergence of the "law-abiding party" in Kimble County. Whether or not Dublin and Potter surrendered to their neighbors because they feared being killed by the Rangers is immaterial. What matters is that the South Llano neighbors collectively asserted themselves against the confederation in an unmistakable declaration against criminal domination.

The next day, Roberts returned to the South Llano and served attachments on Mrs. William Allison and Mrs. John Miller as witnesses in the Pegleg case. On August 12 two Ranger squads started for Austin, one conveying Dublin and Potter to the Travis County jail, the other escorting the two Kimble County women, who were witnesses for the U.S. government, to Austin.[31] The nature of their evidence against the arrested men is not recorded, but the fact that Bill Allison's wife was willing to testify against her Dublin brothers, as well as her husband, indicates that serious dissension existed in the Dublin camp. So far as is known, Mr. and Mrs. John Miller were law-abiding citizens, not affiliated with the confederation.

Captain Roberts spent the next two months conducting various searches of the Dublin and Potter home sites, seeking items of material evidence—such as watches, shirt studs, and buttons—that might match descriptions of personal possessions taken from passengers of stagecoaches that had been robbed over the past three years, and transmitting them to Austin for use in the proceedings against the accused men.[32]

On October 13, 1879, case 888 was filed in U.S. District Court, Western District of Texas, against Mack Potter and Dell Dublin for mail robbery; witnesses for the prosecution included Texas Adjutant General John B. Jones and William Allison. Case 889 was filed on the same day against Roll Dublin, Matthew Wilkins, Reuben Boyce, Mac[k] Potter, Bill Potter, and William Allison for mail robbery; witnesses for the prosecution included the driver and passengers of the stagecoach, plus John Miller.[33]

This time, there would be no release on bail for members of the South Llano confederation. And the jurors that heard their case would not be sympathetic—or intimidated—neighbors.

Rube Boyce employed a more adventurous means of avoiding trial: on January 4, 1880, Boyce, aided by his wife, Adeline, carried out a dramatic escape from the Travis County jail.[34] According to James B. Gillett, Adeline Boyce came to see her husband at the jail with a basket of clean underwear.[35] Under her clothing, she had secreted a pistol, which her husband put in the basket under his exchanged dirty laundry. Boyce then escorted his wife to the end of the corridor to bid her goodbye. As the jailer opened the door, Boyce whipped out the pistol and disarmed him, then ran out through the back yard of the jail, where he mounted a pony that had been hitched there for him, and galloped out of Austin, firing his pistol as he rode. His getaway was complete; Rangers from Companies D and E immediately began to scour his familiar haunts in Kimble County, and then to cast a wider loop throughout the Hill Country, to no avail.[36] He was not captured and returned to jail until the fate of his Kimble County accomplices had been decided.[37]

### The Pegleg Trials

A Travis County grand jury indicted Dell and Roll Dublin, Mack and Bill Potter, Rube Boyce, Matthew Wilkins, and Bill Allison in February 1880.[38] Their trials got underway about August 20, 1880. They were charged with the December 15,

Figure 24. The Travis County jail, next to the Travis County courthouse (in the background), at the corner of 11th and Brazos Streets, Austin, Texas, in about 1900. The jail is where the suspects in the Pegleg robberies—Mack and Bill Potter, Roll and Dell Dublin, Matthew Wilkins, and Rube Boyce—were kept in late 1879 and 1880 while awaiting trial in federal court. With the aid of his wife, Boyce staged a dramatic escape from this jail on January 4, 1880. Courtesy of Austin History Center, Austin Public Library.

1877, robberies of both the westbound and eastbound stagecoaches near Pegleg Station. As James B. Gillett reported, the details of other robberies emerged as the trial progressed, but the defendants pled not guilty to the December 15 crime.

> The Dublin boys were the guiding spirits in the holdups, and worked with great cleverness. Old man Jimmie Dublin's ranch on the South Llano was their headquarters. From the ranch to Pegleg Station on the San Saba it was about sixty miles across a rough, mountainous country. As there were no wire fences in those days the robbers would ride over to the station, rob the stage, and in one night's ride regain their home. Traveling at night they were never observed. Dick Dublin . . . was the leader of the bandit gang. Even the mystery of the tiny footprints was disclosed: they were made by Mack Potter, who had an unusually small foot for a man.[39]

Members of the confederation continued their past patterns of trying to intimidate jurors: on August 25, deputy U.S. marshals guarding the courtroom arrested Joseph Potter—then twenty years old—and George Coburn on charges of "bulldozing witnesses in the Pegleg case."[40]

On the third day of the trial, Matthew Wilkins became convinced that the prosecution's case was so strong that he would be sentenced to life imprisonment. Wilkins changed his plea, accepting a sentence of ten years at hard labor for the crime of robbery of the U.S. mails. Undercut by Wilkins, his fellow defendants eventually caved in and received the same sentence.[41] On August 30, sentence was pronounced by Judge A. P. McCormick. Dell and Roll Dublin, Mack and Bill Potter, and Matthew Wilkins were sent to the state prison of Illinois at Chester, where they were received on September 13, 1880. The fugitive Rube Boyce was convicted *in absentia*. State's witness Bill Allison received a reduced sentence and was placed in the Texas state prison system.[42]

Rube Boyce was back in the Travis County jail in January 1882. He succeeded in getting a new trial set for the following June, claiming the jury had been improperly influenced by court guards. He arranged for Bill Allison, who had received a lesser sentence in exchange for his testimony, to be subpoenaed as a witness and was bailed out of jail by his relatives in March 1882.[43] Eventually Boyce was retried and acquitted.[44]

Writing in late 1880, Adjutant General John B. Jones took obvious pride in the successful prosecution of the Peg leg outlaws:

> Notably among the services rendered by the Frontier Battalion during the last two years [there was no annual report in 1879], is the breaking up of a most notorious band of highway robbers, the largest, most thoroughly organized and successful which has ever existed in Texas, known as the "Pegleg Stage Robbers," who have been engaged in robbing mail coaches and travelers in the highways, robbing stores and residences, and stealing horses and cattle in the counties on the frontier, for the past two years. Of this clan, there have been three killed in attempting to arrest them, and nine have been sent to the penitentiary.[45] This service was performed by detachments from Captain Roberts' Company D, in Menard County, and Lieutenant Nevill's Company E, stationed near Austin.[46]

The law had finally put away the older sons of Jimmy Dublin and Will Potter. But the younger brother of Will and Tom Potter, James K. P. "Jimmy" Potter, was still at large. And the older sons of Tom Potter—the Indian cousins—were still hanging around Kimble County stealing livestock. They would be next on the Rangers' list.

# 11 :: The Cousins

om Potter's name shows up only twice in the official records of Texas Ranger activities in Kimble County. The first occurrence was when he was arrested by Lieutenant Frank Moore and nine other Rangers on March 14, 1877, with Charles Edwin and William Meeks, and charged with theft of cattle.[1] The second mention of his name is in connection with the killing of Dick Dublin at Potter's Cajac Creek homestead on January 19, 1878, by Corporal James Gillett and his ranger squad.[2] Potter was not arrested in that affair, even though he tried to assist Dublin in his ill-fated escape attempt. After that, Tom Potter's name is absent from the Rangers' Monthly Returns, General Correspondence, and lists of suspects and wanted fugitives.

Similarly, Tom Potter's eldest Indian son, Frank, was arrested only once by the Rangers, in connection with the Kimble County Roundup in late April 1877.[3] Frank was probably the third of the "Potter boys" mentioned in the list of fugitives used by the Rangers in the Kimble County Roundup, the others being his cousins, the two eldest sons of Will Potter, Mack and Bill.[4] Only after late July 1880 does Frank Potter's name appear again in Ranger records, and then only as a person of interest.[5]

The name of John Potter, Tom Potter's second son, does not appear in any of the Ranger records in any context until October 1880.[6]

James "Indian Jim" Potter, Tom Potter's third son, does not verifiably appear in the Ranger records until December 15, 1879, when he and his Indian brothers were accused by John Miller of threatening to kill him. Miller was a Kimble County citizen and justice of the peace who had been identified as a witness on behalf of the federal government in the upcoming trials of Roll and Dell Dublin, Mack and Bill Potter, Rube Boyce, and Matthew Wilkins, in federal court in Austin.[7] But "Indian Jim" Potter was certainly known and wanted by the spring of 1880 and was involved in a night-time shoot-out with Rangers in late July 1880 in the South Llano valley, probably near his uncle James K. P. Potter's home site on Chalk Creek.[8] He was then about nineteen years old.

### The Enigma of John Potter

Among all the "Indian Potters," the name of John Potter, the second son among the Indian cousins, is conspicuously absent from any mention at all in the records

of the Kimble County Roundup in late April 1877 or of the repeated Ranger actions and patrols in Kimble County during the next three and a half years. In the
face of the earlier arrests involving his father and eldest brother Frank, his white
Potter cousins and their Dublin partners in crime, and his errant uncle James K. P.
Potter as well as the evident maintained affiliation with the interests of the confederation—revealed by the Indian Potters' threats against putative federal witness John Miller—we may only speculate about possible reasons for this absence.

The obvious and charitable explanation is that John Potter, age twenty-one in
1877, was not engaged in criminal activities but was working with, and perhaps
looking after, his father, and therefore was not a target of the Rangers' interest.
A second explanation is that he was engaged in livestock theft but worked on his
own and was clever and furtive enough to avoid suspicion. A third alternative, as
previously suggested, is that he was regularly absent from Kimble County—possibly was living out of sight in northern Mexico, interacting with the Mexican
Indians and their merchant supporters as an agent for the Kimble County confederation of cattle and horse thieves.[9] The evidence for this explanation is entirely circumstantial: not a single recorded indication or speculation in the official
Ranger records, correspondence, or contemporary newspaper articles attaches the
name of John Potter to such a role.

Evidence does exist, however, that some Texas Rangers may have believed in
1880 that John Potter and his brother Jim had been involved with the Mexican
Indians who murdered the Dowdy young people.[10]

### The Mysterious James K. P. Potter

Understandably, substantial confusion arises in trying to unravel references in
Ranger records to James or Jim Potter during the years 1877 to 1880 in Kimble
County. When James K. P. Potter arrived in the county in late 1876 or early 1877,
he was about thirty years old. His Indian nephew James "Jim" Potter was then
about fourteen, probably too young to have been stealing horses or rustling cattle.
So the "Jim Potter" that was apprehended in May 1877 during the Kimble Coun-
ty Roundup on suspicion of horse theft in Kaufman County was almost certainly
James K. P. Potter. Because the telltale two middle initials appear on the December 1877 Statement of Arrests, there can be little doubt of the identity of the
James K. P. Potter who was arrested on December 27, 1877, with J. A. "Black"
Burt and E. T. Denson for stealing hogs (for which he was acquitted on May 5,
1878).[11]

Similarly, the "James Potter" who, together with newcomer George Cleveland, was arrested on July 11, 1879, with stolen cattle, was also probably James

K. P. Potter, inasmuch as the two men were nearly the same age, grew up together in Mendocino County, California, and later ran together as known cattle rustlers. Potter was tried on August 14, 1879, in Kimble County and probably was acquitted in a justice of the peace proceeding.[12]

Although there may be legitimate uncertainty as to the true identity of the "Jim Potter" who was arrested in Menard County on May 7, 1880, for horse theft—and who later broke jail and escaped—this was also probably James K. P. Potter because his mixed-race nephew and namesake had by then acquired the sobriquet of "Indian Jim" Potter in the Ranger records.[13] In any case, the Rangers knew by year-end 1879 that they were dealing with two James Potters, one a hardened horse thief, then about thirty-three years old, and his nephew, an Indian cowboy a little more than half his white uncle's age.

### George Cleveland Arrives

On July 11, 1879, Sergeant E. A. Sieker and five other Rangers, following cattle thieves, overtook them in the South Llano River valley, where they found James K. P. Potter and George Cleveland in possession of twenty head of stolen cattle. The next day, Sieker and his squad delivered Potter and Cleveland, together with their stolen cattle, to the sheriff of Kimble County.[14] Apparently Potter and Cleveland were released on bail because both were very soon once more at large.

George Cleveland's name was a newcomer to the Ranger Monthly Returns. Aged thirty-one in 1879, he was a previous Mendocino County acquaintance of James K. P. "Jimmy" Potter, the youngest brother of Will and Tom Potter, who had joined his older brothers in Kimble County two or three years after their arrival in early 1874. Cleveland's family were neighbors of two of Jimmy Potter's grown sisters in Mendocino County in 1870, about three years before the Potters departed for Texas.[15]

About December 13, 1872, George Cleveland shot and killed a man named Crowey in Anderson Valley, California. Several young men had abducted a young girl from her parents and then got into a quarrel among themselves about the girl. Crowey, who was not related to the girl, heard the argument and stepped out of his house to ask what the problem was, and was immediately shot and killed by Cleveland.[16] The justice of the peace set a high bail (ten thousand dollars), which was later confirmed by the district court.[17] Cleveland could not pay the required sum so remained in jail until August 4, 1874, when he was convicted of manslaughter and sentenced to five years in state prison.[18]

Apparently, George Cleveland's prison sentence was shortened, perhaps for good behavior, because he married Rebecca Potter Gordon Hildreth, the twice-married sister of Will, Tom, and Jimmy Potter, on September 9, 1877, in Potter

Valley, California.[19] Cleveland was twenty-nine; Rebecca was forty-two. Cleveland did not remain with his new wife long; he left Rebecca newly pregnant, probably in late April or early May 1879, and arrived in Kimble County in late May or June, where he became a confederate of his old friend and new brother-in-law, James K. P. Potter.[20]

## Stolen Saddles

On July 25, 1879, Captain Daniel Roberts and five Company D Rangers made a scout to the South Llano valley in search of stolen saddles, which they recovered and delivered to their rightful owners. They also encountered and arrested George Cleveland, charged with theft of cattle. Three days later, Roberts and two Ranger privates delivered Cleveland to the sheriff of Menard County.[21]

There was much more to the story. As described in Roberts's memoirs, four of his Rangers had been given permission to attend a dance in Junction City. Deputy Sheriff Joe Clements, who was a frequent visitor at the Ranger camp, went with them. The five men hitched their saddled horses to a tree outside the hall, and

> went to the ball room as gay as larks . . . and realized their visions of pleasure, until just before daylight, when they returned to their horses, to come [back] to camp. Lo and behold, two of the Rangers [and Deputy Clements] had lost their saddles. It was fortunate that they could get out of town before daylight to cover the[ir] humiliation.[22]

Roberts questioned his men and the embarrassed deputy as to whom they had seen in the vicinity of the dance, then instructed Clements and the four Rangers to remain quietly in camp all day, and to remain silent about the stolen saddles. Roberts, who by now had acquired a sage understanding of the workings of the Kimble County confederation, realized that a spy would be posted to watch the roads into and out of Junction City, and to warn members of the confederation about the approach of the Rangers. So he waited until nightfall, then took his Rangers and Deputy Clements, rode easterly around the town, crossed the South Llano River, gained the higher ground on the west side of the valley, and proceeded southwest to the camp of the parties he suspected, about ten miles from Junction City, in the South Llano valley.[23]

Roberts and his squad woke up the camp and found one of the suspects there, a young man named Hensley, whom he "invited out to take breakfast with us." They took Hensley a mile or so away and stopped near the road to make breakfast, setting out pickets to either side, with orders to bring any passers-by to camp.

Directly, one of the sentries brought one Charles Beardsley to Roberts, who knew through his spies that Beardsley and Hensley were pals, and that Beardsley was acting as a lookout.

Unable to get anything out of Hensley about the missing saddles, Roberts instructed three of his Rangers to remain by the campfire with Beardsley while he took Hensley into a thicket not far away for a little talk. The Rangers were then to fire their guns, release Beardsley, and come to where Roberts and Hensley waited. Hearing the gunfire, the terrified Hensley said to Roberts, "Captain, they have killed that man."

Roberts replied, "Now if you know anything about those saddles, you had better tell it quick." The frightened young man then broke down and revealed the hiding place of the stolen saddles, and Roberts released him with his promise to seek better company in the future.

The Rangers loaded the saddles on their pack mule and headed northeast toward Junction City on the river road. They had not gone far when they met the "principal actor in the saddle stealing," George Cleveland, whom they also wanted for cattle rustling. He was sent to Menardville, where he was jailed.[24]

Cleveland's trial took place in Menardville, at the spring term of district court (March 22–26, 1880), where he received a two-year sentence for cattle theft. He was placed in irons awaiting transportation to the state penitentiary, but before he could be delivered to prison, he escaped when the Texas Ranger guarding him fell asleep.[25]

### The Llanos Begin to Settle Down

On August 13, 1879, Corporal Gourley and a three-man Ranger squad scouted the South Llano valley for Tom Hensley, James K. P. Potter, and Port Wilkinson but could not find them. The following day Ranger Sergeant L. P. Sieker went to Junction City to attend the justice of the peace trials of Potter and Bud Garland, a neighbor of the Potters and Dublins in the South Llano valley; the results of those trials are not recorded.[26]

On September 6, Ranger Sergeant E. A. Sieker and a nine-man squad made a ninety-mile round-trip scout of the South Llano valley to search for a party of unnamed fugitives reported to be camped in the cedar brakes but did not find them.[27]

The summer and fall of 1879 were extremely dry in Kimble County. During this time, the frequent patrols and arrests of Kimble County outlaws by Company D rangers seemed finally to promise peace and quiet in the long-troubled area. On October 28 Captain Dan Roberts moved the headquarters camp of Company D north to the San Saba River, five miles east of Fort McKavett, where range conditions promised better winter forage for his horses.[28] For the first time in nearly

Figure 25. John A. and Martha B. Miller, about 1905. "Honest John" Miller was elected justice of the peace when Kimble County was organized in early 1876 and served on the first grand jury at the Kimble County Roundup. He and his wife were witnesses for the prosecution of the Pegleg stage robbers in August 1880. Courtesy of Kimble County Historical Commission.

three years, a company of the Frontier Battalion would not be headquartered near Junction City. Nevertheless, Dan Roberts's Rangers would continue periodic patrols southward into the valleys of the Llanos.

### Citizen John Miller Warns of a Plot

As the federal case against the Pegleg defendants in Austin progressed in the fall of 1879, intrigues to combat it were detected by John A. Miller, who lived with his family at the mouth of Johnson Fork, a few miles east of Junction City. Captain Roberts wrote as much to Adjutant General Jones on December 15.[29]

> John Miller [together with his wife Martha, federal witnesses called to testify in the Pegleg case] has been here for some days, waiting to hear from you. He reports [that] the Indian Potters are trying to kill him. I have no confidence in anything he says, and I believe he is trying to play a "double game," and give that clan the best of it, if possible. I didn't let him know anything you wrote me, in regard to what is going on in the interest of those that are in jail. Such a thing may be contemplated, by their friends on the outside, but John Miller [doesn't] know much of it. He couldn't tell me anything about it, more than a man named Robinson was to head it.[30] Didn't know where, or how they proposed to operate. Told me he got his information from Oliver Keese, who lives at Junction City. I told Miller to find out all he could about it and let me know of it. I will watch him at the same time. I believe if he could find out that any

means were being used to catch them, he would inform them of it, as his lot is cast with them, and he is going around unarmed and evidently expects to spend the balance of [his] days in that kind of society.

Captain Roberts's suspicions about John A. Miller notwithstanding, the thirty-one-year-old settler, known locally as "Honest John," was well regarded among respectable Kimble County citizens. Miller had arrived in Kimble County in 1874 with his wife and family. He was a declared early supporter of law and order and was elected justice of the peace for Precinct 4 when Kimble County was first organized. In May 1877 Miller served on the first grand jury to return indictments against criminals belonging to the Kimble County confederation, when that was a courageous undertaking. He also served as jury commissioner for the second term of district court in the fall of 1877.[31]

Furthermore, Miller and his wife, Martha, were serving as witnesses for the state in its case against the Pegleg robbers in federal court, which made them both vulnerable to possible revenge by the confederation, as the Indian Potters' threats demonstrate. Roberts's cryptic reference to what Jones told him about "what was going on in the interest of those that are in jail" suggests that the authorities may have discovered a plot to break the Dublin-Potter group out of the Austin jail, and that Miller may have caught wind of such a plan and was trying to warn state authorities of the scheme. This also would have required commendable fortitude, considering past efforts by the outlaw element to threaten settlers who stood up against it. It may also explain Miller's ambivalent—or cautious?—behavior that Roberts described. Finally, Roberts's general low opinion of early Kimble County settlers is clearly evident.

### Fugitives

On April 8, 1880, two weeks after the adjournment of the spring term of district court in Menardville, Corporal D. W. Gourley and another Ranger made an unsuccessful scout to the head of the San Saba River, looking for the fugitive George Cleveland, who had escaped from the Menardville jail after being sentenced to two years in the state penitentiary for cattle theft. During April 19–23, Corporal H. T. Ashburn and a four-man squad made an equally unsuccessful scout to Kimble County in search of Cleveland and other fugitives.[32]

Captain Roberts and a five-man squad returned to Kimble County on May 7, looking for the notorious escapee Rube Boyce; they did not find him but did run into Jim Potter (probably James K. P. Potter), whom they arrested on charges of horse theft in Menard County and conveyed to the custody of the Menard County sheriff.[33]

James K. P. Potter did not remain in the Menard County jail long, escaping soon after being jailed there. On June 14 Corporal Gourley and two other Rangers were unsuccessfully looking for him around the headwaters of the San Saba River, and during July 24–29, Gourley and a four-man squad were in Kimble County, searching for both Potter and Cleveland on the South Llano.[34] After an exchange of gunfire, their quarry escaped into the brush. Captain Roberts provided more details about this action in his extremely significant August 1, 1880, letter to Adjutant General Jones:

> Sergeant [Ed] Sieker telegraphed me from [Fort] Davis a few days since, that Cleveland was coming in the direction of Kimble County. Consequently, I sent [a] scout over there to watch for him. After watching the Cleveland and Potter camp two nights, during which it rained constantly, a horseman rode up to camp on [the] second night [probably July 27], about eight o'clock. Thinking that [this was] their man, they moved on the camp. They saw James Potter ["Indian Jim"] sitting by firelight, with his gun across his lap. [They] ordered him to surrender, when he "broke for the brush," which was within 20 feet of him. They fired ten shots at him, but couldn't tell whether they hit him or not. During the firing, a party to one side fired on my men, cutting Private Renick's belt . . . but doing no damage. Private Brown saw the blaze come from the gun, and fired two shots at the bulk. My men think it was Frank Potter who fired at them, but were not certain. They examined [the area] next morning to see what they [could], but could find out nothing. Madam Cleveland claimed damage on a nest of milk pans that caught a stray bullet, perforating the lot. Corporal Gourley paid her $1.00, and she seemed happy.
>
> Corporal Gourley and Privates Renick and Brown made the "roundup," leaving Kimbell and Pace to watch the horses. That whole "nest" [of outlaws] are "trimming their sails" to leave here, as soon as the trial of those in Austin [is concluded]. I will try to see who is with them, after several days out.[35]

Although the exact location of this engagement is not identified—other than being somewhere in the South Llano valley—it seems likely that it took place at James K. P. Potter's remote homestead on Chalk Creek, at what is now known as the "Potter Waterhole," because the reference to "Madam Cleveland" (probably James K. P. Potter's wife Evaline) and the "nest of milk pans" suggests a permanent establishment as well as the possibility of young children to feed, and

Figure 26. "Potter Waterhole," upper Chalk Creek, southwestern Kimble County, Texas, looking north. James K. P. Potter and his family are believed to have located near here in 1877, shortly after their arrival in Kimble County. This place is also believed to be the location where Texas Rangers and outlaws of the Potter-Cleveland gang engaged in a gunfight on the night of July 27, 1880. "Indian Jim" Potter was probably under the large oak tree at left when fired on by the Rangers, who were watching the outlaw from the top of the cliff at right. Photo by the author, 2010.

because the Rangers had a specific place in mind when they set up their watch for the fugitives. Also, Kimble County tradition identifies the "Potter Waterhole" with a shoot-out, with the Rangers firing down on the outlaws from a cliff overlooking the outlaws' camp.[36]

More important, Roberts's letter expresses the Rangers' belief that the Indian Potters—Frank, Jim, and, as later events would suggest, John Potter—had by now joined forces with their uncle, James K. P. Potter, and his pal, George Cleveland, both wanted men. It implies that these outlaws were moving back and forth between the Kimble County area and trans-Pecos cattle ranges, and that the Rangers believed that Frank Potter—although not mentioned in Ranger reports from May 1877 to July 1880—was still involved in the criminal activities of the Indian cousins in Kimble County, perhaps as a "transfer agent" in the Pecos River country for onward passage of stolen livestock. Moreover, Sieker's telegram to Roberts also indicates that George Cleveland was by then a known outlaw to the

Rangers in trans-Pecos Texas, and that he represented a link between the Kimble County confederation and more far-flung theaters of criminal activity along the Pecos River.

Finally, and most significantly, Roberts's letter articulates the Rangers' belief that those Potter outlaws who still remained in Kimble County were preparing to leave the area for good, presumably anticipating the conviction and sentencing of their kinsmen in Austin, whose trials for the Pegleg stage robberies were imminent.

### The Demise of Tom Potter

The date of Tom Potter's death is not known. The last record of him alive is contained in a cheerful letter written from Kimble County on December 18, 1878, by his younger brother James K. P. Potter to Moses Carson Briggs, their brother-in-law, in Mendocino County, California, reporting that "Tom Potter and family are enjoying good health. . . . Tom has a good place, and some seventy head of stock."[37]

Kimble County death records during the frontier period are largely incomplete, but the official federal mortality schedule for the period June 1, 1879, to May 31, 1880, does list eight decedents, some of whom were neighbors who lived in the South Llano valley.[38] Tom Potter's name is not among those listed.

Tom's homestead was located about a mile west of his brother Will's family home on Cajac Creek. The 1880 federal census was taken in the Potter neighborhood on Cajac Creek on June 23, 1880. The census record indicates that the three youngest children whom Thomas Potter had brought with him to Texas—Moses, William, and Thomas (Jr.), ages seventeen, fifteen, and twelve, respectively—were then living near the residence of his brother, Will Potter, and his family.[39] All the Potter children—Tom's as well as Will's—of school age are shown to be illiterate. Thomas Potter's name is shown as the head of the family, with "Mrs." added, apparently as an afterthought, above his name. The person designated as "Mrs." was white, female, forty-eight years of age, and a widow. Her given name is not shown. She was literate and was born in Missouri; her parents were both born in Virginia.

The problem with all this is that the same data apply equally well to Tom Potter with the obvious exception of "female" and "widow." No mention is made in Potter family records of Tom Potter having taken a third wife in Texas.[40] Furthermore, the prospect of a mature white woman marrying a middle-aged man with six Indian sons in frontier Texas—where Indians were reviled—seems unlikely, to say the least.

The three younger sons of Tom Potter would probably not have been taken into the home of his brother Will unless Tom had died, was seriously ill, or had abandoned his family. Given his attachment to his children, as manifested by his move to the Round Valley reservation from Potter Valley, during the northern California Indian persecutions of the late 1860s, abandonment seems unlikely. Although his natural death prior to June 23, 1880, is entirely possible, a preferable interpretation, honoring all the facts recorded in the 1880 census—as well as the contemporary federal mortality schedule—is that, when the census was taken, Tom Potter was on his deathbed in the home of his brother Will, together with his younger three sons, and the vital information was provided to the census taker by Will's wife, Mary. If this interpretation is correct, Tom Potter, described in several contemporaneous accounts as "Old Man Potter," was forty-eight years old at the time of his death. Neither the cause of his death nor the location of his grave are known.[41]

This interpretation also suggests that "Indian Jim" Potter had by now transferred his allegiance to his uncle, James K. P. Potter, who apparently had set up a livestock-theft operation involving George Cleveland, Frank Potter, and perhaps John Potter as well, all of whom may have been present at the July 27 gunfight reported by Ranger Captain Dan Roberts, at the "Potter Waterhole" just above James K. P. Potter's homestead on Chalk Creek.[42]

In any case, by June 23, 1880, Tom Potter's three eldest sons were not living at home with their father. Frank, then about twenty-six years old, was—at least part of the time—cowboying with the Hashknife outfit on the Pecos River in West Texas.[43] "Indian Jim," about nineteen, was a fugitive horse thief sought by several county sheriffs as well as the Texas Rangers. The whereabouts of the mysterious John Potter, about twenty-four, are unknown.

Life and Kimble County had not been kind to Tom Potter—the affluence of his golden California days in Potter Valley was long gone, and his Indian consort, Molly Metock, had remained in California and married another man. Tom lived a meager existence in a lonely hollow, his family perceived by his fellow citizens to be part of a vicious criminal confederation. His older sons were gone, or in trouble with the law, or keeping company with his kid brother, Jimmy, a wanted horse thief, and Jimmy's friend George Cleveland, a convicted California murderer and fugitive from justice in Texas. Some of Tom Potter's sons had possibly committed appalling crimes. Two of his nephews were in jail in Austin, awaiting trial for stage robbery. Their father, Tom's brother Will Potter, had been disgraced in the community. Tom's three motherless younger Indian sons were reviled by their frontier neighbors because of their blood. The land on which he had squatted and lived for six years had probably been preempted by other more far-sighted Kimble County citizens, who could enforce their claim by law.[44] His days on Cajac Creek were numbered.

One can imagine many scenarios of accidental injury or illness that might have caused Tom Potter's untimely death. The puzzling silence about his demise, however, implies disreputable circumstances. Perhaps he was an alcoholic. He may have died of advanced syphilis, acquired from long association with California Indian women. Family violence may have been involved, possibly stemming from the increasing influence of his brother James K. P. Potter on Tom's sons John and "Indian Jim."

It is also not unreasonable to wonder if "Old Tom Potter" did not die of a broken heart.

### The Potter Horse Thieves

Following Tom Potter's death, James K. P. Potter, his pal George Cleveland, and Tom's sons John and "Indian Jim" apparently decided to leave Kimble County for good. The manner of their departure was a clear statement of revenge as well as defiance. They targeted a herd of horses that belonged to H. K. Hutchinson, who earlier had filed legally on the Potter homesteads on Cajac Creek. Hutchinson's horse herd was being pastured with others in the North Llano valley, in the vicinity of abandoned Fort Terrett. In late September, the Potter horse thieves struck.

Captain Dan Roberts had established a network of trustworthy cattlemen whom he could rely on to alert him to the presence of suspicious characters on the cattle ranges west of Menardville and Junction City, where Indian or white horse thieves had recently been operating. One of those allies was Sam Merck, who ranched at the head of the North Llano River near old Fort Terrett, just west of the Kimble County line.

Merck arrived at Company D's camp near Fort McKavett on the morning of September 25, 1880, after a thirty-mile ride through torrential rains. He reported that he and his neighbors, chief among them H. K. Hutchinson, had lost a number of horses, and that white men, not Indians, had stolen them.[45]

Roberts immediately formed a six-man squad under Corporal Rush G. Kimbell, ordering him to return with Merck to the scene of the crime, locate the trail of the horse thieves, and "catch them if they stayed on top of the ground." Kimbell did not fail to grasp the intensity of his captain's instructions.[46]

The September 1880 Monthly Return of Company D records an entry for September 25:

Corporal Kimbell [and] six men started to take [the] trail of Horse Thieves at head waters of N[orth] Llano. Supposed to be Cleveland and [the] Potters.[47]

The chase was on.

Figure 27. Corporal R. G. Kimbell, mounted on his favorite horse, Robert E. Lee, in the Texas Ranger camp near Fort McKavett, just before leading his squad in pursuit of the Potter-Cleveland horse thieves, September 25, 1880. Courtesy of Texas State Library and Archives Commission, Austin.

# 12 :: The Chase

Moving out at a purposeful trail-eating trot, Corporal Rush Kimbell's six-man squad rode away from Company D's camp on the San Saba River before noon on September 25. His command included Privates N. J. Brown, Ed Dozier, W. H. "Hick" Dunman, J. V. Latham, "Mac" Smith, and R. C. Roberts, and a pack mule loaded with ten days' rations and assorted gear.[1]

They headed south across the muddy divide toward old Fort Terrett, on the headwaters of the North Llano River (see map 7).[2] Rancher Sam Merck, who had brought word of the horse thefts, led the way.[3] The thieves already had at least a thirty-six-hour head start.[4] Arriving in the narrow, cliff-bound valley of the North Llano by late afternoon on September 25, Merck and the Rangers scoured the muddy ground until they found the trail of the departing outlaws and their stolen horse herd. There Kimbell's squad camped at dusk, making ready for an early start the next morning.[5]

## On the Trail

The Rangers headed out of the North Llano valley at first light, following the trail of the stolen horse herd south about ten miles to the head of Dry Llano Draw, and then struggled up steep, ledgy slopes onto the flat, uninhabited divide between the Llano, Nueces, and Devils Rivers. Here the fleeing outlaws would have made good time over the high-standing, thick-turfed live-oak savanna—but so could their pursuers, and the tracks of their quarry's passing in the wet soil would have been readily visible. Kimbell would have posted outriders on either flank to look out for horse tracks, unwary outlaws, or an ambush by the renegades. Once on top of the plateau, the trail turned west, in the direction of Beaver Lake, at the headwaters of the Devils River. Kimbell pushed his squad hard until dark; then they made a dry camp on the divide on the night of September 26.[6]

Kimbell's command was moving by dawn the next morning, alternating between a fast walk and a trot. The outlaws' trail, clearly visible, stayed on top of the plateau for another twenty miles. Then it descended westerly across the gentle slopes of Buckley Draw, a broad, grassy, west-draining valley that the Rangers followed for another twenty miles to its intersection with the dry upper reaches of the Devils River drainage. There the trail, now becoming fainter with each mile, turned south down the flat alluvial bottom of the gray-cliffed Devils River can-

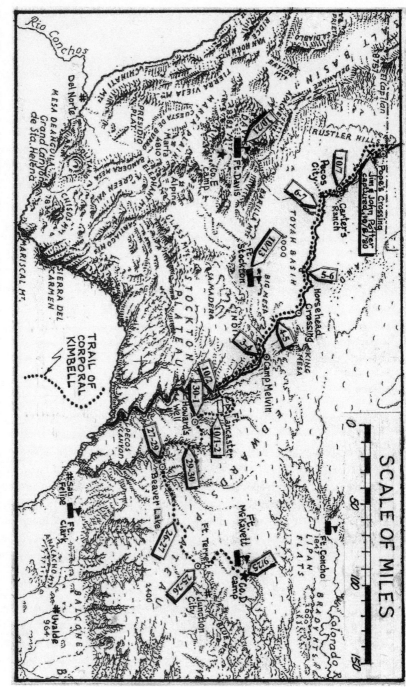

Map 7. The route of Corporal Kimbell's squad in pursuit of the Potter horse thieves, September 25–October 8, 1880. The chase is plotted on Erwin J. Raisz's physiographic map of the United States (1957); used with permission.

yon. After about ten miles it came to Beaver Lake, a shallow pond fed by the head-water spring of the Devils River, and the first living water in more than eighty miles. About three miles downstream, beside another spring, were the ruins of the abandoned stage station that had been built to serve the old southern mail route, connecting San Antonio and El Paso.[7] Kimbell's squad probably camped there on the evening of September 27. And there it rained again, washing out the trail they had followed for the past eighty miles—as well as the trail that lay ahead to wherever it was that their quarry were headed.[8]

The Rangers remained impatiently at the Beaver Lake stage station all day on September 28, waiting for the flooded draws to recede, fearful that the outlaws were increasing their lead. With the trail of the stolen horse herd now washed out, Kimbell had to proceed by educated guesswork, anticipating that the outlaws were headed for the Pecos River, from whence they might take one of several routes. Wagons presently used the old stage road to Fort Lancaster, on the Pecos. This road left the Devils River valley at Beaver Lake and headed northwest for about forty miles, across rough dissected tablelands, to Howard's Well, the next reliable waterhole on the route to the Pecos River.[9]

But Kimbell may have figured that the Potter horse thieves would have preferred another route, one that saw less traffic—meaning fewer people to observe their passage and warn any pursuing Rangers—and also made it easier to keep the horse herd together. Johnson's Run offered such a route, and its upper reaches passed within a dozen miles of Howard's Well, where Kimbell and his squad might surprise the outlaws, or perhaps encounter other travelers who might have seen which way they had gone.

The Ranger column departed Beaver Lake early on the morning of September 29. A mile below the stage station they left the Devils River and turned right at the mouth of Johnson's Run, following its gravelly bottom northwest, confined between bluffs of dark gray limestone for most of that day. Saturated ground made for slow going, and it was only toward late afternoon when they rejoined the old stage road and followed it six miles north to the mouth of a southeast-reaching draw, where they probably camped for the night. The next morning they would have tracked the old ruts northwestward up the draw, onto another divide, and then down into Government Canyon, which the road followed westward about five miles to its intersection with Howard's Draw, a dry, open canyon floored by alluvial gravels and calichified thin soils, and flanked by treeless, ledgy, stratified limestone bluffs.[10] The saddle-sore Rangers probably arrived at Howard's Well on the afternoon of September 30. There they found a squad of buffalo soldiers from General Benjamin Grierson's 10th Cavalry, which had been detached to watch for Indian raiders, incoming from Mexico.[11]

The soldiers reported that, on the day before, they had seen a group of riders a few miles to the west, driving a herd of horses. From a distance, the soldiers thought they were Indians and had so reported to their officers. That news heartened Kimbell and his men—not only had they guessed right and were still on the outlaws' trail, but they had gained about half a day in the bargain.[12]

The tiring Rangers spent the night at Howard's Well, departing early the next day for old Fort Lancaster, the abandoned military outpost built in 1853 to guard the San Antonio–El Paso road, where Live Oak Draw ran into the Pecos River.[13] They followed the old stage road northwestward, up Howard's Draw to a tributary canyon, where it made a steep climb onto a high mesquite-studded tableland.[14] Here the road turned due north for about twenty miles, and the Rangers may have spent some time searching for tracks. Whether they picked up the trail again is not known, but when dusk fell on the evening of October 1, Kimbell would have ordered a dry camp on the tableland.

### Decision at Fort Lancaster

The next day they rode north to the head of Mailbox Draw, where the old stage road made a precipitous, twisty, six-hundred-foot descent to Live Oak Canyon, the Pecos River, and Fort Lancaster. Kimbell's command, men and horses now weary and dust covered, picked their bone-jarring way down the steep, ledgy roadway, past Window Rock, and arrived at the clear thread of Live Oak Creek, where thirsty men and horses refreshed themselves at the first live water since they had left Howard's Well the previous morning. They passed through the shade of the dense oak grove at the mouth of Live Oak Draw and finally pulled up at the stone ruins of Fort Lancaster on the afternoon of October 2. Here "they were informed that, only the day before, men with a bunch of horses, answering [the] description [of the rangers' quarry] had passed that way."[15]

Now Kimbell made a fateful decision—he decided that his squad would ride all night, in an effort to overtake the outlaws.[16] So late on the afternoon of October 2, they splashed across the Pecos, a torpid, alkali-saturated stream, and rode northward along its west bank, the western margin of the Edwards Plateau looming high on their right. At dusk they would have stopped to water their horses at Pecos Spring, at present Sheffield, the west-facing bluffs across the river glowing golden in the reflected last light of the setting sun. It was the last good water they would have for more than two weeks. Then they rode all night, trying to gain a full day on their quarry, knowing there might be a shoot-out with the outlaws the next day.

### The Godforsaken Land of the Pecos

For westward travelers, everything changes at the Pecos River. Left behind to the

east are the extensive high grassy tablelands of the Edwards Plateau and the intervening steep-walled, layered limestone canyons, with their limpid, tumbling
streams and scattered groves of oak and pecan trees in the alluvial bottoms.

The Pecos River heads high in the Sangre de Cristo Mountains of northern
New Mexico. A million or so years ago, the south-flowing Pecos River traversed
the apron of sedimentary outwash reaching out eastward from the foot of the
Rocky Mountains. Because of its steeper gradient, the Pecos cut off and captured
the upper reaches of the Red, Brazos, and Colorado River drainages and then continued its down-cutting through this geologically recent, unconsolidated detritus,
eventually eroding down into older bedrock formations rich in soluble, evaporitic
salts. This geologic history produced the middle stretches of the present Pecos
River valley—a very broad, long valley filled with muddy, endlessly reworked,
alkali-rich sediments. And of course the present arid environment—classed as
Chihuahuan desert—only accentuates the concentration of mineral salts in Pecos
valley soils.[17]

The Pecos is a squalid stream—a sluggish, steep-banked creek that meanders
leisurely across a muddy, alkali-saturated floodplain lined with scrawny desert
willows, mesquite, and salt cedars. Its water is so saturated with alkali that the
banks are stained with a stark white efflorescence of gypsum and salt. Its floodplains and terraces are covered with low-growing tangles of mesquite, creosote
bush, tasajilla, and prickly pear. Going upstream (northwest), the wide, treeless
valley through which the Pecos flows becomes increasingly flat. Much of the
ground surface is covered with powdery caliche. But here and there, between
scattered salt pans, are patches of range grass fit for grazing cattle. More native
grasslands were present in 1880 than today, especially in the floodplain and adjacent terraces, and almost all of the land, then unfenced, was available for the free
grazing of range cattle.

For human beings—as well as horses—water from the Pecos River verges
on undrinkable. Even water wells drilled into the valley alluvium away from the
river have high saturation levels of alkaline salts. The only fresh water is rain
water—and with average annual rainfall of less than twelve inches, there is pre-
cious little of that.[18] Anyone who is personally familiar with the effects of Epsom
salts on the human digestive system will appreciate the consequences, to thirsty
men and horses alike, of their copious and continuing intake of water from the
Pecos River.

### Pecos Station

It is about forty miles from Fort Lancaster to Camp Melvin, the isolated military
outpost that guarded the Pontoon Crossing of the northern stage road, more com-
monly known as Pecos Station. A telegraph station was located there.[19] Having

ridden all night, his men and horses now bone-weary and sick, Kimbell's command probably did not reach Pecos Station until midday on October 3. There they discovered the outlaws had split up, some fleeing west on the Fort Stockton road, the others continuing northwest, up the Pecos, toward New Mexico. Apparently, each group had taken its share of the stolen horses. Kimbell's men needed the remainder of that day to replenish their food supplies, recover some strength, obtain replacement mounts for their exhausted horses, scout out the divergent trails, and decide how to proceed.[20]

Then they were informed that the horse thieves had been identified as the Potter brothers, George Cleveland, and one or more unnamed accomplices, one of whom was almost certainly James K. P. Potter. When the Rangers had first arrived at Pecos Station—before they lost the trail—the departed outlaws were only ten miles ahead.[21] Somehow, word had reached the fugitives that the Rangers were on their trail and closing fast. The outlaws split into two groups and fled with their stolen horses. James K. P. Potter and George Cleveland rode west, on the road toward Fort Stockton. The Indian Potters continued northwest, up the Pecos, toward New Mexico and immunity.[22]

The weary Rangers spent the night at Pecos Station. Early the next morning, October 4, Corporal Kimbell telegraphed the news to Fort McKavett. The message was relayed on to his commander, Captain Dan Roberts, at Company D's headquarters on the San Saba River, six miles east. Roberts passed the news on in turn to Adjutant General John B. Jones in Austin:

> I received a note from Corporal Kimble [Kimbell], in charge of the scout I sent after the Potter delegation, dated Pecos Station, Oct[ober] 4, '80, stating that he was within ten miles of them on [the] 3rd inst[ant], but was then off the trail, and having examined, on the Stockton road, and failed to find it, would start in a few minutes later for Horsehead [Crossing], where I think he will be certain to find them. Only two of them, with five horses.[23]

### The Chase Continues

Kimbell's squad, some now with borrowed horses, pushed on for about twenty miles more before making a dry camp near present Girvin on the night of October 4. About midday the next day, the column of grim, dusty Rangers dragged into the ragged little settlement at the Horsehead Crossing of the Pecos, exhausted, sick from drinking the foul river water, their horses completely worn out. As Kimbell himself recalled fifty-seven years later:

At this point [Horsehead Crossing], I was forced to leave all the Rangers, except ["Hick"] Dunman, as they, or their horses had played out from drinking that horrible water, eating poor food, and with hard work. We were then [with]in a few hours ride of them, whom we now had learned were a part of the renowned, organized bunch of Potters. . . . Here we lost the trail for several hours, and I was forced for the first time to unsaddle my favorite mount, Robert E. Lee, and leave him and get a cow pony, and with Dunman only, we followed the two Potters up the river by which now stands Pecos City.[24]

Leaving their pack mule behind, Kimbell and Dunman rode on, traveling light. They probably camped the night of October 5 on the trail near present Grand Falls, and the next night near the present town of Pecos. On the morning of October 7 they staggered up to J. W. Carter's "West Ranch" headquarters, ten miles northwest of nascent Pecos City, where a young cowhand, one Bill Smith, found fresh horses for them and offered to accompany them in their efforts to overtake and apprehend the Potter boys.[25] Kimbell gladly accepted Smith's offer.[26]

### Encounter at Pope's Crossing

The "West Ranch" headquarters was about forty miles southeast of Pope's Crossing of the Pecos, immediately south of the Texas–New Mexico border (see map 7). Kimbell related in his memoirs that

as it was nearing night, and getting close to our stopping line, the New Mexico border, we had to ride hard, [while] the Potter outlaws had camped [off] the trail, out of sight. . . . [W]e passed them in the night . . . which . . . became known to us when day broke, and we, near the border line, turned back, and with the aid of field glasses, could see them coming several miles distant. As we grew nearer, we saw [that] one was about fifty feet ahead of the other, so I told Dunman to drop behind me about the same distance and meet the first one, at the same time as I'd meet the hind-most one . . . [I told] Smith . . . to just play where he saw he was most needed.[27]

"Indian Jim" Potter was in the lead, and Kimbell, pulling his hat low to prevent recognition, rode past him to come up even with the trailing John Potter and 'pulled down on him,' demanding his surrender. At that moment firing commenced [behind Kimbell], between Jim Potter, Dunman, and Smith, and [John] Potter, pulling at the breech of his [rifle], which was in a scabbard [on] his saddle, Kimbell telling him to turn it loose or he would kill him. John [Potter] jumped off his horse, still pulling at the gun, and Kimbell shot him. . . . At the other end of the fight . . . [Kimbell] saw Jim Potter down, with [two] bullet holes in him, and [two] horses . . . shot.[28]

Kimbell described the fight in his 1937 memoirs:

As I gave the order that we were Rangers and for them to give up, [which was] a term they well knew, every one pulled rifles and the battle was open! After about eight or ten shots, in which both of them, and two horses, one of theirs and one of mine, were shot, I ordered, "Shoot no more." For there was no more danger of them shooting any more.[29]

Well, there I was, over 300 miles from [Company D's camp], men and horses strewn up and down the [Pecos] River for 75 miles, hungry, exhausted and nearly afoot, two wounded men in dying condition, about one thousand miles from "nowhere"!

Figure 28. Corporal R. G. Kimbell, May 1880. Courtesy of Institute of Texan Cultures, University of Texas at San Antonio.

And while we were planning the next move, Dunman looked up the trail in a fog of dust and said, "[Corporal], hell, this thing is just begun, look yonder." And we saw a bunch of about six men coming as fast as possible. Believing they were [from] the same bunch of outlaws, we took no chances, but reloading our empty guns, formed a line of defense to meet any emergency. . . . [A]s they approached, we three stood about ten feet apart, so as not to let them thread more than one of us on one bullet. . . . [I]n the center, I took my hat in my left hand and flagged them down. One of them, Buck Guice [Guyse], whom I had known before I enlisted [in the Rangers] cried out, "Damned if that ain't Rush Kimbell." They were a bunch of [Hashknife Ranch] cowmen, who, having heard our cannonading, believed us to be other cowmen, fighting some of old Chief Victorio's Indian band, which was known to be not over 100 miles from there at that time.

I got [Guyse] to stay with Dunman and take care of the prisoners, while I went to Fort Stockton, a distance, I believe, of 120 to 140 [100] miles, to telegraph Captain Roberts . . . [as to] the results accomplished.[30]

### Journey to Fort Stockton

Corporal Kimbell now set off southeastward, probably in company with J. W. Carter's cowboy, Bill Smith. They would have reached Carter's "West Ranch" headquarters the night of the gunfight, October 8, the two men and their horses all exhausted. Kimbell probably spent the following morning recuperating and obtaining a fresh horse, gear, and supplies sufficient to ride the seventy miles to Fort Stockton. He may have detoured the additional thirty-five miles necessary to reach Horsehead Crossing, where he had left Privates Brown, Dozier, Latham, Smith, and Roberts (as well as his own favorite horse, Robert E. Lee) on October 5. He informed them that the Potters had been captured and instructed them to collect their horses and gear, ride to Fort Stockton thirty-five miles southwest, and await further orders.

In any case, Kimbell did not wait for his men—he started on to Fort Stockton.[31] We do not know whether Robert E. Lee was sufficiently recovered to carry him there.

Rush Kimbell, already worn from his long pursuit and drained by the gunfight at Pope's Crossing, now rode alone across a notably desolate and lonely stretch of western Texas desert, a flat, desiccated, featureless landscape covered by powdery caliche dust, and populated only by ubiquitous creosote bush and scattered dwarf mesquite, interspersed with tasajilla, yucca, and prickly pear. There were no trees, no salving shade. It is a godforsaken region relieved only by the distant silhouettes of the Davis and Glass Mountains far to the west and south. He arrived at Fort Stockton either the night of October 12 or around noon the following day, exhausted, parched, and dust covered. On October 13, he telegraphed Captain Roberts the news of his capture of Jim and John Potter. As Kimbell reported later, his commanding officer replied:

> "Return to your [prisoners], I am wiring [Ranger] Lieutenant Charles Nevill, at Fort Davis, to render you assistance, with wagon and rations, follow his instructions."[32]

> That October night, in Fort Stockton, I was royally entertained by the Post Commander. I was given nice bedding, on a pool table from the Officers' Quarters, the most expensive bed I'd ever slept on in my life.

> When I told the Post Surgeon that one of them was shot [once] through the lungs, and the other one twice, one ball through the thigh [and another through the kneecap], he told me that he expected I'd find the one shot through the thigh dead, but the other one might live, and so it was.[33]

### Kimbell's Return

When Corporal Kimbell got back to the site of the shoot-out on October 16, he found that both prisoners had been moved to a nearby cow camp, probably in a ranch wagon, where "Indian Jim" Potter, shot twice, once in the hip and once in the kneecap, had died several days after the fight. His brother, John Potter, shot through the left lung, was still alive.[34] Lacking tools, Dunman and Guyse had scratched out a shallow grave in the calichified gravel with a hoe and a butcher knife, and covered Jim Potter's corpse with rocks to protect it from wolves, coyotes, and vultures.[35]

There was one more surprise. Among Buck Guyse's group of Hashknife cowboys was Frank Potter, who claimed to be unaware of his younger brothers' presence in the area, or of their horse-stealing expedition.[36] Frank Potter had remained with his two wounded brothers, nursing them as best he could, until Jim died. Afterward, he accompanied John Potter on to Fort Davis.[37]

Corporal L. W. Rodgers and two Company E privates arrived with a wagon at Pope's Crossing on October 16, the same day Corporal Kimbell returned from

Fort Stockton. The next morning they lifted John Potter into the arms of his brother Frank in the bed of the wagon and headed for Fort Davis. Buck Guyse went with them, hoping to enlist in the Rangers, trading on Rush Kimbell's good recommendation to Lieutenant Nevill. They arrived on October 21. There the wounded prisoner was placed in the infirmary, attended by the post surgeon, and cared for by his older brother.[38]

In his report to Adjutant General Jones on October 23 from Fort Davis, Lieutenant Charles Nevill, Commander of Company E, summed up the results:

> Your dispatch with regard to Kimbell is received. The prisoner is severely and dangerously wounded[.] [T]he Doctor says he [must] be kept quiet, he is shot through the left lung, the ball coming out near the backbone. [T]his is John Potter[;] Jim died from his wounds. Frank Potter is here waiting on his brother[.] I don't think he is wanted[:] he was not with the others when overtaken. Jim was wanted as indicted for horse stealing, and John will be held for the stolen horses found in their possession when arrested. [W]ill start them [back] as soon as I can.[39]

In his October 13, 1880, letter to Adjutant General Jones, Captain Dan Roberts, who had pursued most of the Potter family outlaws off and on since 1877, reflected on the results of Kimbell's scout:

> That, I think, will put an end to the Potter raiding in Kimble County. They have cost the State of Texas a great deal, and terrorized the section of country in which they stayed.[40]

# 13 :: The Return

Shot "through-and-through" his left lung, John Potter's gunshot wound remained professionally untreated for twelve days. The last four of those days he was being transported about 110 dusty, bone-rattling miles in the bed of a wagon to the post hospital at Fort Davis. Lieutenant Charles Nevill had recently established the headquarters camp of Company E near the army post.

It is a testament both to Potter's frontier-tough constitution and will to live as well as the primitive care he received from his brother Frank and the Rangers that he survived the journey.

### To Fort Davis

Leaving Pope's Crossing on October 17, the Rangers' route would probably have taken them southeast, along the southwest bank of the Pecos, past J. W. Carter's "West Ranch" headquarters, where they might have spent the night. By midday of the next day they, and the five stolen horses they had recovered from the Potters, would have passed newly established Pecos City. There they would have

Figure 29. Lieutenant Charles Nevill, commander, Company E, Frontier Battalion, Texas Rangers, about 1881. Courtesy of the Chuck Parsons Collection.

turned south across the alkali plains, passed Toyah Lake, and made a dry and dusty camp amidst the creosote bush and low mesquite shrubs. They probably nooned the next day at the desert oasis of Balmorhea Springs and camped in the foothills near Barrilla Springs that evening. They started the final leg of their journey on October 20, up through the glowering, reddish-black volcanic cliffs of Limpia Canyon to Fort Davis.

After delivery of the prisoner to the post hospital on the evening of the twentieth, the post doctor reported to Lieutenant Nevill that John Potter was "severely and dangerously wounded, and [that he] must be kept quiet." Accordingly, he was placed under guard in the hospital for eighteen more days, during which time he began to gradually recover. His eldest brother, Frank Potter, remained with him, attending to his needs as best he could.[1]

Adjutant General Jones had instructed Lieutenant Nevill to "let [the] prisoner recover sufficiently to travel without danger."[2] By early November, the post doctor advised Nevill that Potter would be able to travel "in a wagon, but not by horseback for some time."[3]

### Return to Fort McKavett

On November 7 Corporal Kimbell departed from Fort Davis with his prisoner, John Potter, in a wagon, accompanied by four of the six Ranger privates (Ed Dozier, J. V. Latham, R. C. Roberts, and "Mac" Smith) he had started out with from Fort McKavett six weeks earlier.[4] All the Rangers had by now recovered their own horses and were also driving the five horses that had been stolen by John and Jim Potter, all of which had benefited from more than two weeks of rest and grazing. Frank Potter remained at Fort Davis, where he was employed by Lieutenant Nevill as Company E's teamster; Kimbell's friend, Buck Guyse, who had accompanied them to Fort Davis, enlisted in Company E as a private.[5]

Kimbell's return route is reasonably certain. It would have followed the existing stagecoach road eastward, especially since the squad was now escorting a wagon used to carry their wounded prisoner.[6] Presumably, their eastward journey would have been much easier than their intense, west-bound pursuit six weeks before: they would have been able to carry food, cooking gear, and bedding in the wagon with the prisoner, as well as limited fresh water, and the weather was now cooler. They would have been able to stop at scattered stage stations along the way. Two or three Rangers would have been able to ride in the wagon at a time, hitching their horses to the wagon's tailgate. They had a wounded prisoner whom they wanted to deliver to their Captain, alive and ready to stand his trial for horse theft—but in reality already suspected of participating in a horrific crime two years earlier in Kerr County. It is not unreasonable to suppose that his captors may have asked John Potter about his part in the Dowdy murders. Whether he was innocent or guilty, John Potter may have sensed that—quite aside from his gunshot wound—his life was in mortal danger at the hands of the legal system.

They averaged between twenty and twenty-five miles per day on their return journey. They would have left behind the bare highlands and dark-cliffed canyons of the Davis Mountains by the end of the first day, camping at Barilla Springs. The next day, they turned east down dusty Barilla Draw, making a dry camp the next night in caliche scablands on the low divide crossing over toward the drainage of Coyanosa Draw. The third day would have seen them on the dusty desert plains again, finally pulling into Fort Stockton and passing the night at Comanche Springs just south of town. On the morning of November 10, they would have headed due east across the desiccated plains, making two dry overnight camps. On November 12 they crossed the Pecos River on the pontoon bridge at Pecos Station, where Kimbell had telegraphed Captain Roberts more than five weeks earlier with the news that he was headed up the Pecos after the Potter boys.

Now their road headed north, flanking the mass of the Edwards Plateau to the east and south, and rising steadily (see map 7). They passed a dry night on the powdery, creosote-bush desert east of Table Top Mesa and Rattlesnake Butte, and then continued on during the morning of November 13, crossing the broad divide between the Concho and Pecos drainages about midday. It is possible that they swung south to camp that night at Grierson's Spring, south of the head of Centralia Draw, where they may have encountered more buffalo soldiers of the 10th Cavalry, patrolling for Indian raiders inbound to the Texas settlements from Mexico or outbound, on their way back across the Rio Grande.

As they rode east, the desert was beginning to give way to scrubby, rolling prairie with scattered juniper clumps, small mesquite trees, and sparse range grasses. On November 14 a bone-chilling wet norther blew in, with snow and sleet, making their eastward journey miserable.[7]

For the next three frigid days they rode east, hunched over against the sleety wind, hats pulled down over their ears. They rode down broad, open, windswept Centralia Draw, passing stage stations at Head of Concho, Camp Charlotte, and Camp Johnson.[8] All along the way, they could see the distant, flat profile of the Edwards Plateau on the southern skyline. Three of the stolen horses, already weakened from their long run with the fleeing Potter boys, died from the cold.

At the mouth of the south fork of the Concho they turned south, following that spring-fed, clear-water stream up to the lush, dark, oak-sheltered bottoms adjacent to the little river, at present Christoval. Here they probably camped on the night of November 17, finally finding shelter from the biting north wind in the first grove of trees they had seen since leaving the Davis Mountains. They were back in home country.

Early the next morning, the wind would have dropped and the temperature begun to moderate. They would have headed southeast on the "Toenail Trail," over familiar live-oak savannas, and made a dry camp that night on the divide between the South Concho and San Saba Rivers.[9] They rode into Company D's headquarters camp on the San Saba River on the afternoon of November 19, 1880. Captain Roberts wrote Adjutant General Jones the next day: "Kimbell has returned with his prisoner, their horses terribly used up."[10]

Corporal Kimbell and his squad had been gone fifty-six days and logged 1,118 miles.[11]

## Back to Kimble County

On November 21 Kimbell and a squad of three Rangers left Company D's headquarters to deliver John Potter to the sheriff of Kimble County. The first night out, the Rangers probably made camp on the headwaters of Bear Creek. Now back in familiar territory, John Potter made a sudden attempt to escape. He was being taken from the hack in which he was being carried when he began to run.[12] "Private Latham fired at him three times, and finally 'rounded him up'," as Captain Roberts reported to Adjutant General Jones.[13] Potter's immediate recapture may also have been related to his still-weakened physical condition.[14]

The Rangers proceeded on the next day, November 22, to Junction City, where John Potter was transferred into the custody of Sheriff John Garland. Kimbell and his squad returned to their camp on the San Saba the next day.[15]

It is unlikely that a Kimble County grand jury had indicted John Potter in absentia for horse theft during the fall 1880 term of the district court—such a proceeding would have to have taken place in late October, only a few weeks after Potter's capture had been announced, and there was legitimate concern that he might soon die of his wound. Moreover, such short notice would have made it difficult to assemble necessary documentation and testimony.

It is more likely that a habeas corpus hearing would have been held in Junction City soon after Potter's delivery into custody, with testimony by Sam Merck, Corporal Kimbell, and at least one of the owners of the stolen horses, H. K. Hutchinson. Bail would probably have been set high enough that his relatives and friends would not have been able to meet it. Junction City did not have a jail, and Potter still had friends among the dwindling Kimble County outlaw confederacy who might try to liberate him, so Sheriff Garland probably transported him promptly to San Antonio, transferring him into the custody of the sheriff of Bexar County. This would have given the district attorney time to line up his witnesses and prepare his case, present it to a grand jury at the beginning of the spring term of district court, obtain an indictment, and try Potter toward the end of the spring term of court, in May of 1881, on charges of horse theft and resisting arrest. It is doubtful that the state had compelling evidence tying John Potter to the Dowdy murders.

### Portentous Journey

John Potter—probably confined now in handcuffs and leg irons because of his attempted escape from the Rangers en route to Junction City—was conveyed by wagon to San Antonio by the Kimble County sheriff's office, possibly by Sheriff Garland himself and one or more of his deputies, Joe Clements, S. S. Jobes, or Manny Kimbreau, during the last week of November or the first week of December 1880.[16]

They would have left Junction City before daybreak, following the ruts of a rough wagon road about fifteen miles southeastward, up the Johnson Fork of the Llano River, then climbing easterly onto a high, flat, waterless fifteen-mile stretch on the divide between the Llano and Guadalupe drainages. The road then veered southwest, descending into the upper reaches of the watershed of Johnson Creek, south-flowing tributary of the Guadalupe River.

In the early afternoon, they would have passed within a few hundred yards of where the Dowdy young people had been murdered a little more than two years earlier. Just beyond, they probably drew up before Tom and Susan Dowdy's new store, near the original Dowdy home site of 1878. Here they would have stopped for refreshment before resuming their southeastward travel, down the Johnson Creek valley toward Kerrville, the midpoint of their journey to San Antonio. It is not recorded whether the Kimble County law officers may have asked their prisoner, John Potter, about the appalling acts that had occurred nearby, or whether Tom Dowdy or his wife may have come out of the store to confront him as to his guilt.

Two miles farther on, the road passed beside the new Sunset Cemetery, the first graves of which contained the bodies of Alice, Martha, Susan, and James Dowdy. Six miles beyond, it passed beside the new home of James and Susan Dowdy and their surviving family, Dick, Mary, and George, who still lived with their parents on the west side of Johnson Creek.

We do not know if the officers pointed out the Dowdy graves to John Potter or elicited his response about them, or if any of the Dowdy family came out to see the prisoner pass by their new home, or celebrate his capture.

It is more than just possible that John Potter may not have even grasped the irony of his presence along that tragic route.

### The New Cellmate

When John Potter was placed in the Bexar County jail, his new cellmate tuned out to be a tall, dark, twenty-year-old cowboy who had killed a young man named John Condy in Kimble County nearly two years before, and who was awaiting trial for murder in Junction City at the spring 1881 term of district court.[17]

John Potter's new cellmate was William M. "Bill" Dunman, no known relation to William H. "Hick" Dunman, the Ranger who had killed his brother "Indian Jim" in the gunfight on the Pecos about two months earlier.

It is not unlikely that the two prisoners had been acquainted previously, or knew of one another, especially if John Potter had been in Kimble County frequently during 1879 when Dunman killed Condy. Certainly they would have known some of the same Kimble County people, and that might have encouraged John Potter to talk with his new cellmate.

# 14 :: Meeting at Mountain Home

### Bill Dunman

In the spring of 1879, Bill Dunman was working as a cowboy for Creed Taylor at Taylor's ranch on the headwaters of the James River in eastern Kimble County. Dunman was then about nineteen years old. Another cowboy named John Condy worked for Taylor's neighbor, Jim Davis, who lived about three or four miles away. Bad blood had developed between the two young men, and Dunman challenged Condy to a duel at a certain time and place.[1]

Davis counseled Condy not to risk the sought-for fight: "If you go out there this morning, I'll have to take my oxen and haul you in." Apparently, on April 15, 1879, as Condy approached the appointed dueling ground, Dunman shot him off his horse.[2] Dunman fled to avoid arrest by Kimble County law officers.

Early in 1880, the Kimble County sheriff learned that Bill Dunman was living with relatives in Goliad County and asked Texas Ranger Captain Dan Roberts for help in arresting him and bringing him back to Kimble County for trial. On February 16, 1880, Ranger Privates Moore and Sheffield started to Goliad County after the fugitive. On March 9 Moore and Sheffield returned to Company D's headquarters camp having captured the wanted man, marched five hundred miles during their mission, and lodged Dunman in the Gillespie County jail at Fredericksburg for safekeeping.[3]

Bill Dunman was indicted for the murder of John Condy,[4] probably at the fall 1880 term of district court, and then sent to San Antonio to be held in the Bexar County jail pending his murder trial in Junction City at the spring term of court in May 1881.

### The Dunman Connection

Daniel C. Dunman, born in 1832, married Katherine (Kate) Martin in 1857 in Refugio County, Texas. The couple had two sons, William M. "Bill," born in 1860, and Daniel J. "Dan," born in 1861. Their father enlisted in the Confederate army and died of measles in Walker County in 1862.[5] Their widowed mother later married a John Nelson in Refugio County in 1865.[6] Whether the marriage failed or Nelson died is not clear, but by 1882 she was again living under the name of Katherine Dunman, in San Antonio, Texas.[7]

What is clear, however, is that both Bill and Dan Dunman were nonmilitary casualties of the Civil War, having had little or no fatherly guidance during their growing up.[8] But Kate Dunman continued to intercede for them all her life—and with good reason, as both her sons were in and out of trouble with the law for most of their adult lives.[9]

Recognizing the pervasive affinities and loyalties within nineteenth-century frontier families, it is likely that Bill and Dan Dunman maintained contact with their relatives in Refugio and Goliad Counties, for that was where Bill Dunman fled after he killed John Condy in Kimble County.[10] Among those relatives were his paternal aunt, Sara Dunman Reeves, and her husband, William Reeves, residents of Goliad County. Aunt Sara was Bill Dunman's late father's older sister.[11] Her daughter, Susan, had married Thomas A. Dowdy and gone with him to Kerr County in late 1878 to care for his bereaved parents and surviving siblings after the brutal murders of Alice, Martha, Susan, and James Dowdy.

Figure 30. Tom and Susan Reeves Dowdy, about 1890. Tom Dowdy was acquitted of the murder of the prisoner John Potter on May 12, 1883, in the 24th Judicial District Court, Kerrville, Texas. Susan Dowdy was a first cousin of the liberated prisoner, Bill Dunman. Courtesy of W. C. Dowdy. (Images digitally enhanced, with permission.)

Susan Reeves Dowdy, sister-in-law of the murdered Dowdy youngsters, was Bill Dunman's first cousin.

### The Revelation

John Potter and Bill Dunman shared a cell in the Bexar County jail for about five months. Potter might have been suspicious of his cellmate, since he bore the same family name as the Ranger who had mortally wounded his brother Jim in the gunfight at Pope's Crossing the previous October. On the other hand, Potter may well have known, or known of, Dunman as a wild cowboy from their earlier Kimble County days. Either way, it probably would have taken some weeks for Dunman to worm his way into Potter's confidence. But sometime, probably around February or March 1881, perhaps through a private interview with his brother, Dan Dunman, or in a letter to his Dowdy relatives in Kerr County,[12] he conveyed stunning news: Bill Dunman claimed that John Potter had admitted to having been involved in the murders of the Dowdy youngsters.[13] We do not know how this news was communicated, or what subsequent plans derived from that revelation, but they were instrumental in deciding the fate of John Potter.

### Return for Trial

The spring 1881 term of district court for Kimble County was scheduled for the first week in May in Junction City. Two accused men were being held in the Bexar County jail in San Antonio because Kimble County did not have a secure jail. Sheriff H. J. Garland sent his senior deputy, Joe Clements, and two other

Figure 31. Joseph H. Clements, probably taken in one of the Kansas trail towns, early 1870s. Joe Clements was the Kimble County deputy sheriff from whom the prisoners John Potter and Bill Dunman were taken by four armed and masked men near Mountain Home, Texas, on May 8, 1881. Potter was executed and Dunman released. Image courtesy of Western History Collection, University of Oklahoma.

deputies, M. Kimbreau and Sam Jobes, to San Antonio in a hack to escort the two defendants, Bill Dunman and John Potter, back to Junction City to stand their trials for murder and for horse theft and resisting arrest, respectively.[14]

The three lawmen departed Junction City before dawn on Tuesday, May 3, bound for San Antonio via Mountain Home, Ingram, Kerrville, Comfort, and Boerne. They covered the first sixty miles in about fourteen hours, rolling into Kerrville at dusk on Tuesday evening. There they spent the night.[15] The next morning they would have again departed very early in order to cover the remaining seventy miles to San Antonio, arriving in the city about sundown on Wednesday, May 4.[16]

The next day Deputy Sheriff Clements began to conduct himself in a most extraordinary manner:

> He stayed here several days and took the prisoners [Dunman and Potter] around with him, drinking at saloons, the reporter is told by Sheriff McCall, and giving every one a chance to find out his business.[17]

Early on Saturday morning, May 7, the Kimble County lawmen took permanent custody of the two prisoners and departed for Junction City in their hired hack. Both prisoners were handcuffed and placed in leg irons. The party arrived in Kerrville after dark, where they spent the night. Whether Dunman and Potter were placed overnight in the Kerr County jail, or the officers took turns sitting up with them in a hotel room, is not known.

### Somber Interview

The next morning, Sunday, May 8, the officers again departed Kerrville early with their prisoners. The hack wheeled briskly northwest, up the bluff-bound valley of the Guadalupe River. It was high spring and still cool: the scissortails fluttered in the soft air, and the valley was cloaked in its annual finery of wildflowers. They would have passed through the village of Ingram at about 9:00 a.m., crossing to the west side of cypress-lined Johnson Creek where it joins the Guadalupe and then continuing northwesterly up the Johnson Creek valley road. Two and a half miles farther on, the road passed by the new dog-run home of James and Susan Dowdy, set in a grove of sheltering live oaks. Here they were met by a woman in the road who waved them down.

She was Susan Cassell Dowdy, the mother of the slain Dowdy youngsters, then about fifty-one years old. Four of her children had been slaughtered two years and seven months earlier, at their then new homestead on the headwaters of Johnson Creek. Prostrate with grief, she and her husband James had moved to a new location farther down Johnson Creek valley, near his brother Gib Dowdy's land at the mouth of Henderson Creek. Accounts do not indicate that Susan Dowdy was accompanied by any other family member when she stopped the hack.[18]

> It is reported that, as [Deputy] Clemen[t]s was going up Johnson's Creek, and passing by Mr. Dowdy's . . . Mrs. Dowdy came out to the hack where the prisoners were and entreated Potter to tell her what [were] the last words that her children [had] said, as she knew that he helped kill them, and was one of the party. Potter said he knew nothing about her or her children and they started on.

The heartbreaking interview with Susan Dowdy concluded, Deputy Sam Jobes drove on. About eight miles farther northwest, the road curved past the new Sunset Cemetery, the final resting place of the Dowdy youngsters (see map 8). The officers continued on, past the cluster of little houses newly collecting at the confluence of Johnson and Contrary Creeks, the nascent community of Mountain Home.

Figure 32. Site of Susan C. Dowdy's confrontation of the prisoner John Potter on May 8, 1881. After the murders of four of their children, James E. and Susan C. Dowdy moved about nine miles southeast of the site of the murders, where they built a dog-run house on land they acquired in the valley of Johnson Creek. The original house was divided into two separate buildings sometime after the death of Susan C. Dowdy in 1913. Mary Dowdy lived out her life as a recluse in the small cabin in the background. Author's photograph of a watercolor painting by Clarice Akin Holloway, about 1965, from an earlier photograph. Courtesy of W. C. Dowdy.

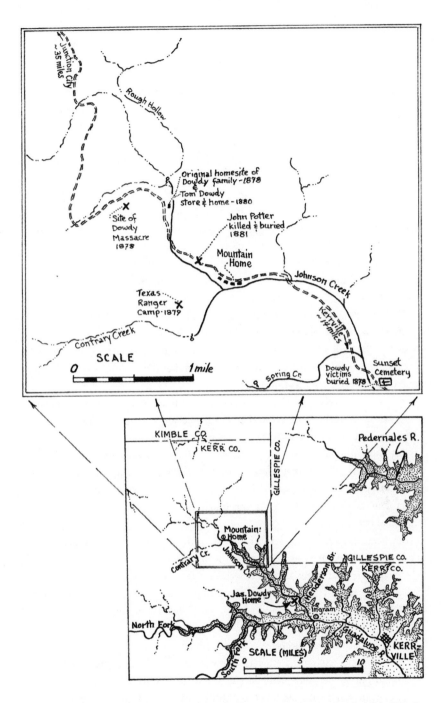

Map 8. The Mountain Home location of the original home site and events involving the Dowdy family, 1878–81. The stippled areas show outcrop areas of the Trinity Formation; the white areas are Edwards Limestone.

### The Execution

Shortly after noon, about a quarter of a mile beyond Mountain Home, the hack drew even with a narrow, dark, tree-filled gully north of the road. As reported in the *San Antonio Weekly Express Supplement*, four hooded men came suddenly out of the draw and stood in the road, their guns trained on the lawmen in the hack. One of the men told Deputy Joe Clements that they wanted both of his prisoners. Looking into a battery of trained gun muzzles, Clements said "Take them."

One of the four men then told Bill Dunman, "Take Joe's pistol," which Dunman did, and clambered awkwardly out of the hack, leg-irons rattling. Lawman Clements then asked if he could not take his other prisoner, John Potter, onward. "No, he's our meat." After Dunman assisted Potter out of the hack, the three officers were ordered to drive on, but before the hack started moving, Dunman said to Deputy Clements, "Joe, you go on two or three hundred yards and stop and wait a little bit, and I will come to you."

Clements did as he was told, driving the hack out of sight. Shortly after starting off, the three officers heard three shots in quick succession behind and off to the side of the road. Clements stopped the hack, "I guess they have killed Potter."

A few minutes later, Bill Dunman approached the hack. Clements said, "Well, you got the drop on me this time."

"Yes, but you have treated me fair and square, and I won't hurt you," replied Dunman. Additional conversation then ensued between Dunman and Clements, which was not revealed to the newspaper correspondent.

The lawmen then started for Junction City. As they were crossing the divide several hours later, they met some freighters on the road. Deputy Sheriff Clements gave one of them a note to deliver to Louis Nelson, who lived at Mountain Home. The note related what had transpired as well as Clements's fears that John Potter had been killed.

But Clements's note did not find its way to Louis Nelson until Monday evening, more than twenty-four hours after the prisoners had been freed. Nelson and his son went immediately to the site, where they found the corpse of John Potter beside the road. The neighbors held an inquest the next morning, following which John Potter's body was buried with the chains still on him.

> Your correspondent has learned that Dunman, who was confined in the San Antonio jail with Potter, is a cousin of the Dowdys, and that he found out while there with him all about the matter. There is a great deal of mystery connected with the affair, particularly who the releasing party were, and why they killed Potter, who was on his way to Kimble

County to be tried for horse-stealing, while Dunman was to be tried for murder.[19]

Scattered among various sources are additional scraps of information—some of which conflict—that allow a fuller picture to be drawn of John Potter's execution.

Potter's body remained beside the road where he had been shot for several days (map 8), and no one in the Mountain Home community reported the murder to Kerr County authorities. This suggests community sympathy—if not complicity—with the murder, or intimidation—which implies awareness of who the murderers were. Potter's body was buried on the north side of the road near where he was shot. The otherwise unmarked grave was covered with rocks.[20]

Captain Dan Roberts reported the murder to Adjutant General J. B. Jones:

John Potter was taken from Deputy Sheriff Clemen[t]s of Kimble County as he was bringing him up from San Antonio jail to trial for theft of horses, by four masked men near [the] head of Johnson [Creek] of [the] Guadalupe in Kerr County and carried a short distance from the road and literally riddled with buckshot. Dunman, charged with murder, was released at [the] same time. Clemen[t]s' pistol has since been returned to him."[21]

According to Kimble County historian O. C. Fisher, "the two prisoners were taken . . . into a live oak thicket. There Dunman was liberated and never rearrested, and John Potter was cut and shot to death."[22]

## Rumors

In the aftermath of John Potter's execution, the old rumors—expectedly—began to resurface and circulate about his possible participation in the massacre of the Dowdy young people in October 1878. Potter's known involvement in the late September 1880 horse-stealing raid on the North Llano, the notoriety of his criminal relatives and confederates, who lived and operated just thirty miles away in the South Llano valley, and were widely rumored to have raided disguised as Indians, the facts of his own Indian ancestry, and the known mixed-race nature of the Mexican Indian raiders, all served to reinforce the public perception of his guilt.

Subsequent rumors as to a possible prior romantic connection between John Potter and one of the Dowdy daughters, either Mary, the oldest, or Alice, the next

Figure 33. Mary Dowdy, circa 1877, when she was about twenty-one years old. She was the sole surviving daughter of the James Dowdy family; after the massacre of her siblings, she lived with her parents until their deaths, and afterward as a recluse until she died in 1945. Courtesy of W. C. Dowdy. (Image digitally enhanced, with permission.)

oldest sister, probably originated with Bill Dunman, as related to his relatives, the Dowdy family, either in his original communications with them from the San Antonio jail or after the four hooded men set him at liberty. Most of these rumors were hard to reconcile with the fact that the Dowdys had been resident on Johnson Creek only a few days when the murders occurred, which therefore seemed to indicate that any prior contact must have occurred when the Dowdys lived in Goliad County. That of course suggests some incidental contact when John Potter was traveling far from home on some horse-trading—or horse-stealing—expedition. Tom Dowdy's wife Susan may have been alluding to this, in her later claim that she had encountered John Potter previously, when he stole some horses from her family.[23]

Later interviews with Dowdy family members and long-time area residents may contain the original basis of Dunman's claims: Leo Dowdy, who was raised by his grandfather, Tom Dowdy, reported that "John Potter wanted to marry Alice Dowdy, but she rejected him."[24] And Ned B. Estes, long-time resident of Mountain Home, stated that Bill Dunman claimed to the Dowdys that John Potter said the oldest Dowdy daughter wouldn't have anything to do with him.[25]

Certainly Mary Dowdy's lifelong reclusive behavior after the execution of John Potter and the subsequent ambivalence of her three surviving brothers toward her could not help but contribute to such community rumors: Myrtle Dowdy, widow of George Dowdy's son Bill, said that there may have been some connection between John Potter and Mary Dowdy: "She never got over the tragedy—she became a recluse, lived a fearful, separate life from the rest of the Dowdy family [after the deaths of her parents], always wore a long black dress."[26] And Jasper Moore, another long-time Mountain Home native, said that Mary Dowdy was a recluse after the murder of John Potter, and that her brothers [Tom, Richard, and George] didn't have much to do with her.[27]

On the other hand, other specific comments indicating the Dowdy family's affection for Mary Dowdy can be found among early documents and interviews with first-generation Dowdy descendants: her nephew, Solon Dowdy, son of Mary's brother Tom, described his Aunt Mary as "the smartest woman he ever knew. She took care of all her parents' business [affairs until they died]. Children loved her. Many adults thought she was 'off,' but she was not. She just couldn't get over her grief."[28]

Her niece, Nina Dowdy McCall, attributed Mary Dowdy's subsequent behavior to the combined shocks of being stood up at her wedding in Goliad County, moving away from her familiar home to a new place, and the murders of her four siblings.[29] She was described in a 1928 history of Kerr County families as having devoted her life to her "grief-stricken parents, made her home with them as long as they lived . . . [and] tried to make up for the three beloved young sisters whose tender lives had been so brutally snuffed out."[30]

Soon after the execution of John Potter, a new rumor surfaced among the Mountain Home community, one eminently logical and to many settlers completely justified—that the men who had taken the prisoners away from the Kimble County law officers were avenging angels of the Dowdy family, administering their own implacable justice.

### Complicity of Kimble County Law Officers

The culpability—not to say outright connivance—of Kimble County Deputy Sheriffs Clements, Kimbreau, and Jobes in the execution is manifest. Joe Clements, in particular, had worked very closely with Dan Roberts's Company D Rangers and doubtless understood, or even shared, some of their experiences with, and opinions about, Kimble County juries, especially their propensity to return "not-guilty" verdicts for accused members of the confederation.[31]

His behavior in taking his prisoners Dunman and Potter bar-hopping in San Antonio on the eve of their return journey to Kimble County for trial was obviously a prior attempt to expand the number of possible suspects in the subsequent investigation of the crime. Moreover, Clements's compliance with Bill Dunman's instructions to "go on two or three hundred yards and stop and wait a little bit, and I will come to you" certainly suggests that the two men had an understanding.

### Motivations and Rationales

We can readily grasp that Kimble County law officers—and citizens—may not have been confident that John Potter would be found guilty of horse theft at the impending spring term of district court in Junction City and sent to the penitentiary. Given the past record, it was entirely conceivable that he might well be set free on the charge by yet another friendly—or intimidated—Kimble County jury, resulting in the suspected, but uncharged, murderer of the Dowdy young people escaping punishment for his awful crime. Of course, it is also possible that even baser motivations were working—that the Dowdy family paid off Deputy Clements and his colleagues Sam Jobes and Manny Kimbreau in order to free their kinsman, Bill Dunman, and cynically obscure the real motive by executing John Potter.[32]

No hard evidence can today be found that John Potter had indeed been involved with the Mexican Indians who murdered the Dowdy youngsters on October 5, 1878. But it seems clear that in May 1881, some of the Texas Rangers, the Kimble County law officers, and certainly the Dowdy family, thought—or pretended to think—that he had been.

Of course, the devastating grief suffered by the Dowdy survivors can readily be understood to have demanded some explanation—a mere random act of such horrific violence was unfathomable. Also, the virulent fear and hatred of Indians by Texas frontier settlers certainly would have fanned the coals of suspicion and rumor into a blaze of revenge.

Although the story Bill Dunman told his Dowdy relatives may indeed have been true—that John Potter admitted to him that he had been involved in the Dowdy murders—it is also true that Dunman's story could as well have been only a clever ruse by which he might engineer his own escape from an impending murder trial with the aid of his kinsmen. It is the old question about the reliability of testimony offered by a tainted witness who stands to benefit from its acceptance.[33]

Today we have documented knowledge about John Potter's experiences as a youngster in the merciless ethnic cleansing that he and his Indian brothers experienced in northern California at the hands of American settlers in the 1860s. We can understand why he might have developed an unquenchable enmity toward all white people. Was John Potter recognized to harbor such a racial animus by law officers and settlers of the region during the late 1870s and early 1880s, or was it just stereotypically assumed? The judgment of Kerr County pioneer Ann Morriss, derived in the decades after Potter's execution and conveyed years afterward (during the 1930s and 1940s?) to her granddaughter, certainly suggests that Potter was thought to bear such a murderous enmity: "a discontented half-breed . . . who hated white men and raised his hand against them whenever he could with no provocation other than that his victims were white."[34]

It is indisputable that John Potter was a member of an extended family that contained many criminals and that they were part of a coercive criminal confederation that dominated Kimble County, their home county. They preyed on the surrounding region for many years, raiding and stealing in adjacent counties, including Kerr County, severely testing the forbearance of Kerr County settlers.[35] It is indisputable that this confederation was widely rumored to conduct some of its raids disguised as Indians and that it trafficked in livestock stolen in Texas and traded in Mexican markets, necessitating some representatives to interact with their Mexican receivers and partners. It is indisputable that many Mexican Indians took part in repeated raids into adjacent Texas, feeding the Mexican markets, and that Texas settlers held a profound, unreasoning hatred of all Indians. It is indisputable that John Potter was an Indian and a horse thief.

It is also indisputable that he was lynched, as surely as if he had been hanged on an elm tree on the road near Mountain Home. Whether or not he was guilty of the appalling crime of which he was suspected remains an unanswered question.

### The Reckoning

John Potter's death marked the end of the Dublin-Potter outlaw gang in Kimble County. The families had been a malignant blight on the settlement, development, and prosperity of the entire region of the eastern Edwards Plateau beginning with their arrival in early 1874. Bringing them under control had required four separate campaigns by the Texas Rangers, with gradually growing support from area citizens:

- Major Jones's Kimble County Roundup of April and May 1877;

- Lieutenant N. O. Reynolds's aggressive campaign with Company E Rangers during December 1877–May 1878;

- Captain Dan Roberts's capture of the Pegleg robbers by Company D Rangers, assisted by Kimble County citizens, in July and August 1879; and

- the heroic pursuit and arrest of Jim and John Potter on the Pecos River in the fall of 1880 by Corporal R. G. Kimbell and his squad from Company D.

Now, seven years after the Dublins and Potters arrived in Kimble County, order had finally been established—if very irregularly—and the rule of law could begin. The reckoning was long in coming, serially executed, brutally effective, and like the people of the region, highly imperfect.

# 15 :: The Trial

## The Legacy of John B. Jones

Less than three months after John Potter was executed near Mountain Home, Adjutant General John B. Jones died in office on July 19, 1881, aged forty-six.[1]

The Frontier Battalion had been his life's work.[2] In 1874, as Major Jones, he had organized and staffed it, set its priorities and standards, and guided it through the next five turbulent years of frontier unrest and lawlessness.[3] He had started off focused almost entirely on suppressing Indian raiders incoming from North Texas, which threat was largely eliminated during the next three years. The incidence of Indians raiding from Mexico gradually diminished during his tenure but mostly because of actions by the U.S. military. Starting in 1875, the Frontier Battalion increasingly tried to control bands of outlaws operating along the advancing western frontier of Texas, even as East Texas political interests continually tried to reduce or eliminate it.[4]

Jones continued to oversee the Rangers as adjutant general beginning in January 1879 when the incumbent, William Steele, resigned. But times were changing—by the time of Jones's death, the only areas in which large standing bodies of Rangers were regularly operating were in the Trans-Pecos region of far West Texas and the remote plains of the northwestern panhandle.[5] Sensing that the Texas frontier was disappearing, most of the senior officers of the Frontier Battalion were resigning their commissions and moving on to other positions and careers. Lieutenant N. O. Reynolds and Captain Pat Dolan had both resigned in the spring of 1879.[6] Captain Dan Roberts ran unsuccessfully for sheriff of Menard County in fall 1880 and then resigned his commission to go into private business in New Mexico on September 1, 1881.[7]

John B. Jones served the citizens of his adopted state with determination and distinction. He was a primary force in the establishment of order and law in frontier Texas, and it is strangely fitting that his death coincided closely with the demise of one of the last of the notorious border renegades. He probably would not have approved of the extra-legal manner of John Potter's death, but he would not have been surprised.

On July 25, 1881, Governor Roberts appointed W. H. King to be the new adjutant general of Texas, replacing the late John B. Jones.[8]

Figure 34. Richard B. and Lee Ella McKeen Dowdy, about 1920. Richard (Dick) Dowdy was acquitted on May 14, 1881, of the murder of prisoner John Potter in the 24th Judicial District Court, Kerrville, Texas, by instructed verdict from Special Judge Leo Tarleton. According to Dowdy family tradition, Dick Dowdy killed John Potter with a shotgun. Image courtesy of W. C. Dowdy. (Image digitally enhanced, with permission.)

## Arrests, Indictments, and Proceedings

Richard B. (Dick) Dowdy, Tom Dowdy's younger brother, had a crippled leg from childhood.[9] This may have contributed to his identification by Kimble County Deputy Sheriff Joe Clements as one of the four masked men who had stopped his hack near Mountain Home on May 8, 1881, taken his two prisoners, Bill Dunman and John Potter (as well as his two pistols), murdered Potter, and liberated Dunman.[10] In late May or early June 1881, Kerr County Sheriff F. J. Hamer arrested Dick Dowdy and jailed him in Kerr County on suspicion of taking part in the murder of John Potter. The other three participants remained at large.[11]

On November 7, 1881, a Kerr County grand jury separately indicted Tom Dowdy, Dick Dowdy, Bill Dunman, and Dan Dunman for the murder of John Potter. The same grand jury also indicted Tom and Dick Dowdy together for the theft of Deputy Sheriff Clements's two six-shooters and for aiding the escape of prisoner Bill Dunman from the Kimble County law officers. Bill and Dan Dunman were indicted together for assault of Deputy Sheriff Joe Clements as well as the theft of his two revolvers.[12]

Grand jury witnesses were Kimble County law officers Joseph H. Clements, M. Kimbreau, and S. S. Jobes, and Kerr County residents H. L. Nelson, Allen S. Nelson, P. C. Smith, James Summers, Martin Reeves, and Mrs. Martin Reeves.[13]

H. L. (Louis) Nelson was the Mountain Home settler to whom Clements had sent a note about the incident by some teamsters whom he encountered on the divide, after being relieved of his prisoners and resuming his return journey toward

Junction City. Louis Nelson did not receive the note until the next evening but then went to the site with his son, Allen, and found Potter's corpse lying beside the road.[14]

P. C. Smith and James Summers were neighbors of the Dowdys. Martin Reeves was the older brother of Tom Dowdy's wife Susan; he and his wife had come to live at Mountain Home about 1880. It is hard to imagine that any of these would have been zealous witnesses for the prosecution.

On November 22, following the indictments, Tom Dowdy gave bond in the amount of $7,500, pledged by eleven of his friends and neighbors; there is no record of a counterpart bond being given by his brother Richard or by their kinsman Dan Dunman.[15] Bill Dunman was a fugitive from justice; his brother Dan was in prison. Richard Dowdy was not a fugitive.

Their trials were docketed for the spring term of district court, 1882, scheduled for the week of May 10–14. Apparently the trials were continued for one year because they were finally held during the week of May 11–15, 1883, in Kerrville, presided over by Leo Tarleton, a San Antonio criminal attorney who had been appointed by Texas Governor Oren Roberts to serve as special judge for the 24th Judicial District of Texas.[16]

Tom Dowdy's attorney was Wesley Thigpen, a maternal first cousin whose family had been neighbors of the Dowdys back in Goliad County.[17] Tom's murder trial was the first of the eight proceedings.[18] It turned out to be the linchpin that held all eight cases together.

**Trial and Verdicts**

No record of the courtroom testimony survives, only Judge Tarleton's instructions to the jury. Those instructions explain murder, first-degree murder, murder with express malice, group offenses, circumstantial evidence, presence at the scene of the crime, witness credibility, and presumption of innocence.[19]

We do not know if, or how, Tom Dowdy's attorney, Wesley Thigpen, managed to introduce into the jury's consideration the rumored involvement of the murdered man, John Potter, in the horrific slaughter of Tom Dowdy's four younger siblings in October of 1878. We do not know if they were made aware of the profound suffering those deaths caused the Dowdy family afterward, or of the pain that attended the early deaths of Tom and Susan Dowdy's two infant sons in the two years following their arrival in Kerr County to assist the survivors of Tom's desolated family. We do not know whether the known crimes of John Potter and his notorious family were formally made known to the jury.

We do know, as a moral certainty, that by May 1883 every man on that jury, all residents of Kerr County, had had four and a half years to ponder the Dowdy murders. They had, by then, heard repeatedly about the accumulating notoriety of the Kimble County confederation, their reputed raiding disguised as Indians, John Potter's imputed involvement in those activities, and the neighborhood rumors of his participation in the Dowdy raid. The fact of John Potter's Indian ancestry, together with the long history of known Mexican Indian raiding in the region, would only have added fuel to the fires of retribution. So it may well be that Tom Dowdy's attorney did not even have to bring any of those topics forward.

We do not know what the jury's rationale was for their verdict. We can speculate, however, that questions about circumstantial evidence and proof of Tom Dowdy's presence at the scene of the crime may have provided a plausible rationalization in their minds. But perhaps it was as simple as the traditional perception in many frontier murder trials—the murdered man needed killing, and the community owed the perpetrator their thanks for taking care of an unpleasant task.

Whatever their reasons, on May 12, 1883, a jury of Tom Dowdy's Kerr County peers found him not guilty of the murder of John Potter.[20]

The following day, the district attorney did not offer any evidence to sustain Dick Dowdy's murder charge, so on the next day, May 14, Judge Tarleton instructed the jury to return a verdict of not guilty.[21] Following the same rationale, the two Dowdy brothers were found not guilty of aiding the escape of a prisoner, and of stealing Deputy Sheriff Joe Clements's two six-shooters, by Judge Tarleton's instructed verdicts.[22]

On the same day, Bill and Dan Dunman also benefited by the "not guilty" verdict handed down in Tom Dowdy's murder trial—again, the district attorney did not offer any evidence to sustain their murder and theft charges, so Judge Tarleton again instructed their juries to return "not guilty" verdicts.[23]

### Complicity of District Attorney in Acquittals

The district attorney of Kerr County, W. R. Wallace, was as complicit in Tom Dowdy's acquittal as the law officers of Kimble County had been in John Potter's lynching. As an elected official who must have been sensitive to the sentiments of his constituents, the district attorney's legal strategy and tactics foreordained the "not-guilty" verdict returned by Tom Dowdy's jury. By not moving earlier for a change of venue for this sensational trial, nor offering sustaining evidence in any of the related subsequent cases against the Dowdys and the Dunmans, the district attorney practically guaranteed the acquittal of all accused parties.

The whole story is an Old Testament tragedy, reeking of vengeance. The death of John Potter was classic eye-for-an-eye, tooth-for-a-tooth retribution, delivered up in a way that would have warmed the hearts of the unforgiving Anglo-Celtic frontiersmen who constituted the bulk of the citizenry of Kerr County—and Tom Dowdy's jury.

## A Community Judgment

Beginning in 1877, a series of blows had been delivered to the Kimble County criminal confederation, mostly by forces of the Frontier Battalion. The Rangers assisted inconstant and often ineffective county law-enforcement officers who were nevertheless increasingly supported by courageous citizens desirous of bringing civil justice to their community. Long-suffering citizens of adjacent counties welcomed the gradual demise of the Kimble County outlaw organization. John Potter's capture, jailing, and execution was the final, and perhaps symbolic, reckoning.

The subsequent acquittal of the Dowdys and the Dunmans, with the connivance of the incumbent legal officials, expressed the Kerr County community's satisfaction with the concluding violent act, and the ultimate outcome of the judicial process.

Justice had been served. Order had been established. Now the rule of law could begin to take root in the communities around the Edwards Plateau.

# 16 :: Afterward

The dramatic events and remarkable coincidences associated with the main characters who figured in "The Reckoning" did not cease with the execution of John Potter in May of 1881, or the acquittal of Tom and Dick Dowdy, and Bill and Dan Dunman, two years later. Indeed, the lives of these disparate individuals continued to be filled with surprising twists and turns, unforeseen relationships, and fates ranging from tragic to heroic.

## The Dowdys

James and Susan Cassell Dowdy lived out their lives on the section of land they filed on in 1879, located in the valley of Johnson Creek near the home place of James's brother Gib Dowdy.[1] James died in 1900, aged eighty-two, and Susan followed him in 1913, aged eighty-three.[2]

Tom and Susan Reeves Dowdy operated the first store and post office in the Mountain Home community at the original Dowdy homestead. Later, they moved their family to Ingram, about twelve miles southeast, where they founded another store. After they lost two infant sons during the 1878–80 crisis, Tom and Susan had four sons and two daughters. Their second surviving son was named Tarleton Leo, after the special judge under whose jurisdiction Tom was acquitted of the murder of John Potter. Their fourth and youngest son was named Wesley Thigpen Dowdy, after Tom's defense attorney.[3] Tom Dowdy died in 1919 as a result of falling under a threshing machine. He was sixty-five. His wife, Susan, died in 1936, aged seventy-seven.[4]

Mary Dowdy is a tragic figure. After her mother died in 1913, her brothers separated the old dog-run house into two separate buildings and relocated the larger portion on the premises. The smaller part, a single room about twelve feet by sixteen feet, became Mary Dowdy's own cottage, in which she lived, alone and fearful, for the rest of her days, pitied by her community. She was very quiet and reclusive, thought by many to be of unsound mind, and her brothers had little interaction with her other than to supply her material needs.[5] She lived to be eighty-eight years old, dying in 1945.[6] She was the last of her siblings to go.

Richard Dowdy and his wife, Lee Ella, also lived out their lives in the area. Dick Dowdy, suffering from a brain tumor, died in 1938, the result of being shot in the back of the head with a .44 caliber pistol by his wife. This may have been a "mercy killing," as Mrs. Dowdy, after initially being charged with murder, was never prosecuted. He was eighty-two years old.[7] His wife died in 1953, aged ninety-two.[8]

The youngest Dowdy sibling, George, married Georgia Lamb. They had two children and lived in the Mountain Home area most of their lives. George died in 1935, aged sixty-four; his wife died in 1960, aged eighty-six.[9]

All the Dowdys were buried in the family plot at the Sunset Cemetery, just two miles southeast of the original Dowdy home site. The lives of many of their descendants, some of whom still live in Kerr County, appear to have become hostage to the Dowdy tragedy, which continues to be a favorite topic of discussion among area residents.

### The Dunmans

After he helped the Dowdy brothers free his brother Bill in May 1881, Dan Dunman was frequently in trouble with the law, usually in regard to stolen horses, usually in some sort of claimed "stock-detective" capacity. He was convicted of theft of geldings in Travis County on May 3, 1882, but pardoned on May 7, 1884, officially at the request of his mother, Kate Dunman,[10] but more likely at the urging of Bexar County law enforcement officials, who wanted to employ him as a stock detective and informant against a gang of horse thieves then active around Austin and San Antonio.

On May 11, 1886, Dan Dunman was again convicted of horse theft, this time in LaSalle County, and sentenced to fifteen years in Huntsville prison. In this case, Dunman informed on two prominent citizens, Joe and John Sheely. Joe Sheely was a former Texas Ranger captain; his brother, John Sheely, was an active horse dealer in South Texas. Dunman was convicted, mostly because his name was on the bill of sale of the subject horses. John Sheely was also convicted but pardoned in 1890. Dan Dunman was pardoned two years later, on November 19, 1892, by Governor J. S. Hogg.[11]

Bill Dunman apparently remained a fugitive for about twelve years after the Dowdy brothers liberated him from Kimble County law officers in early May 1881. By 1893 he had married a woman named Maggie and had an infant son, Burt, and was living in San Antonio. But sometime in 1893 he and his brother Dan were arrested and indicted on multiple counts of horse theft and burglary in Bexar County.[12]

Word of Bill Dunman's capture reached the Kimble County sheriff's office, and he was indicted on November 1, 1893, for the 1879 murder of John Condy.[13] His trial was scheduled for the spring 1894 term of district court in Junction City.[14] However, the Bexar County sheriff refused to deliver Dunman to the Kimble County authorities until the conclusion of his trial in San Antonio. In that proceeding, Bill and Dan Dunman were both convicted on two counts of horse theft, and each sentenced to twelve years. They were received together at the Texas state prison at Huntsville on April 20, 1894.[15] Recognizing that Bill Dunman was already serving a lengthy sentence, and that many of the state's witnesses in the Condy murder trial were no longer available, the district attorney for the 33rd Judicial District (Kimble County) moved on October 26, 1895, to dismiss the case.[16]

Kate Dunman, by then living in San Antonio, began a campaign to get her eldest son pardoned, and a substantial correspondence ensued, the gist of which was that Bill Dunman had been framed. His request for pardon was refused on April 14, 1896. The request was reinstituted immediately, with additional support and verification from the previous clerk and district attorney of the 37th Judicial District (Bexar County), Henry Umschied and W. R. Camp, respectively, and former sheriff of Bexar County, John M. Campbell, as well as State Senator J. A. O'Connor. In addition, the prison physician at the Rusk prison affirmed to Senator O'Connor that Dunman was in ill health and recommended executive clemency. Bill Dunman was pardoned and released on April 26, 1897.[17]

Dan Dunman was released from Huntsville prison on January 26, 1901.[18] The further fates of the Dunman brothers, and of their loyal mother, Kate, are not known to the author.

## The Dublins

Roll and Dell Dublin pled guilty to the December 15, 1877, robbery of the stagecoach near Pegleg Crossing, were sentenced to ten years at hard labor, and delivered to prison at Chester, Illinois, on September 13, 1880. Afterward, the James Dublin family and their neighbors, the William Potter family, each of whom now had two sons incarcerated for the Pegleg crime, moved to Backbone Valley in southern Burnet County, probably in early 1881.[19]

By that time, Jimmy Dublin would have been sixty-one years of age; his wife Nancy was thirty-five. The Dublin offspring that made the move would probably have included Caroline (sixteen), G. A. (fifteen), Charles A. (fifteen), Sallie (twelve), Jennie (ten), George (eight), M. (six), and Maggie May (two). Whether the eldest Dublin daughter, Catherine, married to the incarcerated Bill Allison (who had informed on his former accomplices), went with her parents and sisters is not known.

But in December 1886—more than six years after the Dublin and Potter brothers had been imprisoned—both families received electrifying news. A fellow inmate at Chester Prison, one Tom Moody, who had been received at the prison only a few months after the Dublins and Potters, had confessed to the authorities that it was he and one other accomplice—and not the Dublins and Potters—who had robbed the stagecoach at Pegleg Crossing on December 15, 1877.[20] Moody provided numerous details about the robbery that convinced the authorities that he had indeed been the perpetrator. The Dublins and the Potters were pardoned and released on December 13, 1886.[21] So was their inconstant accomplice, Matt Wilkins, whose plea agreement with the trial prosecutors had broken the united front of the Pegleg defendants and effectively forced them all to abandon their original "not-guilty" pleadings.

After Roll Dublin managed to find ranch work in southeastern New Mexico, he and Elizabeth Lee (Lizzie) Potter became engaged. A group of friends and relatives escorted them from Burnet County about 150 miles north to the new town of Baird, in Callahan County, where they were married on July 3, 1887, before boarding the train to Midland. Dublin subsequently worked for John Scharbauer in the ranching business before buying his own ranches in Gaines and Ector Counties, Texas.[22]

That apparently started the relocation of the Dublin and Potter families to West Texas. Dell Dublin married Mary Ellen Potter, Lizzie's sister, in 1887. Subsequently, he was engaged in ranching in eastern New Mexico and western Texas, possibly with his brother Roll. Charles A. Dublin married Roberta M. Potter in 1890 in Coleman, Texas; in 1900 they were living in Midland. Charles's mother, Nancy Fondren Dublin, was living with them. The youngest of the Dublin siblings, Maggie May, married Bill Potter in 1896 in Midland. George Dublin was also in Midland by 1900, married to a woman named "Prude."[23] She was not one of the Potter daughters. In addition, other Dublin cousins seem to have congregated in the Midland area in the 1890s.[24] The fates of the rest of the Jimmy Dublin family are not known to the author—the dates and locations of Jimmy Dublin's death, or of his wife, or of eight of their nine daughters.

Dell Dublin had six children by his wife Mary Ellen Potter. They were living in Midland in 1900 and 1910, where they were staunch members and supporters of the First Christian Church. Mary Ellen died in a house fire during a visit to Kimble County in 1912. Dell Dublin died in Midland in 1915.[25]

Roll Dublin prospered in West Texas. He and his wife Lizzie had six children. They lived in Midland during the school year but stayed on the family ranch during the summers. Roll Dublin was vice president of the Midland National Bank at the time of its founding and a director when he died. According to family tradition, he and his brother Dell gave the land on which was built the First Christian Church in Midland, provided lumber and supplies to construct the building, and paid all the church's bills until it could support itself. Roll Dublin died a wealthy man in 1919, aged sixty-three;[26] his wife, Lizzie Potter Dublin, died in Midland in 1958, aged ninety.[27]

Figure 35. Mack and Lizzie (Veach) Potter, probably in their wedding photo, in late August 1887, when he was about thirty-five years old and she was about fifteen. Courtesy of Mary Lou Midkiff.

## The Potters

**The White Potters.** Will and Mary Gordon Potter left Kimble County with their family, probably in early 1881, after their two oldest sons, Mack and Bill, were convicted in federal court of robbing the Pegleg stage, along with their accomplices, Roll and Dell Dublin, Bill Allison, and Matthew Wilkins. By then Will's brother Tom had been dead for six months or more, and Tom's orphaned Indian sons Moses (age eighteen in 1881), William (sixteen), and Tom, Jr. (thirteen) were probably living with their Uncle Will's family.

They moved about ninety miles east to Backbone Valley in southern Burnet County near their Kimble County friends the Jimmy Dublin family.[28] Will and Mary Potter were fifty-six and forty-four, respectively. Their Texas dreams had been dashed, the family disgraced. Once again, the Potters were starting over.

Son Jeff Potter died in Backbone Valley on September 29, 1883, of causes unknown. He was twenty-one. His parents and siblings continued to reside in Backbone Valley until at least early 1887.[29] By January of 1888, Will Potter and part of his family were in Toro, Callahan County, Texas.[30] He probably gave his daughter Lizzie away on July 3, when she married Roll Dublin in the nearby town of Baird.[31] The Potter family then moved to Midland County, Texas, where their siblings were congregating, many of them married to Dublin offspring.

Will Potter died on April 15, 1896, in Midland, aged seventy-one. His wife,

Mary Evaline Gordon Potter, followed him on February 24, 1904, aged seventy.[32] In retrospect, William Potter may be seen as a traditionalist, a well-meaning but naive and ineffective man who was easily manipulated by others. From a distance of 130 years, his wife appears to have been the power figure in the family.

After Mack and Bill Potter were pardoned and released from Chester Prison, they both eventually migrated to the western Texas–eastern New Mexico area, where they worked as cowboys and stockmen. Mack hung around Illinois long enough to marry Elizabeth Veach on August 27, 1887, in Vienna, about sixty miles southeast of Chester; she returned with him to the Southwest. They had seven children. Mack Potter died in Elkins, New Mexico, in 1903, aged fifty. Bill Potter married Maggie May Dublin in 1896, and sired one son, Jeff. He was working on a ranch in Winkler County north of Kermit, Texas, when he died on December 31, 1898, aged forty-two.[33]

The other children of William and Mary Potter—Joseph, John Hildreth, and Hattie May, the youngest, all lived the rest of their lives in the Midland area.[34]

James K. P. Potter, after separating from his nephews John and "Indian Jim" Potter at Pecos Station on October 3, 1880—leaving them to their fate at the hands of Corporal Kimbell and his Rangers—escaped west and north to southeastern New Mexico with his pal, George Cleveland. The pair was located by Texas Ranger Lieutenant Charles Nevill, commanding Company E, just after Corporal Kimbell had departed for Kimble County with his wounded prisoner, John Potter.[35] On November 21, 1880, Nevill sent Corporal L. W. Rodgers and three men in search of Potter and Cleveland, suspected of cattle rustling. Rodgers returned on December 3, having encountered the fugitives on Black River, southeastern New Mexico, where the Rangers

> gave Cleveland a run of six miles and exchanged shots with him. [Cleveland] succeeded in making his escape. [We] saw Potter leave a ranch some distance ahead of us while in pursuit of Cleveland. Our horses being run down, he also escaped.[36]

James K. P. Potter became associated with John H. Slaughter, the notorious Texas cattleman and range pirate, probably after 1880 but conceivably as early as 1878, when Slaughter was reputed to be operating in the Devils River country, only about seventy-five miles west of the Potter-Dublin neighborhood on the South Llano River.[37]

Slaughter had been indicted for cattle theft in Atascosa County on September 9, 1876, and was listed in the official Texas Rangers 1878 List of Fugitives from Justice, which indicated that he might be operating in the vicinity of Fort Concho.[38] He began to move his operations into the outlaw-ridden Seven Rivers region of southeastern New Mexico in April 1879. On arrival in New Mexico, however, he almost immediately found himself wanted for murder and cattle theft. Without delay, Slaughter immediately set out for southeastern Arizona with a herd of cattle, which he sold in Tombstone, then returned to New Mexico, got married, and returned to Tombstone with a second herd.[39]

In 1881 James K. P. Potter accompanied Slaughter's third and final cattle herd to Cochise County, Arizona, from Texas. After a fifth child, Ruben C., was born in Texas about 1881, Potter's wife, Evaline, and their children followed him to Arizona. Potter, his son William, and his nephew John Hildreth worked for Slaughter in Arizona for many years afterward. Slaughter was noted for hiring hard cowboys, many of whom may have become outlaws later. James K. P. Potter died in Bisbee, Arizona, in 1912; Evaline died sometime afterward.[40]

In hindsight, James K. P. Potter appears to have been a reckless, self-interested, opportunistic man with little conscience or sense of responsibility, especially with regard to his Indian nephews, John and "Indian Jim" Potter, whom he exploited and then callously abandoned in order to escape from Corporal Kimbell's pursuing Ranger squad.

**The Indian Potters.** After his younger brother John was carried back to Junction City by Corporal Kimbell's Ranger squad in November 1880, Frank Potter worked as a teamster for the Texas Rangers at Fort Davis before being terminated by Lieutenant Charles Nevill in March 1881 for unspecified reasons.[41]

Frank Potter may have been involved with ranching interests in Arizona over the next ten to twelve years through his connection with his uncle, James K. P. Potter, who worked there for rancher John H. Slaughter. But Frank Potter eventually made his way back to Mendocino County, California, by late 1892 or early 1893.[42] In 1895 he was a minor player in a Mendocino County cattle war.[43] He married a Jessie Gray, probably in 1896, by whom he had three children. Frank Potter died before 1915 in Mendocino County.[44]

Tom Potter, Jr., the youngest of Tom Potter's sons by Mollie Metock, was about twelve years old when his father died, probably in 1880. Presumably, he and his brothers Moses and William were looked after by their Uncle Will after their father died, the three oldest Indian Potter brothers, Frank, John, and Jim, not being at home. But like his brother Frank, Tom Potter, Jr., eventually made his way back to his people in Mendocino County by late 1892 or early 1893. In 1905 he married an Agnes Costello in Mendocino County and raised a family.[45]

Moses and William Potter were both old enough (seventeen and fifteen, respectively, in 1880) to go with their brother Frank after their father died, if he had been inclined to look after his two young brothers. But Frank Potter may have been living a hard and dangerous life. It seems unlikely that they would have been able to go to Arizona with their uncle, James K. P. Potter, and his family because of his previous apparent indifference to the welfare of their two older brothers, Jim and John Potter. In any case, what became of these two young Indian sons of Tom Potter is simply unknown.

**George Cleveland.** After George Cleveland split off from John and Jim Potter at Pecos Station on October 3, 1880, fleeing from Corporal Kimbell and his Texas Rangers, Cleveland continued west with his wife's brother, James K. P. Potter. The pair were sought as suspected cattle thieves by Lieutenant Charles Nevill, commander of Company E, Frontier Battalion, stationed at Fort Davis.[46]

As previously noted, James K. P. Potter went from the Pecos country to Cochise County, Arizona, with John H. Slaughter's third cattle herd in 1881. It is not known whether George Cleveland went with him. Perhaps not coincidentally, however, George Cleveland's wife, Rebecca (Potter), also went from California to Arizona with her infant son, William Jasper Cleveland, in the same year, eventually ending up in Bisbee.[47] Whether Rebecca went to Arizona to be with her husband, George Cleveland, or her youngest brother, James K. P. Potter, is left for the reader's speculation, but by 1897 she was living with James K. P. Potter in Tombstone, Arizona.[48]

In April 1887 George Cleveland stole a horse from the Grand Central Mine near Bisbee, Arizona. He was pursued and captured by deputies of the then-sheriff of Cochise County, John H. Slaughter. At trial, Cleveland claimed that he had bought the horse from a Mexican who was on his way to Mexico, a time-worn alibi which earned him a year in Yuma Prison.[49] In 1892 George Cleveland returned to California. Whether he and his wife, Rebecca Potter, were legally divorced is not known but in 1898 he remarried and in 1900 at age fifty-two was keeping a saloon in Calpella, Mendocino County, California. George Cleveland died sometime after March 24, 1913, probably in Mendocino County.[50]

### The Kimble County Citizens

By early 1881, the Dublin-Potter gang was gone from Kimble County. Most of their criminal accomplices were either in jail, on the run, or had forsaken the region for more lawless surroundings. The region around the forks of the Llano was settling down. As reported a year later, in the *Galveston Daily News,*

Kimble County has heretofore borne rather a bad reputation, but the bad element has all been removed, and at present a more peaceable law-abiding people are seldom found in any portion of the State; they are social, refined, and hospitable. Any party looking up a location to settle would do well to give this section a call. Junction City, the county seat, has about 300 inhabitants, is located immediately at the junction of the north and south forks of the Llano, has a good courthouse and jail, two stores, general merchandise, and a furniture store, all doing a profitable business. There is lumber on the ground for the construction of a Christian Church. The Methodists are also on the eve of building. A good school will be opened the first Monday in next month, and still the city is only in its fourth year.[51]

Of the handful of courageous early settlers who resisted the outlaw confederation in Kimble County during the turbulent years 1874–80, most did not linger long in the community they had helped to civilize and stabilize.

After the Kimble County confederation was subdued, cattleman Felix Burton remained on Bear Creek with his family until about 1882, when he resumed his earlier wandering life. He took his family first to New Mexico, then on to Oregon about 1890, settling finally in Sonoma, California, around 1896, where he died sometime after 1910.[52]

Dr. E. K. Kountz brought his family to the forks of the Llano in 1874, when he was forty-six years old. In 1879 he built the first public building in Junction City, in which was located the post office, county clerk's office, drug store, and general store. His wife, Harriet, was the first postmistress. Kountz died in 1884 in Del Rio, Texas; Harriet Kountz died in 1890. Both were buried in Junction City. Their son, John C. Kountz, and his wife, Laura, lived out their lives in Kimble County. He died in 1929; she died in 1939.[53]

W. F. Gilliland remained in Kimble County until 1887, when he and his family moved to New Mexico in search of open range and land to homestead. He died in Alamogordo, New Mexico, in 1913.[54]

John A. Miller had come to Kimble County in 1874 with his family, settling near the mouth of Johnson Creek, where he took up land and became a stock farmer. "Honest John" Miller was known as a man of strong moral character, who would not put his brand on any animal he was not certain that he owned. He and his wife lived in Kimble County for the rest of their lives. Miller died in 1926, his wife four years later. Most of their children continued to live in Kimble County.[55]

N. Q. Patterson, who was the first county treasurer in 1876, succeeded the resigned William Potter as county judge in 1877. He had arrived in Kimble County with his family in late 1875, when he was forty-six years old. Patterson's first wife died in 1885; two years later he remarried. In 1890 N. Q. Patterson moved to New Mexico, where he died in 1897.[56]

Ben Pepper had brought his family to Kimble County in about 1875, when he was fifty-three years old, and immediately became involved in community affairs. In 1880 Pepper built one of the first stone, two-story houses in Kimble County, on his ranch property, a wide alluvial terrace in the South Llano valley, about four miles southwest of the confluence of the Llanos. He was a capable and progressive stock farmer, introducing improved breeds of livestock and setting up irrigation systems to water his fields. In 1902, at the age of seventy-nine, he sold his ranch and moved with his family to Ramona, California, where he and his wife lived out their days. Ben Pepper died in 1916, age ninety-six.[57]

John E. Temple lived with his family in Junction City until 1885, when he moved to Lampasas, Texas, with his third wife. He died in Lampasas County in 1899 at age seventy-seven.[58]

### The Rangers

Captain Dan W. Roberts resigned his commission on September 1, 1881, whereupon he and his wife, Luvenia Conway, moved to Nogales, New Mexico, where Roberts was involved in mining and stock-raising ventures. The couple was childless. They returned to Texas in 1912, settling in Austin, where Roberts published his Ranger memoirs in 1914. He was prominent at Texas Ranger reunions during the 1920s. Roberts died in Austin on February 6, 1935, aged ninety-four.[59] Dan Roberts was a steady, prudent, scholarly, well-organized commander, primarily an Indian fighter, one of the legendary officers of the Frontier Battalion, who served for more than nine years, mostly around Kimble and Menard Counties. When he joined the Rangers, their clear priority was controlling Plains Indians raiding from the north and Mexican Indians raiding from the west. By the time Dan Roberts resigned, the Indian raids were over and the Rangers had cleaned out the last of the outlaw confederation that had plagued the margins of the Edwards Plateau.

Pat Dolan resigned from the Frontier Battalion in April 1879 and went with his family to Zavala County, where he was in the cattle business until 1884, when Dolan moved his family and his herd of graded Durham cattle to a ranch in the Davis Mountains. In 1887 he became the first sheriff of newly created Jeff Davis County. He sold his ranch in 1898 and moved to Marfa, where he opened a saddle shop, and then moved back to Uvalde briefly. By 1902 the Dolans were living in El Paso. He and his wife, Margaret Jane Cook Dolan, raised seven children, four of whom predeceased their parents. Pat Dolan died in El Paso on February 12,

1930, aged eighty-six.[60] In trying to anticipate and locate trails and stopping places of raiding Mexican Indians, Pat Dolan explored the rough Devils River and lower Pecos River country of southwest Texas. Dolan's Creek and Dolan's Falls on the Devils River are named in his memory.

After he left the Frontier Battalion in February 1879, Lieutenant Nelson O. ("Maje," for "Major") Reynolds became a saloon keeper in San Marcos. In early 1882 he moved to Lampasas, where he had won plaudits during his earlier Ranger service, and opened another saloon. In September 1882, Reynolds married Irene Temperance Nevill, the younger sister of his old Ranger sidekick Charles Nevill. Their two daughters were born in Lampasas. Reynolds was town marshal in 1883, and Lampasas county sheriff from 1886 to 1889. He then relocated his family to Angleton, in Brazoria County, where he was in the shoe and boot business. In 1899 the Reynolds family moved to Lockhart, Texas, where he opened another saloon. By 1910 Reynolds and his wife were living in Orange, Texas, where the old Ranger was the night watchman and assistant manager at a paper mill. In 1920 Reynolds retired and moved to the town of Center Point, in eastern Kerr County, which was also the home of another old Ranger colleague, Captain Neal Coldwell. On March 1, 1922, Reynolds died of pneumonia, aged seventy-seven. Irene Nevill Reynolds lived on at Center Point until her death in 1947, aged eighty-four. Nelson O "Maje" Reynolds was the most widely respected Ranger officer of his time, recognized for his courage, energy, relentlessness, and leadership.[61] J. B. Gillett described him aptly as "Reynolds, the Intrepid."[62]

Corporal James B. Gillett transferred to Company C (later Company A), commanded by Lieutenant George W. Baylor, on July 28, 1879, and accompanied the new commander and his family on their journey to Ysleta, El Paso County, far west Texas. Gillett served there with distinction, rising to sergeant before he resigned at the end of 1881 to take a position as chief of railroad guards for the Santa Fe Railroad. He had married Helen Baylor, the daughter of his commander, in early 1881. In 1882 Gillett became El Paso town marshal, serving until 1885, when he resigned to take a position as manager of the Estado Land and Cattle Company ranch in Brewster County, Texas.[63] His first marriage having failed, Gillett married Lou Chastain in San Marcos in 1889, by whom he had seven children. He acquired his own ranch in 1890, after which he pursued personal business interests in West Texas and eastern New Mexico. Gillett wrote his memoirs in 1921. He retired in 1923 and lived at Marfa, Texas, until his death in 1937, aged eighty.[64] Although he never made lieutenant or captain as a Texas Ranger, Jim Gillett was the consummate fearless, tenacious man hunter that helped to establish the reputation of the Texas Rangers as an effective law enforcement organization among the criminal element on both sides of the border.

Corporal Rush G. Kimbell resigned from the Frontier Battalion in October 1881, almost a year after he had returned with the wounded prisoner John Potter and delivered him to the sheriff of Kimble County. As he explained in his 1937 memoir, he had originally enlisted on September 10, 1878, following through on a promise made to his sweetheart in Limestone County, Texas:

> One moon-light night, in September, 1878, while at her home, in the yard, sitting on the old-fashioned well-curb . . . I asked her if I might hope. She told me that there was another contender, who said he loved her well enough to die for her, and so I answered that that could then be easily solved—just let him die for her, and I would live for her, and we would all be happy. She said on one condition, only, would she consent, and that was that if I would agree to prove my love and loyalty to her and to Texas, by joining the Ranger service, and serving three years, and bring back an honorable discharge. We closed the deal, and I left her that night and was sworn into the service . . . [on] September 10, 1878, at the Capitol, at Austin. . . .
>
> Now, as the time of service agreed upon with my "Yellow Rose [of Texas]" was fast approaching . . . I told my Captain of my future plans, and that I would like for him to give me a discharge . . . [and] he was soon able to hand me my discharge, as he said with sadness and regrets and best wishes for me and "The Yellow Rose of Texas's." And in October [1881], I went to her, threw my record in her lap and asked if she were ready to comply with the contract, to which she answered in the affirmative. We were married and started [a] life in happiness on a different plane.[65]

Rush Kimbell and Emma N. Love, his "Yellow Rose of Texas," were married on October 20, 1881, in Stephens County, Texas.[66] He was twenty-six years old; she was seventeen. They raised a family of seven at Groesbeck, Limestone County, Texas, before she died sometime between 1895 and 1900.[67] He remarried in 1908 and moved to Altus, Oklahoma, where he died on January 18, 1954, aged ninety-eight.[68] He was buried in Altus. Rush Kimbell manifested exemplary courage and dedication in his Ranger service, and his memoirs express an unquenchable optimism and an engagingly whimsical sense of humor.

Lieutenant Charles Nevill continued as commander of Company E in the Fort Davis area, distinguishing himself and his command. In January 1881, Nevill joined his Company E forces with Captain Baylor's Company A to eliminate the last band of Apache raiders in West Texas, a hold-out segment of Victorio's band.[69] On September 1, 1881, Nevill was promoted to captain. He resigned his Ranger commission on November 7, 1882, having been elected sheriff of Presidio County, a post at which he served for three two-year terms. He married Sallie Crosson at Fort Davis on June 4, 1883; they had eight children. He participated in ranching ventures in the late 1880s. The Nevills moved to San Antonio in 1889, where he became chief deputy sheriff and subsequently held other offices. He was district clerk of Bexar County at the time of his death on June 14, 1906, aged fifty-one.[70] Charles Nevill served with the Frontier Battalion for more than eight years. He absorbed and applied the teachings and traditions of his mentors, John B. Jones, Dan Roberts, and Nelson O. Reynolds, as well as his long-time colleague and friend, Jim Gillett.

Lieutenant Frank M. Moore, a long-time resident of Kerr County, served as sheriff from 1882 to 1892. He was Kerr County sheriff during the 1883 trials of the Dowdys and Dunmans for the murder of John Potter, whom Moore probably remembered from 1877, when his Ranger command, Company D, had been stationed on Bear Creek in Kimble County before and after the Kimble County Roundup. In November 1892, at age sixty, Frank Moore declined to run again for sheriff and retired, living out his days in the area. He died in 1909, aged seventy-seven, and was buried in the Center Point Cemetery, Kerr County. Frank Moore never married.[71]

### Deputy Sheriff Joe Clements

Joe Clements, who knew his way around hard men in a hard country, served for several years as deputy sheriff under Sheriffs John Gorman and H. J. Garland. Afterward, he became a successful stockman in Kimble County, developing several ranch properties before selling out and moving to Chavez County, New Mexico, in 1899, where his business interests expanded to include more than one hundred thousand acres of land by 1924. Joe Clements was a founder and first president of the Bank of Commerce of Roswell, New Mexico. He died on March 16, 1927, aged seventy-seven.[72]

### The Military

Ranald S. Mackenzie was transferred from Fort Clark, Texas, to the Los Pinos, Colorado, Indian agency in October 1879, where, with six companies of cavalry, he successfully settled an uprising by the Ute Indians. In September 1881, he was ordered to move his cavalry to Arizona, and bring the Apache Indians under control. After a brief, successful campaign, he was given command of the Military District of New Mexico, where he also settled restive Apache and Navajo tribesmen. Mackenzie was promoted to brigadier general in October 1882. By this time, however, his health was broken, both physically and mentally. Nevertheless, he was assigned command of the Department of Texas, and took command on November 1, 1883. Very soon afterward, his behavior became erratic, sometimes violent, and he was ordered by the U.S. secretary of war to be admitted to the Bloomingdale Asylum in New York City. Mackenzie did not respond to treatment and was retired from the U.S. Army on March 24, 1884. After June 1884, he was looked after by family and friends, first at his boyhood home in Morristown, New Jersey, and then at New Brighton, on Staten Island, New York, where his sister Harriet cared for him until his death on January 19, 1889, from "general paresis." He was forty-eight years old.[73] Ranald Mackenzie was a man of action, a driven and demanding personality, and a soldier of great personal courage and determination. He was certainly the most effective high-level army officer to serve on the Texas frontier and along the Mexican border during the decade of the 1870s.

John L. Bullis, commander of the Seminole Scouts, made his last raid into Mexico in the spring of 1881, pursuing Lipan Indians who had murdered a woman and a young man on April 19 at the McLauren ranch in the Frio Canyon, north of present Leakey, Real County, Texas. Bullis, stationed at Fort Clark, was informed of the murders on April 26, crossed the Rio Grande with his Seminole Scouts, and caught up with the raiders on the morning of May 2, deep in the Serranía del Burro, about sixty miles west of present Del Rio, Texas. They killed more than half the raiders and scattered the rest. They also recovered an American woman and a small boy not known to be missing, plus twenty-one horses and mules. On April 7, 1882, the Texas Legislature, in a joint resolution, commended Bullis for his services "in behalf of the people of the frontier of this State, in repelling the depredations of Indians and other enemies of the frontier of Texas."[74] In 1882 he was transferred to Camp Supply, Indian Territory, where he served until 1888, when he rejoined his old regiment in Arizona and was appointed to act as agent for the Apaches at the San Carlos Reservation. In 1893 he was sent to Santa Fe, New Mexico Territory, where he acted as agent for the Pueblo and Jicarilla Apache Indians. In 1897 he returned to Fort Sam Houston, Texas, as Major Bullis. He saw additional service in Cuba and the Philippines from 1898 to 1902. He was promoted to brigadier general by President Theodore Roosevelt in 1904, following which he retired. In 1885 he had entered into a partnership with William Shafter and John Spencer to open the Shafter silver mining district in Presidio County, Texas, which made Bullis a wealthy man. He had married Alice Rodriguez in San Antonio in 1872; she died in 1887. In 1891 he married Josephine Withers in San Antonio; this union produced three daughters. John Bullis died in San Antonio on May 26, 1911, aged seventy. Camp Bullis, the military training base established north of San Antonio just before the United States entered World War I, was named in his honor. John Bullis was a dedicated combat soldier all his life, from when he enlisted as a corporal in the 126th New York Volunteer Infantry at age 21, to service on the southwestern frontier, and concluding with his service in Cuba and the Philippines. He was an authentic American hero and a legend in his own time.[75]

## The Judges

The Honorable W. A. Blackburn served as district judge of the 17th Judicial District of Texas for twenty years, beginning in 1876. A native of Tennessee, he married Sarah Graham there in 1857 and then served in the Confederate army throughout the Civil War. In July 1865, Blackburn came to Burnet, Texas; his wife and family followed him the next year. After practicing law in Burnet for nearly ten years, Blackburn was elected judge of the 17th Judicial District, in which Burnet was then located. The Blackburns had four children, three of whom survived their parents. Judge Blackburn retired from the bench in 1896 and lived out his days in Burnet. He died on June 2, 1908.[76] Through his long judicial service to the 17th district, W. A. Blackburn oversaw the establishment of order and then the rule of law in the turbulent Hill Country region. He provided much-needed continuity in jurisprudence to a society that found the evolution to lawful stability challenging and gradual. He was a courageous, stalwart, long-serving, wise, and pragmatic frontier judge.

After the "not-guilty" verdicts of Tom and Dick Dowdy, and Bill and Dan Dunman, were delivered by the Kerr County jury, attorney Leo Tarleton returned to San Antonio, where he practiced law for the next thirty-eight years. His service in the 1883 Kerr County trials apparently earned him the subsequent sobriquet in San Antonio legal circles of "Judge," by which title he was even described in his obituary. He was a founding member of the San Antonio Bar Association and an active member of the legal community. Leo Tarleton and his wife, Mary, had three children during the 1880s, but his family apparently left San Antonio after 1900, as he was living by himself in a boarding house in 1910.[77] He died on September 21, 1921, aged seventy-six. The 37th District Court adjourned the day after his death "out of respect and in memory of Judge Leo Tarleton. . . . The court appointed . . . a committee to draft and present appropriate resolutions on his death." His widow and two surviving children were living in New York at the time of his death.[78]

# 17 :: Judgments and Insights

Istarted this project with the intent of weaving together and tying up the various loose ends of a fascinating larger story that—inescapably—had been described incrementally in the literature of the time as eight separate incidents: the Kimble County confederation, Major John B. Jones's Kimble County Roundup, the killing of Dick Dublin by Corporal Jim Gillett, the murders of the Dowdy youngsters, the capture and trials of the Pegleg robbers, Corporal Rush Kimbell's heroic pursuit and capture of Jim and John Potter, the execution of John Potter, and the subsequent acquittal of his murderers, the Dowdys and Dunmans.

### Judging John Potter

I naturally expected to come to a clearer perception of John Potter's innocence or guilt in the Dowdy murders. Because there is no direct evidence placing Potter at the scene of the massacre, any assessment must rest on informed, objective judgment. The historical evidence is still circumstantial, still equivocal.

The case for John Potter's guilt begins with the fact that he was a twenty-year-old Indian man who probably harbored violent resentment against white people, arising from his own family's mistreatment at their hands in California during the 1860s, when Potter was growing up. The brutal assaults upon the Dowdy young people were perpetrated by Mexican Indians on a horse-stealing raid on October 5, 1878. A contemporary newspaper report, supported by Dowdy family tradition, indicates that, just before Alice Dowdy died, she was able to inform her mother, Susan Cassell Dowdy, of the name of a white man who was with the Indians who assaulted her; her mother's subsequent confrontation of the prisoner, John Potter, on May 8, 1881, in the presence of Kimble County law officers, supports that report. Tracks made by moccasins as well as boots were found at the scene of the crime.

Raids on frontier settlements around the periphery of the Edwards Plateau were not uncommon during the 1870s; such raids supplied clandestine markets in Mexican border towns, at which were traded horses, cattle, booty, and, occasionally, captives. John Potter was a member of a family-related criminal confederation headquartered in the South Llano river valley, only about thirty miles northwest of the Dowdy home site. This gang traded regularly in the Mexican livestock markets and was widely rumored to have conducted raids themselves, disguised as Indians. Indian raids and horse thefts were reported frequently in the South Llano valley during 1875–80.

Such an outlaw ring would have found it useful to have had one of their own in Mexico, acting as a representative to facilitate interactions with Indian raiders and Mexican traders. During 1875–80, when his father, two oldest brothers, two uncles, and two cousins were involved in the criminal activities of the Kimble County confederation, it is likely that John Potter himself was frequently absent from the South Llano valley, possibly in Mexico, serving as an agent on behalf of his family.

John Potter and his outlaw brother "Indian Jim" Potter were horse thieves who engaged in a gunfight with Texas Rangers before being taken into custody on October 8, 1880. Jim Potter was mortally wounded; John Potter, shot through the right lung, recovered. On November 21, 1880, the day before being returned to the custody of the sheriff of Kimble County, Potter attempted unsuccessfully to escape from his Ranger escort.

On hearing of the massacre, Tom Dowdy, the elder brother of the murdered young people, immediately left his home in Goliad County and traveled to Mountain Home with his wife, Susan Reeves Dowdy, to assist his parents and surviving siblings. She claimed afterward that John Potter had stolen horses from her family in Goliad County, sometime prior to the murders of the Dowdy youngsters.

Upon being delivered to the Bexar County jail for safekeeping, awaiting his May 1881 trial in Kimble County for horse theft and resisting arrest, John Potter was placed in a jail cell with Bill Dunman, who was also awaiting trial in Kimble County, for an 1879 murder. The two prisoners may have known one another previously in Kimble County. Sometime in spring 1881, Bill Dunman reported to the Dowdy family that John Potter had admitted to being involved with the Dowdy murders and that "the eldest daughter wouldn't have anything to do with him."[1] The reclusive, possibly guilt-ridden, lifetime behavior of the only surviving Dowdy daughter, and her brothers' apparent antipathy toward her, may suggest her possible indirect involvement with John Potter.

The Dowdy family, and subsequently many Kerr County neighbors, believed that John Potter had been involved in the Dowdy murders. Ranger Captain Dan W. Roberts very badly wanted the Potter brothers captured in September 1880, and Ranger Corporal Rush Kimbell articulated in his 1937 memoirs his belief that John Potter had been involved in the Dowdy murders. Kimble County law officers who colluded in the execution of John Potter had a legitimate fear that a Kimble County jury would acquit John Potter of horse theft at his impending trial, thus releasing a dangerous murderer.[2] From a distance of 125 years, it is unwise to dismiss out of hand the "group knowledge" held by law enforcement officers about John Potter, even though it may not have constituted legitimate legal evidence sufficient to arrest or indict.

On the other hand, there are additional facts, logical inferences, and rumors that argue against John Potter's involvement in the Dowdy murders, or at least negate much of the evidence so far delineated. First, there is no evidence that John Potter served as his family's "Mexican connection," facilitating traffic in stolen livestock with Indians raiding from Mexico, or traders operating clandestine markets in Mexican border towns. Moreover, the South Llano valley was a well-known outlaw hangout during the 1875–80 period. The fact that John Potter's father and brothers were part of that criminal confederation does not prove that he was also. Until he was wounded and arrested by Texas Ranger Corporal Kimbell on October 8, 1880, John Potter's name had never appeared on any reports or correspondence of the Rangers as a suspect, fugitive, or person of interest.

John Potter and his younger brother "Indian Jim" may only have been assisting their uncle James K. P. Potter and his friend George Cleveland, both wanted rustlers, in getting out of Kimble County following their father's death. They were losing their home site, it having been filed upon by other settlers, and they were anticipating the final exodus of the William Potter and Jimmy Dublin families from Kimble County, following the conviction of their cousins and neighbors for the Pegleg stage robberies.

The Dowdy family had been in Kerr County less than two weeks, and at their homestead on Johnson Creek for only three or four days, when the murders occurred, which would make any prior connection with John Potter unlikely. Newspaper reports indicate that, more than two years afterward, when confronted by Susan Cassell Dowdy, mother of the murdered youngsters, John Potter replied that he knew nothing of her, or her murdered children. The only surviving Dowdy daughter, Mary, may have been traumatized by three other recent events: (a) her jilted wedding in Goliad County, (b) her family's recent move from her childhood home, and (c) the violent murder of her four siblings.

It is not clear whether John Potter's name was attached to the crime immediately after it was committed or sometime later, just before his cellmate, Bill Dunman, told the Dowdys that Potter had admitted to his involvement in the massacre. Dunman was a tainted witness in that he was a kinsman of the Dowdy family (first cousin of the wife of Tom Dowdy, the older brother of the murdered young people). Dunman also had a strong motivation to find a way to obtain his freedom in the face of his impending murder trial in Kimble County, which his story certainly facilitated by motivating the Dowdys to liberate both prisoners from the Kimble County law officers. Furthermore, Dunman's subsequent extensive criminal record makes him an unreliable witness against his cellmate, John Potter.

Any family so traumatized by the brutal murder of four of its children would have great difficulty accepting such a crime as a random event and would understandably search for, accept, or invent any credible explanation or perpetrator, and John Potter would have filled that need. Finally, the fear and loathing of Indians by frontier Texas settlers was palpable and—by their lights—merited, which would have rendered the imputed family beliefs about the Indian, John Potter, entirely understandable, and their objective judgment correspondingly biased.

John Potter may indeed have been involved in the brutal murder of four innocent young people at their new home on Johnson Creek in October 1878. However, the evidence that we can access 130 years later, applied under contemporary constitutional standards, would almost certainly result in a not-guilty verdict.

Perhaps a more nuanced judgment is appropriate. Scottish criminal procedure allows three verdicts: guilty, not guilty, and not proven.[3] In the case of John Potter, "not proven" would probably be more apt.

**Enduring Verities**

The whole integrated story presents larger issues and conclusions beyond the guilt or innocence of the executed John Potter. Although some of these were unique to the frontier period, and therefore are not applicable to the American situation today, other verities may be germane and insightful.

One such verity is the silent yet profound influence of geology on our history and our lives, especially during the period of the American frontier. A good example is the Edwards Plateau region of west-central Texas. Until the mid-1880s, the high-standing, waterless expanse of the Edwards Plateau was a wilderness savanna adjacent to a westward-expanding frontier, uninhabited precisely because there was no permanent water on top. Numerous strong springs around its peripheral margins, however, formed the headwaters of all the rivers and tributaries in west-central Texas. The plateau's dissected margins provided secluded, spring-fed coves and hollows that offered abundant hiding places for law-shy settlers pushed west by the post–Civil War advance of organized, thus lawful, society. The dry plateau uplands formed formidable barriers, causing early roads to be diverted around the plateau, isolating the forks of the Llano from adjacent towns and established counties to the northwest, northeast, east, and southeast.

Because the divides were unpopulated, they were used as wilderness pathways for frequent raids from the west by Mexican Indians, and from the northwest by Plains Indians until 1875. These continuing raids themselves intimidated prospective settlers, thereby retarding the establishment of county governments and thus law. This geologically induced combination—ample water around the margins, and no permanent water on top—made the Edwards Plateau a barrier to settlement until the technology of deep-well drilling and windmills brought reliable water to the plateau uplands, and barbed wire allowed stockmen to enclose their pastures and manage their livestock. Even so, the Edwards Plateau region is still sparsely populated today, still dependent on ranching as the primary industry, still dependent on groundwater lifted from the plateau aquifer by windmills and down-hole pumps—and still governed by the inexorable constraints of geology. The region's geology—and climate—still determine preferred ranching methods and favored livestock, still control where uncommon arable soils and better grazing lands exist, and where durable pasture roads can best be laid out.[4] Although the plateau is now served by a network of widely spaced, mostly paved highways, many large areas remain essentially in the same isolated condition that existed in the 1870s.

Another verity concerns the consequences of a vast, sparsely populated, lightly governed, common grazing area exploited by individuals operating under a vague range law. Such conditions were almost guaranteed to result in unmitigated competition, rampant cattle theft, and environmental abuses. The blessing was that, romantic as it certainly was, the free-range period lasted only about twenty-five years.

### Tribalism

The social organization of Texas frontier settlers was fundamentally tribal, governed primarily by loyalty to, and cooperation with, extended family members and their friends. Family alliances were common, such as the remarkably resilient connection between the James Dublin and William Potter families. Such social patterns descended from their Anglo-Celtic roots as surely as did their cattle-droving proclivities.[5] Reaching even further back, tribalism surely had survival value to primitive humans.

It requires no imagination to see that traditional interactive family networks, operating in lightly populated areas, could well be perceived by state law officers as criminal conspiracies engaged in extortionary and coercive activities. Conversely, law officers sent to bring order were resented as intrusive and unwelcome agents of a distant, powerful, and indifferent state. Local elected county law officers were easily cowed and influenced by the real and perceived wishes of their constituencies. In such circumstances, it was often nearly impossible to obtain a witness who would testify, or a jury that would convict.[6] Law-abiding settlers of the emerging community were understandably intimidated, as they were constantly threatened by sudden violence, akin to modern terrorism. The first inescapable principle here is that tribalism is the mortal enemy of progressive, representative, commercial society, such as the modern Western state. But the members of the Kimble County confederation were not dealing with unfamiliar language, customs, and law. English was their native tongue, their culture was Anglo-Celtic, and they were familiar with American and British traditions of law.

The second lesson is that the power of tribalism is pervasive, resilient, and extraordinarily stubborn, suggesting that *Homo sapiens* may well be hard-wired for it.

### Supporting Markets

The most effective force in sustaining criminal confederations like that in Kimble County during the 1874–82 period was the continued existence of livestock markets in Mexico,[7] which made theft of Texas horses and cattle a profitable ongoing business in the same way that a ready means to dispose of stolen automobiles in Mexico today sustains automobile theft in U.S. border states. Eliminate the markets, and the criminal behavior diminishes. This principle has applications to contemporary American society—and to international geopolitics—too obvious and numerous to mention. But the familiar pattern of Mexican criminal enterprises benefiting from illicit trade with American customers—reinforced by criminal activity of Mexicans in the United States, a weak Mexican government, and a palpably porous border—is an enduring one.

Did the Dublins and Potters carry out horse-stealing raids disguised as Indians? No proof exists, but the published widespread rumors should not be ignored. Furthermore, one must acknowledge that a certain perverse genius attends an adopted strategy of conducting horse-stealing raids disguised as Indians: suspicion could be diverted from Anglo-Celtic settlers—such as the Dublins and Potters—to a widely despised and feared traditional enemy on the western frontier: the Mexican Indians.

### The Potters Turn to Crime

The Potter brothers were in declining fortunes when they arrived in Kimble County in 1874. As far as we know, the family had no reputation for lawlessness before they came to Texas. Within a few years of their arrival, however, Will Potter, the patriarch of the family, had been forced to resign as Kimble County's first county judge, accused of being in league with a powerful criminal confederation. His two oldest sons, Mack and Bill, had been arrested repeatedly and finally sent to the federal penitentiary (in error, as it turned out) for robbery of the U.S. mails. Will's brother Tom and his oldest Indian son, Frank, had both been arrested for theft. So had James K. P. Potter, the youngest brother of Will and Tom Potter. Tom's second and third Indian sons, John and Jim, may have been led into criminal acts by their uncle, James K. P. Potter—both young men were shot while resisting arrest by Texas Rangers for a rustling raid led by their uncle. "Indian Jim" Potter died of his wounds, while his brother John recovered, only to be executed later by private citizens on suspicion of his having participated in an appalling massacre of four innocent young people several years earlier in neighboring Kerr County.

Certainly, cash money was in short supply, and jobs were scarce in Kimble County in the late 1870s. For young men like the Potter boys, there was little or no regular paying work aside from gathering cattle, either by individual enterprise, or working for other cattlemen. But many young cowboys worked as cowboys without also becoming criminals, so it is difficult to argue that financial privation led to their criminal behavior.

The young Potter men saw that Will Potter, the head of the family and the head of county government, was involved in criminal activities. Did they see that involvement as condoning livestock theft and stage robbery? Their reckless uncle James K. P. Potter, closer to their own ages, had taken on the criminal ways of the confederation—did that encourage them to fall into a criminal web spun by their Dublin neighbors and the wider confederation? Did Dick Dublin's powerful personality seduce them into participating in a criminal gang? Certainly there was no effective law enforcement for three years after they first arrived in Kimble County, during which time the confederation became entrenched. Can the Potter boys—Mack, Bill, Jim, and John—be seen as 1870s counterparts to urban gang members in the United States today?

**The Drift toward Order**

Gradually—but ultimately—the collective will of the law-abiding citizens of western Texas, and of Kimble County, asserted itself through the Frontier Battalion, backing up the district courts and the sheriffs of Kimble and adjoining counties. Reviewing all the Texas Ranger Monthly Returns, Reports of Scouts, correspondence, memoirs, and contemporary newspaper reports, I have been continually struck by how dedicated these young Rangers were, and how very difficult and dangerous their work was, to bring order to a lightly populated region in which many of the residents were actively or passively resisting their efforts. It is also clear that they had a strong affection for and loyalty to the State of Texas—Texas was their country. Allegiance motivated their strong sense of duty.

In contrast to strident criticism of the Texas Rangers expressed in recent books by revisionist historians such as Gary C. Anderson and Michael Collins, which portrayed the Rangers of the 1820–75 period as bigoted and brutal, I found no example of such undisciplined or unprovoked racial violence by Rangers in any of the official or unofficial contemporary accounts of events in the Edwards Plateau region during 1874 to 1882.[8]

From the original handful of courageous settlers who publicly stood up against the criminal confederation, Kimble County citizens gradually gained confidence and strength, supported by the Texas Rangers. But most of the early community leaders did not linger long enough in the new community that was growing at the forks of the Llano for their families to benefit from living in a lawful society. They moved on, looking for new land, new opportunity. So we must conclude that their motives for resisting the Kimble County outlaw confederation were probably more self-interested than altruistic, short-term rather than long-term, pragmatic rather than philosophical—most of all, they were trying to protect their property.

Organized, economically progressive societies require civic order and a just, visibly functioning rule of law by which grievances can be settled, property protected, and offenders punished. Only then can commercial ventures, development, and stable social conditions take root and flourish, and societies prosper. The flowering of the Scottish mercantile economy, and the Scottish Enlightenment, did not take place until the power of the Scottish clans was finally broken at the Battle of Culloden in 1746.[9] It was a rough suppression—but it worked. Similarly, economic progress did not start in Kimble County until the Dublin-Potter criminal confederation had been eliminated.

## Imperfect Justice

To impose order on the lawless, resistant, tribal network of Kimble County required the support of the community and the persistently imposed force of the state, which is inevitably a blunt tool. We can today decry the mistaken imprisonment of the Pegleg stage robbers and give thanks for the constitutional protections advanced over the last 130 years. We can condemn the execution of John Potter, even as we can understand how and why it happened—and why the Kerr County community silently condoned it.

The police power of the state was imperfect. After the Dublins and the Potters—and their criminal accomplices—were gone, however, Kimble County immediately became a much more peaceful community and grew gradually more prosperous during the 1880s and 1890s. Livestock thefts were much reduced, and reports of Indian raiders ceased. The last stage robbery at Pegleg Crossing took place in 1881.

There will always be those who claim that although the Dublins and Potters—and their sidekicks—may not have been guilty of the December 15, 1877, robbery of the U.S. mail at Pegleg Crossing, they were guilty of plenty of other crimes, and will thus rationalize the imperfect prosecution of the law. Also, it must be admitted that the Pegleg gang did eventually plead guilty, even though today their admission of guilt carries the strong taint of legal coercion. Moreover, newspaper accounts of their trial, and Ranger Gillett's memoirs, state that they did freely admit other stage robberies—just not the one they were indicted for.[10]

The subsequent results in Kerr, Kimble, and Menard Counties—an end to rampant theft, robbery, and intimidation—seem to offer support for the pragmatic, though constitutionally unacceptable view that justice, though highly flawed, was served. In any case, the punishment had the desired effect: the Dublins and Potters who were imprisoned and then pardoned and released from Chester prison in December 1886 thereafter seem to have lived lawful and variably successful lives, especially Roll Dublin.

### Order and Law

"Law and order" is today a mantra, a cliché, having both good and bad implications among Americans belonging to different economic and social strata. In its theoretical sense, almost all of us want law and order to prevail in our communities. But before we can have the rule of law, we must first have order. Texas Rangers of the Frontier Battalion, reinforcing fragile county governments and their law enforcement officers in nascent, sparsely populated counties, and supporting an intimidated but increasingly determined citizenry, gradually brought order to the region adjacent to the forks of the Llano. An exasperated society had finally said, "Enough!" and had demanded a reckoning. The rule of law followed.

# Notes

**Series Editor's Preface**

1. See, for example, on Wyoming, John W. Davis, *A Vast Amount of Trouble: A History of the Spring Creek Raid* (Niwot: University Press of Colorado, 1994) and John W. Davis, *Goodbye, Judge Lynch: The End of a Lawless Era in Wyoming's Big Horn Basin* (Norman: University of Oklahoma Press, 2005).

2. Rose contrasts the work of Robert Utley and other recent books following Walter Prescott Webb's *The Texas Rangers* (1935) with Gary Clayton Anderson's *The Conquest of Texas* (2005) and Mike Collins's *Texas Devils* (2008) in the preface, giving readers an excellent understanding of the work of historians on the issue.

3. Also see Robert C. Ellickson, *Order without Law: How Neighbors Settle Disputes* (Cambridge: Harvard University Press, 1994). The author focused on ranchers in Shasta County, California, and their transactional society. The author did not have enemy deviants raiding livestock herds, but the law and economics study may interest some.

4. James Willard Hurst, *Law and the Conditions of Freedom in Nineteenth-Century United States* (Madison: University of Wisconsin Press, 1956); *The Growth of American Law: The Law Makers* (Boston: Little, Brown, 1950); *Law and the Social Order in the United States* (Ithaca: Cornell University Press, 1977); and for the hearty reader of legal history, *Law and Economic Growth: The Legal History of the Lumber Industry in Wisconsin, 1836–1915* (Cambridge: Harvard University Press, 1964). I once asked Willard who he wrote the last book for and he replied, "For the five people who can understand it." It is a deeply researched book on how law at the local level operates to solve social and economic problems.

5. John Phillip Reid, *Law for the Elephant: Property and Social Behavior on the Overland Trail* (San Marino: Huntington Library Press, 1980), 335.

6. John Phillip Reid, *Policing the Elephant: Crime, Punishment, and Social Behavior on the Overland Trail* (San Marino: Huntington Library Press, 1997), 192.

7. Bruce Thornton, *Searching for Joaquin: Myth, Murieta, and History in California* (San Francisco: Encounter Books, 2003), 159.

8. Ibid., 145.

9. Rose specifically delineates the recent scholarship on the Texas Rangers. Looking at Michael L. Collins's *Texas Devils: Rangers and Regulars on the Lower Rio Grande, 1846–1861* (Norman: University of Oklahoma, 2008), readers will immediately note that the time and place of the two studies are quite different.

10. Thornton, *Searching*, 146.

11. James M. Smallwood, Barry A. Crouch, and Larry Peacock, *Murder and Mayhem: The War of Reconstruction in Texas* (College Station: Texas A&M University Press, 2003), 127.

## Author's Preface

1. Peter R. Rose, "Regional Perspectives on the Edwards Group of Central Texas: Geology, Geomorphology, Geohydrology, and Their Influence on Settlement History," in *Edwards Water Resources in Central Texas: Retrospective and Prospective*, ed. Sue Hovorka (Austin: Texas Bureau of Economic Geology, 2004), CD-ROM, 12, 16.

2. Mary Hall Paterson, "I Remember," 1947, unpublished manuscript in the author's personal collection, 73.

3. From the *Fort Worth Gazette*, April 27, 1884, found in Frederica B. Wyatt, "Newspaper Excerpts," in *Families of Kimble County*, vol. 2 (Junction, TX: Kimble County Historical Commission, 1998).

4. The historians' works are Ovie C. Fisher, *It Occurred in Kimble and How: The Story of a Texas County* (1937; repr., San Angelo, TX: Talley Press, 1984), and Walter P. Webb, *The Texas Rangers: A Century of Frontier Defense* (1935; repr., Austin: University of Texas Press, 1977). The memoirs are Dan W. Roberts, *Rangers and Sovereignty* (1914; repr., Austin, TX: State House Press, 1987), and James B. Gillett, *Six Years with the Texas Rangers, 1875–1881* (1921; repr., Lincoln: University of Nebraska Press, 1976).

5. Mary Paterson Rose, Paterson family tradition communicated to the author, n.d.

6. Peter R. Rose, "Edwards Group, Surface and Subsurface, Central Texas," in *Report of Investigations, No. 74* (Austin: Texas Bureau of Economic Geology, 1972), 198.

7. Rose, "Regional Perspectives," 1–18.

## Chapter 1

1. Theodore R. Fehrenbach, *Lone Star: A History of Texas and the Texans* (New York: Collier Books, 1968), 572–73.

2. Charles M. Robinson, *Frontier Forts of Texas* (Houston: Lone Star Books / Gulf Publishing Company, 1986), 81–84.

3. Elizabeth Cruse Alvarez and Robert Plocheck, eds. *Texas Almanac, 2008–2009* (Dallas: Dallas Morning News, 2008), 231, 236, 244, 289, 324, 335, 340, 345.

4. Robert M. Utley, *If These Walls Could Speak*: Historic Forts of Texas (Austin: University of Texas Press, 1990), 12–13.

5. William H. Leckie, with Shirley A. Leckie, *The Buffalo Soldiers: A Narrative of the Black Cavalry in the West*, rev. ed. (Norman: University of Oklahoma Press, 2003), 71–72, 142, 238–40.

6. Claudia Hazlewood, "Menard, Texas," *Handbook of Texas Online*, accessed Aug. 19, 2009, http://www.tshaonline.org/handbook/online/articles/hjm12; see also Vivian Elizabeth Smyrl, "Menard County," *Handbook of Texas Online*, accessed Aug. 17, 2009, http://www.tshaonline.org/handbook/online-articles/hcm11.

7. Fisher, *It Occurred in Kimble*, 66–74, 183, 188.

8. Rose, "Regional Perspectives," 1, 5–6, 12.

9. Ibid., 12–13.

10. "The Texas Border Troubles," Misc. Doc. No. 64, House Reports, 45th Congress, 2nd Session, 1878 (1820), 285; see also A. M. Gibson, *The Kickapoos: Lords of the Middle Border* (Norman:

University of Oklahoma Press, 1963), 216–17; and Michael L. Collins, *Texas Devils: Rangers and Regulars in the Lower Rio Grande, 1846–1861* (Norman: University of Oklahoma Press, 2008), 72.

11. Rose, "Regional Perspectives," 13.

12. Ibid., 12–13; see also Fisher, *It Occurred in Kimble*, 151–58, 215–20.

13. Webb, *Texas Rangers*, 329–30.

## Chapter 2

1. Rose, "Regional Perspectives," 5–16.

2. Robert T. Hill and T. Wayland Vaughan, "Geology of the Edwards Plateau and Rio Grande Plain Adjacent to Austin and San Antonio, Texas, with Reference to the Occurrence of Underground Waters," *U.S. Geological Survey* 18, no. 2 (1898): 193–321.

3. An unconfined aquifer is open to the atmosphere, thus it has a water table above which water does not rise in a well bore drilled into the aquifer. This type of aquifer is in contrast to a confined (or artesian) aquifer, which is both overlain and underlain by impermeable formations so that the confined groundwater is under pressure inherited from a higher entry point; consequently, water rises in a well bore drilled into the aquifer, in some cases, even above the surface of the ground, so that the well flows.

4. Rose, "Regional Perspectives," 5–6.

5. Ibid.

6. Walter P. Webb, *The Great Plains* (1931; repr., Lincoln: University of Nebraska Press / Bison Books, 1981), 333–48; see also Henry D. McCallum and Frances T. McCallum, *The Wire That Fenced the West* (Norman: University of Oklahoma Press, 1965), 130–39, 202–14.

7. Theodore R. Fehrenbach, *Comanches: The Destruction of a People* (New York: Knopf, 1989), 365–553; see also Fehrenbach, *Lone Star*, 530, 536.

8. David LaVere, *The Texas Indians* (College Station: Texas A&M University Press, 2004), 203–6.

9. J'nell Pate, "United States–Mexican Border Conflicts, 1870–1880," *West Texas Historical Association Yearbook* 28 (1962): 175–94.

10. Robinson, *Frontier Forts of Texas*, 36; see also Utley, *If These Walls Could Speak*, 10–12.

11. Rupert N. Richardson and Harold B. Simpson, *Frontier Forts of Texas* (Waco, TX: Texian Press, 1966), xviii–xix.

12. Grover C. Ramsey, "Camp Melvin, Crockett County, Texas," *West Texas Historical Association Yearbook* 37 (1961): 137–47.

13. Ernest Wallace, *Ranald S. Mackenzie on the Texas Frontier* (College Station: Texas A&M University Press, 1993), 128–49; see also Leckie, *Buffalo Soldiers*, 113–41; and Robert M. Utley, *The Indian Frontier of the American West, 1846–1890* (Albuquerque: University of New Mexico Press, 1984), 174–78.

14. Wayne R. Austerman, *Sharps Rifles and Spanish Mules: The San Antonio–El Paso Mail, 1851–1881* (College Station: Texas A&M University Press, 1985), 211–12.

15. Ibid.

16. William C. Pool, *A Historical Atlas of Texas* (Austin, TX: Encino Press, 1975), 120–22.

17. David Johnson, *The Mason County "Hoo Doo" War, 1874–1902* (Denton: University of North Texas Press, 2006), 20, 36–37.

18. Peter R. Rose, "Setting the Stage of the Hoo Doo War: Land, People, and History of Settlement" in *The Hoo Doo War: Portraits of A Lawless Time*, eds. Peter R. Rose and Elizabeth E. Sherry (Mason, TX: Mason County Historical Commission, 2003), 10.

19. Webb, *Great Plains*, 17–21.

20. George W. Bomar, *Texas Weather* (Austin: University of Texas Press, 1983), 54–62.

21. Robert A. Caro, *The Path to Power: The Years of Lyndon Johnson* (1981; repr., New York: Random House, 1990), 11–14.

22. Rose, "Setting the Stage," 13.

23. Fisher, *It Occurred in Kimble*, 183–206.

## Chapter 3

1. LaVere, *Texas Indians*, 204.

2. Webb, *Texas Rangers*, 133–36.

3. Collins, *Texas Devils*, 72.

4. John M. Goggin, "Mexican Kickapoo Indians," *Southwestern Journal of Anthropology* 7, no. 3 (1951): 314–27.

5. T. F. Smith, *From Dominance to Disappearance: The Indians of Texas and the Near Southwest, 1786–1859* (Lincoln: University of Nebraska Press, 2005), 200–209, 215–17.

6. T. F. Schilz, *Lipan Apaches in Texas* (El Paso: Texas Western Press, 1987), 57–58.

7. "Texas Border Troubles," Misc. Doc. No. 64, House Reports, 201.

8. Gibson, *Kickapoos*, 200.

9. LaVere, *Texas Indians*, 205.

10. Gibson, *Kickapoos*, 193–207.

11. LaVere, *Texas Indians*, 205; see also Gibson, *Kickapoos*, 193–207.

12. LaVere, *Texas Indians*, 205; see also Gibson, *Kickapoos*, 208–21.

13. Gibson, *Kickapoos*, 198.

14. Ibid., 216–17.

15. Collins, *Texas Devils*, 72.

16. "Texas Border Troubles," Misc. Doc. No. 64, House Reports, 201.

17. LaVere, *Texas Indians*, 205; see also Ernest Wallace, *Ranald S. Mackenzie*, 94.

18. Frederick Wilkins, *The Law Comes to Texas: The Texas Rangers, 1870–1901* (Austin, TX: State House Press, 1999), 10.

19. Ibid.

20. James M. Callahan, *American Foreign Policy in Mexican Relations* (New York: Macmillan, 1932), 346.

21. Ibid., 348.

22. Pate, "United States–Mexican Border Conflicts," 179.

23. Richard A. Thompson, *Crossing the Border with the 4th Cavalry: Mackenzie's Raid into Mexico, 1873* (Waco: Texian Press, 1986), 12–43; see also Ernest Wallace, *Ranald S. Mackenzie*, 95–96.

24. Thompson, *Crossing the Border*, 39–40; see also Robert G. Carter, *On the Border with Mackenzie* (1935; repr., Denton: Texas State Historical Association Press, 2007), 431–60; Kenneth W. Porter, *The Black Seminoles: History of a Freedom-seeking People* (Gainesville: University Press

of Florida, 1996), 182–84; and Edward S. Wallace, "General John Lapham Bullis, the Thunderbolt of the Texas Frontier, II," *Southwestern Historical Quarterly* 55 (July 1951): 80–81.

25. Thompson, *Crossing the Border*, 47–51; see also Ernest Wallace, *Ranald S. Mackenzie*, 98–99.

26. Ernest Wallace, *Ranald S. Mackenzie*, 100–101.

27. Thompson, *Crossing the Border*, 59–65.

28. Ernest Wallace, *Ranald S. Mackenzie*, 102–4.

29. Ibid., 105.

30. Ibid., 106–9; see also Gibson, *Kickapoos*, 246–52; and Schilz, Lipan Apaches, 61. Schilz says that forty Lipan prisoners were also taken in Mackenzie's Remolino raid and that they were sent to the Mescalero reservation in the Sacramento Mountains of New Mexico, where they joined about three hundred of their tribesmen and more Mescalero and Mimbreno Apaches.

31. Carter, *On the Border*, 475; see also Ernest Wallace, *Ranald S. Mackenzie*, 106–10.

32. Kit Fuller, "Putting the Potters in Perspective." Unpublished paper presented at the annual meeting of the Edwards Plateau Historical Association, April 26, 2008, 4–5.

**Chapter 4**

1. Kit Fuller, interviews with the author, August 28, 2007, and September 21, 2007. Ms. Fuller, the great-great-great niece of William and Thomas Potter, has assembled extensive, documented genealogical data and histories of the Potter family as well as the Dublin family, with whom the Potters later intermarried; see also Fuller, "Potters in Perspective," 4–5, and Fisher, *It Occurred in Kimble*, 217. Neither Fuller nor Fisher provide supporting data for this date; however, U.S. census data (U.S. Federal Census, 1870, California, Mendocino County, Calpella Township, p. 186, Dwelling 90, Family 94, enumerated July 19, 1870; and U.S. Federal Census, 1880, Texas, Kimble County, Precinct 1, p. 9, Supervisor's District 6, Enumeration District 95, Dwelling 67, Family 72, enumerated June 23, 1880) indicate that William and Mary Potter's daughter Roberta was born on March 4, 1872, in Mendocino County, California, and their next (and last) daughter, Hattie, was born on July 1, 1876, in Kimble County, Texas. Assuming that Mary Potter did not choose to take an infant on such an arduous (but elective) journey, it seems likely that the Potters would not have left Mendocino County until perhaps the fall of 1872, which might have put them in Kimble County in the spring of 1873 at the very earliest. More likely, they would have left in the late summer of 1873, traveling the largely desert portion of their route through Arizona and New Mexico in the fall, arriving in Kimble County in early 1874. Also, William Potter applied for affiliation with the McCulloch Lodge no. 273 (the Masonic Lodge in Mason, Texas) on August 8, 1874, and was accepted on September 12, 1874 (Wilburn Shearer, interview with the author, February 7, 2008). Whether the Potters were able to get their horse herd safely through to Texas is not known.

2. Fuller, interview, August 28, 2007; see also Fuller, "Potters in Perspective." 4–5. The fact that they named their fourth son Jefferson Davis Potter (born 1862) indicates their political leanings.

3. U.S. Federal Census, 1850, California, Mendocino County, p. 104a, Dwelling 6, Family 7, enumerated November 12, 1850; U.S. Federal Census, 1860, California, Mendocino County,

Calpella Township, p. 813, Dwelling 212, Family 211, enumerated June 16, 1860; U.S. Federal Census, 1870, California, Mendocino County, Calpella Township, p. 186, Dwelling 90, Family 94, enumerated July 19, 1870; U.S. Federal Census, 1880, Texas, Kimble County, Precinct 1, p. 9, Supervisor's District 6, Enumeration District 95, Dwelling 67, Family 72, enumerated June 23, 1880. See also Fuller, "Potters in Perspective," 7.

4. N. O. Reynolds to J. B. Jones, January 22, 1878, Frontier Battalion Correspondence, Texas Ranger Records, Adjutant General's Records, Archives and Information Services Division, Texas State Library and Archives Commission (the commission's Adjutant General's Records collection is hereafter abbreviated as AGR); see also Gillett, *Six Years*, 93. "Cajac" is a local spelling of the term "kyak," vernacular for "packsaddle" in the southwestern United States. The described location of the Potters departs from existing Kimble County understanding, which has heretofore placed the Potters adjacent to Bailey Creek, immediately south of the James Dublin family. But the Ranger records cited here, as well as the sequence of enumeration in the 1880 census, disproves this earlier understanding. We know where the Dublins lived because the 1879 Kimble County Land Ownership Map shows their location on the north side of Bailey Creek (Kimble County Land Ownership Map, 1879, Texas State Land Office Archives, Austin). Twenty dwellings, containing twenty-two families, intervene in a southerly (upstream) direction between the James Dublin family and the Will Potter family on the 1880 census. Tom Potter's family follows the Will Potter family on the census listing, and we know where Tom Potter lived, at the headwater spring of Cajac Creek. We also know that the locations of the subsequent enumerated families on the census list were around Little Paint Creek, the next tributary south from Cajac Creek (Frederica B. Wyatt, correspondence with the author, September 1, 2007).

5. U.S. Federal Census, 1860, California, Mendocino County, Calpella Township, p. 813, Dwelling 213, Family 212, enumerated June 16, 1860; U.S. Federal Census, 1870, California, Mendocino County, Round Valley Township, p. 216, enumerated July 26, 1870; U.S. Federal Census, 1880, Texas, Kimble County, Precinct 1, p. 9, Supervisor's District 6, Enumeration District 95, Dwelling 67, Family 72, enumerated June 23, 1880; see also Fuller, "Potters in Perspective," 7.

6. See n. 4.

7. Fuller, "Potters in Perspective," 7.

8. Dorothy J. Hill, "James John Morehead, 1828–1885: A California Pioneer," in *Ripples Along Chico Creek: Perspectives on People and Time* (Chico, CA: Butte County Branch, American League of American Pen Women, 1992), 141–42.

9. U.S. Census records (U.S. Federal Census, 1850, California, Butte County, p. 31, Family 368, enumerated September 30, 1850) show John Potter living with four daughters and one son, James, age four, but Nancy Potter is absent from the Potter household.

10. Hill, "James John Morehead," 141–42.

11. Fuller, "Potters in Perspective," 5.

12. Ibid.

13. Ibid., 5–7.

14. Delight C. Shelton, *From Acorns to Oaks* (Willits, CA: Golden Rule Printing, 1986), 11.

15. Julia Moungovan, ed. *The Potter Valley Story* (Ukia, CA: Mendocino County Historical Society, 1972), 1–5. The valley is about four miles wide and eight miles long, with about ten thousand acres of flat bottomland adjacent to the north fork of the Russian River, which bisects the valley.

16. Moungovan, *Potter Valley Story*, 2–5; see also Shelton, *Acorns to Oaks*, 9, 116.

17. Lynnwood Carranco and Estelle Beard, *Genocide and Vendetta: The Round Valley Wars of Northern California* (Norman: University of Oklahoma Press, 1981), 403; see also Moungovan, *Potter Valley Story*, 3; and Shelton, *Acorns to Oaks*, 2.

18. Moungovan, *Potter Valley Story*, 5; see also Shelton, *Acorns to Oaks*, 116. Both sources reference William Potter's good relations with local Indians. See also Fuller, "Potters in Perspective," 6. Ms. Fuller refers to "Tribes of California," by William Powers (1877), in which Powers reports interviewing William Potter in 1871 or 1872. Potter apparently spoke several of the Pomo dialects and was very knowledgeable about the Pomo people and their customs.

19. Shelton, *Acorns to Oaks*, 7, 11.

20. Ibid., 7, 11, 117; also Kit Fuller, correspondence with the author, August 31, 2007.

21. U.S. Federal Census, 1860, California, Mendocino County, Calpella Township, p. 813, Dwelling 212, Family 211, enumerated June 16, 1860; U.S. Federal Census, 1860, California, Mendocino County, Calpella Township, p. 813, Dwelling 213, Family 212, enumerated June 16, 1860.

22. Moungovan, *Potter Valley Story*, 6; see also Shelton, *Acorns to Oaks*, 12–15.

23. Carranco and Beard, *Genocide and Vendetta*, 304–27. This well-documented account is a depressing record of the lethal, largely condoned campaign of early California settlers and quasilegal militias to exterminate the indigenous Indian population over a ten-year period between 1856 and 1865.

24. Carranco and Beard, *Genocide and Vendetta*, 321–26.

25. Ibid., 324–26.

26. Ibid., 323, 325.

27. Ibid., 327.

28. Fuller, "Potters in Perspective," 6; also Kit Fuller, correspondence with the author, November 30, 2007.

29. Fuller, "Potters in Perspective," 6; also Kit Fuller, Potter family genealogical lists, provided to the author, September 10, 2007.

30. Based on California land and tax records, Tom Potter was actively involved in mining and land investments, and he had a reported net worth in 1865 of nearly five thousand dollars (Kit Fuller, correspondence with the author, August 31, 2009).

31. Fuller, "Potters in Perspective," 6; see also U.S. Federal Census, 1870, California, Mendocino County, Round Valley Township, p. 216, enumerated July 26, 1870. With the exception of Tom Potter's eldest son, Frank, all his children of school age—John, Rebecca, and James—could read and write.

32. Fuller, "Potters in Perspective," 6; see also U.S. Federal Census, 1870, California, Mendocino

County, Round Valley Township, p. 216, enumerated July 26, 1870.

33. U.S. Federal Census, 1870, California, Mendocino County, Round Valley Township, p. 216, enumerated July 26, 1870; see also n. 33. Tom Potter was clearly not destitute; however, he sold land and livestock (probably his Potter Valley holdings) to one Lewis Gassey on June 6, 1871, for $4,000 and declared personal property worth $4,850 on the Mendocino County tax rolls (Fuller, correspondence, August 31, 2009).

34. U.S. Federal Census, 1870, California, Mendocino County, Calpella Township, p. 186, Dwelling 90, Family 94, enumerated July 19, 1870. All of William Potter's children of school age were literate.

35. Kit Fuller, correspondence with the author, April 24, 2008.

36. Shelton, *Acorns to Oaks*, 11, 105, 142.

37. Ibid., 11–15.

38. Ibid., 117; see also Fuller, "Potters in Perspective," 6–7; and U.S. Federal Census, 1880, Texas, Kimble County, Precinct 1. It remains stubbornly unresolved as to what connections brought the Potters to Kimble County. The Isaac Boyce family, including eldest son Reuben ("Rube"), then twelve years old, moved from Burnet County, Texas, to California in 1865 and returned in 1870, later settling in Kimble County; however, they settled in central California before moving to southern California in 1870, making it unlikely that they would have come to know the Potter family (see Frederica B. Wyatt, "The Boyce Family," in *Families of Kimble County* [Junction, TX: Kimble County Historical Commission, 1985], 68). Other Potter relatives were in Kimble County by 1879: The niece of William Potter's wife, Mary Evaline (Gordon) Potter, Lucy Gordon, married Richard O. Smith. The Smiths were living in Kimble County in the North Llano River valley at least by July 1, 1880, with Richard's brother Enoch and sister Ann. A May 9, 1879, letter from a Potter daughter, Margaret, living in northern California, to her parents, William and Mary Evaline Potter, indicates her belief that Lucy (Gordon) Smith was now living in Kimble County with her husband and in-laws (Kit Fuller, correspondence with the author, April 14, 2008).

39. Fuller, "Potters in Perspective," 7; see also U.S. Federal Census, 1880, Texas, Kimble County, Precinct 1, p. 9, Supervisor's District 6, Enumeration District 95, Dwelling 67, Family 72, enumerated June 23, 1880.

40. Fuller, "Potters in Perspective," 7; see also U.S. Federal Census, 1880, Texas, Kimble County, Precinct 1, p. 9, Supervisor's District 6, Enumeration District 95, Dwelling 67, Family 72, enumerated June 23, 1880.

41. Fisher, *It Occurred in Kimble*, 59–65, 93–94, 167.

42. "U.S. Federal Census 1870" and "U.S. Federal Census 1880," in *Families of Kimble County* (Junction, TX: Kimble County Historical Commission, 1985), 462–76. About fifteen settler families were living in Kimble County, all in the eastern half of the county, none in the South Llano River valley. By July 1880 about forty families were living in the South Llano valley, southwest of and beyond the town limits of Junction City; probably half of these lived within two miles of the outskirts of town.

43. William Potter applied for affiliation with the McCulloch Lodge no. 273 (the Masonic Lodge

in Mason, Texas) on August 8, 1874, and was accepted on September 12, 1874. He was dropped from membership on October 11, 1879, for nonpayment of his five-dollar dues (Shearer, interview).

## Chapter 5

1. J. Fred Rippy, *The United States and Mexico* (New York: Knopf, 1926), 290.
2. Callahan, *American Foreign Policy*, 346.
3. Pate, "United States–Mexican Border Conflicts," 184; see also Bernarr Cresap, *Appomattox Commander: The Story of General E. O. C. Ord* (San Diego: A. S. Barnes, 1981), 304–6.
4. Paul H. Carlson, *"Pecos Bill": A Military Biography of William R. Shafter* (College Station: Texas A&M University Press, 1989), 88–112.
5. Pate, "United States–Mexican Border Conflicts," 184; see also Cresap, *Appomattox Commander*, 304–6.
6. "Texas Border Troubles," Misc. Doc. No. 64, House Reports, 188–96.
7. Porter, *Black Seminoles*, 182–207; see also Edward S. Wallace, "General John Lapham Bullis," 84; and Michael L. Tate, "Bullis, John Lapham," *Handbook of Texas Online*, accessed April 11, 2008, http://www.tshaonline.org/handbook/online/articles/BB/fbu19.html.
8. Rippy, *United States and Mexico*, 288.
9. Theodore R. Fehrenbach, *Fire and Blood: A History of Mexico* (1973; repr., Cambridge, MA: DaCapo Press, 1995), 451–54.
10. Pate, "United States–Mexican Border Conflicts," 193.
11. Cresap, *Appomattox Commander*, 308–20; see also "Corralling the Braves, Mexican Troops Making Arrests among the Indians," *Galveston (TX) Daily News*, December 28, 1878; and "Beyond the Bravo: What General Trevino Has Done for the Border," *Galveston (TX) Daily News*, December 28, 1878, 1, 3.
12. Pate, "United States–Mexican Border Conflicts," 184–93; see also Cresap, *Appomattox Commander*, 324–25.
13. "Texas Border Troubles," Misc. Doc. No. 64, House Reports, 190.
14. *Cedar brake*: A dense grove of cedar trees and bushes (actually Ashe juniper) common in tributary canyons of rivers in the Edwards Plateau; analogous to cane brakes in low-lying areas of the Deep South.
15. "Texas Border Troubles," Misc. Doc. No. 64, House Reports, 197–98.
16. Ibid., 198.
17. Ibid., 191.
18. Fisher, *It Occurred in Kimble*, 25.
19. Carlson, *"Pecos Bill,"* 88–112.
20. Fehrenbach, *Lone Star*, 529–51.
21. Mike Cox, *The Texas Rangers: Wearing the Cinco Peso, 1821–1900* (New York: Tom Daugherty Associates / Forge Press, 2008), 208, 212; see also Webb, *Texas Rangers*, 307, and Wilkins, *Law Comes to Texas*, 23–28.
22. Wilkins, *Law Comes to Texas*, 25–56.

23. Webb, *Texas Rangers*, 307–18.

24. Ibid., 324.

25. Frontier Battalion Monthly Returns, 1874–75. Texas Ranger Records, AGR.

26. Webb, *Texas Rangers*, 324.

27. Wilkins, *Law Comes to Texas*, 72.

28. Roberts, *Rangers and Sovereignty*, 71; see also Gillett, *Six Years*, 34–45.

29. Robert M. Utley, *Lone Star Justice: The First Century of Texas Rangers* (New York: Oxford University Press, 2002), 151; see also Utley, *Indian Frontier*, 174–78; and S. C. Gwynne, *Empire of the Summer Moon: Quanah Parker and the Rise and Fall of the Comanches, the Most Powerful Indian Tribe in American History* (New York: Scribner, 2010), 274–87.

30. Wilkins, *Law Comes to Texas*, 76.

31. Frontier Battalion Monthly Returns, 1875–1876, Texas Ranger Records, AGR.

32. Frontier Battalion Monthly Returns, 1876, Texas Ranger Records, AGR.

33. Wilkins, *Law Comes to Texas*, 83.

34. Frontier Battalion Monthly Returns, 1876.

35. Fisher, *It Occurred in Kimble*, 169–78.

36. Frontier Battalion Monthly Returns, 1877, Texas Ranger Records, AGR.

37. Ibid.

38. Ibid.

39. U.S. Military Division of the Missouri, *Record of Engagements with Hostile Indians within the Military Division of the Missouri from 1868 to 1882* (Washington, D.C.: Government Printing Office, 1882), 67.

40. Frontier Battalion Monthly Returns, 1877.

41. Ibid.

42. Ibid.

43. J. Frank Dobie, *A Vaquero of the Brush Country* (1929; repr., Austin: University of Texas Press, 1981), 126–27.

44. P. Dolan to J. B. Jones, December 15, 1877, General Correspondence, AGR.

**Chapter 6**

1. "Correspondence from Kimball County," *San Antonio Weekly Express Supplement*, [November 13, 1875], December 2, 1875. This source is a travelogue that describes the primitive living conditions of settlers along the Johnson Fork of the Llano River in eastern Kimble County.

2. U.S. Federal Census, 1880, Texas, Kimble County, Precinct 1, pp. 6 and 9, Supervisor's District 6, Enumeration District 95, Dwellings 47 (Dublins) and 67 (Potters), enumerated June 19 and June 23, 1880; see also Kimble County Land Ownership Map, 1879.

3. Fisher, *It Occurred in Kimble*, 215–16; see also Gillett, *Six Years*, 87–89, who states that the Dublins arrived in the fall of 1874; and see also U.S. Federal Census, 1880, Texas, Kimble County, Precinct 1, p. 6, Supervisor's District 6, Enumeration District 95, Dwelling 47, Family 57, enumerated June 19, 1880. See also correspondence from Fuller (April 8, 2011) indicating that Charles A. Dublin's mother was Nancy Fondern [Fondren].

4. U.S. Federal Census, 1880, Texas, Kimble County, Precinct 1, p. 6, Supervisor's District 6, Enumeration District 95, Dwelling 47, Family 57, enumerated June 19, 1880; U.S. Federal

Census, 1880, Texas, Travis County (Jail), p. 6, Supervisor's District 5, Enumeration District 136, enumerated June 2, 1880. See also Gillett, *Six Years* , 89; and also Fuller, genealogical lists, September 10, 2007. James Dublin and his family have proved difficult to trace, being absent from the 1850, 1860, and 1870 U.S. federal censuses. When, and by what route, Jimmy Dublin came to Texas from Alabama, I have not discovered, but Dublins were in Cherokee County (eastern Texas) in the 1850s and 1860s, and they had been born in Alabama (U.S. Federal Census, 1850, Cherokee County, Texas, p. 823B, Dwelling 139, Family 129, enumerated October 2, 1850; see also U.S. Federal Census, 1860, Cherokee County, Texas, p. 458, Dwelling 621, Family 621, enumerated July 9, 1860). Jimmy Dublin and his first wife were in Williamson County, Texas, when son Roll was born in 1857. Jimmy apparently married his second wife, Nancy Fondren, in Texas about 1861. She was in San Augustine County (eastern Texas) in 1850 (U.S. Federal Census, 1850, San Augustine County, Texas, p. 347, Dwelling 222, Family 222, enumerated September 27, 1850). Fondrens were also living in nearby Cherokee County during the 1850s and 1860s (U.S. Federal Census, 1850, Cherokee County, Texas, p. 49, Dwelling 326, Family 326, enumerated October 25, 1850; U.S. Federal Census, 1860, Cherokee County, Texas, p. 477, Dwelling 866, Family 866, enumerated July 20, 1860). Jimmy Dublin and his family were in Hamilton County in 1867 when son Charles Albert Dublin was born, and they probably were in Coryell County about 1873, when Dick and another man, Ace Langford, killed two men in that county. From their ages and the four-year gap between Dell and eldest daughter "C." (for Catherine) Dublin, it would appear that Nancy Dublin gave birth to her first child and eldest daughter in 1862, at age nineteen. The next two children were also daughters, Caroline and G. A., born in 1865 and 1866, respectively, followed by Charles (1867), who is absent from the 1880 census in Kimble County. The next three daughters are designated on the 1880 census as B. (1868), Sallie (1869), and Jennie (1871). In addition to son George, born in 1873, the last Dublin children were two more daughters, M. (1875) and Maggie May (1879).

5. Richard Dublin, arrest warrant, June 20, 1874, Arrest Warrants, AGR; see also Chuck Parsons and Donaly E. Brice, *Texas Ranger N. O. Reynolds, the Intrepid* (Honolulu: Talei Publishers, 2005), 94–109.

6. Gillett, *Six Years*, 87–88.

7. Fisher, *It Occurred in Kimble*, 215.

8. H. B. Waddill to Major J. B. Jones, February 27, 1877, Frontier Battalion Correspondence, Texas Ranger Records, AGR.

9. Wilkins, *Law Comes to Texas*, 72; see also J. B. Jones to William Steele, September 28, 1875, Frontier Battalion Correspondence, Texas Ranger Records, AGR.

10. J. B. Jones to Lieutenant Neal Coldwell, October 25, 1875, Company F, Frontier Battalion Correspondence, Texas Ranger Records, AGR.

11. Fuller, "Potters in Perspective," 4–5.

12. Fuller, genealogical lists, September 10, 2007.

13. Ibid; see also Frontier Battalion Monthly Returns, 1877; and Fuller, correspondence, August 31, 2009, including Potter family letters. The evidence for J. K. P. Potter's arrival date in Kimble County, Texas, is based upon (1) the birth of his son John "Tuck" Potter in the first half of 1876 in California; (2) his recorded arrest (as James Potter) by Texas Rangers in

May 1877 on suspicion of horse theft in Kaufman County, as well as a second arrest (as James K. P. Potter) for theft of hogs on December 29, 1877; and (3) Potter family letters indicating that he had settled near his brothers on the South Llano: (a) a December 18, 1878, letter to his brother-in-law, M. C. Briggs, describing a good life with his family in Kimble County (from Kit Fuller, correspondence with the author, citing a newspaper clipping from the *Ukiah City Press*, January 31, 1879, titled "From Texas"); and (b) a Potter family letter, dated May 9, 1879, to William and Mary Potter from their married daughter Maggie Potter Marders, indicating that James K. P. and Evaline Hopper Potter were in Texas living nearby. The evidence for where he located his family is less certain, depending mostly on a local landmark known as the "Potter Waterhole," a crescent-shaped pond in Chalk Creek at the foot of a towering amphitheater-like cliff, bordered by an open, narrow, alluvial bench. Several hundred yards downstream were, until the flood of 1957, the remains of a substantial log house with a dirt floor, as reported by the long-time owner of the pertinent ranch property, Ms. Jo Fred Burt Evans (interview with the author, March 15, 2010).

14. Frontier Battalion Monthly Returns, 1877–1881, Texas Ranger Records, AGR.
15. Ibid.
16. D. W. Roberts to J. B. Jones, May 18, 1880, General Correspondence, AGR.
17. Frontier Battalion Monthly Returns, 1877–1880, Texas Ranger Records, AGR.
18. Ibid.
19. Frontier Battalion Monthly Returns, 1880, Texas Ranger Records, AGR; see also D. W. Roberts to J. B. Jones, August 1, 1880, General Correspondence, AGR.
20. Frontier Battalion Monthly Returns, 1875, Texas Ranger Records, AGR.
21. Wilkins, *Law Comes to Texas*, 76.
22. Fisher, *It Occurred in Kimble*, 185; Jordan A. "Black" Burt (born in Georgia in 1848) was married to Mary Moore, daughter of long-time cattleman Rance Moore, who operated in the area around Big Saline Creek in the Llano valley northeast of Junction City (Frederica B. Wyatt, communication with the author, November 24, 2009); see also "U.S. Federal Census, 1880," in *Families of Kimble County*, 475.
23. Parsons and Brice, *Texas Ranger N. O. Reynolds*, 94; see also Fisher, *It Occurred in Kimble*, 183–87, 238. Knowing the subsequent record of intimidation and coercion of Kimble County residents by the criminal element, it is perhaps natural to speculate that Frank Latta resigned the office of sheriff under credible threat and was succeeded by the man he had narrowly defeated in the original election.
24. Fisher, *It Occurred in Kimble*, 187, 189; a second election was held later in 1877, in which Junction City was officially designated.
25. Fisher, *It Occurred in Kimble*, 191–92.
26. Kit Fuller, correspondence with the author, September 25, 2007.
27. Fisher, *It Occurred in Kimble*, 185; see also H. B. Waddill to Major J. B. Jones, February 27, 1877. For a full copy see also Parsons and Brice, *Texas Ranger N. O. Reynolds*, 95–96. Waddill stated that "implicit confidence could be placed in Gilliland, and Kountz, as well as [John E.] Temple, and [Ben F.] Pepper" (neither of the latter two were elected officers).
28. L. R. Mudge, "Ezekiel Kiser Kountz and Harriet (Lindamood) Kountz" and "John Cook

Kountz and Laura (Turner) Kountz," in *Families of Kimble County* (Junction, TX: Kimble County Historical Commission, 1985), 224–25; see also "U.S. Federal Census, 1880," in *Families of Kimble County*, 463, 467.

29. H. G. Patterson, "N. Q. Patterson Family," in *Families of Kimble County* (Junction, TX: Kimble County Historical Commission, 1985), 290; see also "U.S. Federal Census, 1880," in *Families of Kimble County*, 468.

30. M. V. Pendergrass, "William Franklin Gilliland Family," in *Families of Kimble County* (Junction, TX: Kimble County Historical Commission, 1985), 158.

31. U.S. Federal Census, 1860, California, Yolo County, Cottonwood Township, Buckeye P. O., p. 106, enumerated July 17, 1860, Dwelling 848, Family 848; U.S. Federal Census, 1870, New Mexico Territory, Grant County, Silver City, p. 21, enumerated August (n.d.) 1870, Dwelling 24, Family 24; and "U.S. Federal Census, 1880," in *Families of Kimble County*, 468; also Frederica B. Wyatt, correspondence with the author, October 19, 2009.

32. M. P. Lee, "Benjamin Franklin Pepper," in *Families of Kimble County* (Junction, TX: Kimble County Historical Commission, 1985), 294–95; also "U.S. Federal Census, 1880," in *Families of Kimble County*, 465.

33. Catherine Randolph, "Joseph Jackson Ramsey," in *Families of Kimble County* (Junction, TX: Kimble County Historical Commission, 1985), 310–11; for data on George E. Stewart, see "U.S. Federal Census, 1880," in *Families of Kimble County*, 464.

34. Bob Alexander, *Winchester Warriors: Texas Rangers of Company D, 1874–1901*, (Denton: University of North Texas Press, 2009), 114.

35. Frontier Battalion Monthly Returns, 1876.

36. Fisher, *It Occurred in Kimble*, 208.

37. Ibid.; see also Webb, *Texas Rangers*, 330; and Wilkins, *Law Comes to Texas*, 126.

38. Frontier Battalion Monthly Returns, 1876.

39. "U.S. Federal Census, 1880," in *Families of Kimble County*, 467.

40. Frontier Battalion Monthly Returns, 1876.

41. "Topics in the Interior," *Galveston (TX) Daily News*, July 7, 1878: two related articles report that the July 6, 1878, robbery is "the fourth time the mail has been robbed here in two years." See also the *Burnet (TX) Bulletin*, January 26, 1877: "news of another stage robbery, which happened on last Saturday morning [January 19, 1877] to the stage running between San Antonio and Fort Concho. The robbery, which occurred about daylight . . . at what is known as the Pegleg Crossing of the San Saba River between the towns of Mason and Menardville, and within ten miles of the latter place." Taken together, the language suggests that at least one robbery must have occurred in the last half of 1876, presumably the first of many. See also Alexander, *Winchester Warriors*, 340, which indicates a total of five robberies occurred, the last one on July 6, 1878.

42. Parsons and Brice, *Texas Ranger N. O. Reynolds*, 95–96, 98; see also Webb, *Texas Rangers*, 329; and Alexander, *Winchester Warriors*, 121–22.

43. Austerman, *Sharps Rifles*, 290–93, 322; see also *Burnet (TX) Bulletin*, February 9, 1877.

44. Frontier Battalion Monthly Returns, 1877; see also Frank M. Moore to J. B. Jones, February 6, 1877, Frontier Battalion Correspondence, Texas Ranger Records, AGR.

45. Moore to Jones, February 6, 1877.

46. Felix Burton to John B. Jones, February 22, 1877, Frontier Battalion Correspondence, Texas Ranger Records, AGR.

47. This episode can be pieced together from the following references: (1) Ray McGuffin, "Scabtown, U.S.A." in "Interesting Places and Unusual Names" by Anys Whitley Godfrey, in *Menard County History: An Anthology* (San Angelo, TX: Anchor, 1982), 31; (2) Frontier Battalion Monthly Returns (Company D), February, 1877; Texas Ranger Records, AGR; and (3) Lt. F. M. Moore to Major John B. Jones, March 22, 1877, Frontier Battalion Correspondence, Texas Ranger Records, AGR.

48. H. B. Waddill to Major J. B. Jones, February 27, 1877. For a full copy see also Parsons and Brice, *Texas Ranger N. O. Reynolds*, 95–96.

49. About J. E. Temple, see R. L. Temple, "John E. Temple Family," in *Families of Kimble County* (Junction, TX: Kimble County Historical Commission, 1985), 365; see also "U.S. Federal Census, 1880," in *Families of Kimble County*, 465. John E. Temple was born in 1828 in Mississippi. He and his first wife, Mary Hicks, came to Texas in 1853 with their family. After Mary's death, Temple married a widow, in 1869, named Susan Crim Pearce (born in 1829 in Tennessee). They brought a large merged family to Kimble County in about 1873, settling along the North Llano River above the future site of Junction City, where Temple was a stock raiser. He became county treasurer on April 1, 1878, succeeding John C. Kountz, who had resigned to take the vacant county clerk position. Temple's eldest son, Lewis Temple, was a deputy under Sheriff John B. Gorman.

50. Fisher, *It Occurred in Kimble*, 198, quoting Burton to Jones, February 22, 1877.

51. Frontier Battalion Monthly Returns, 1877; see also Frank M. Moore to J. B. Jones, March 22, 1877, Frontier Battalion Correspondence, Texas Ranger Records, AGR.

52. Frontier Battalion Monthly Returns, 1877; see also "U.S. Federal Census, 1880," in *Families of Kimble County*, 466. Tom Doran was probably the husband of E. I. Doran, a single woman with three young children who was apparently Will Potter's nearest neighbor to the east, according to the 1880 census. Tom Doran's name does not appear on the census roll because he had been killed in a gunfight in December 1878 in Junction City.

53. Frank M. Moore to J. B. Jones, March 22, 1877.

54. Frontier Battalion Monthly Returns, 1877.

55. M. A. McFarland to J. B. Jones, March 26 and 27, 1877, Frontier Battalion Correspondence, Texas Ranger Records, AGR.

56. J. B. Jones to Henry M. Holmes, March 31, 1877, Frontier Battalion Correspondence, Texas Ranger Records, AGR.

57. H. M. Holmes to J. B. Jones, April 7, 1877, Frontier Battalion Correspondence, Texas Ranger Records, AGR.

58. Fisher, *It Occurred in Kimble*, 208, quoting Blackburn-Jones correspondence, March 30–April 6, 1877.

59. Webb, *Texas Rangers*, 330–31, quoting Frontier Battalion correspondence.

60. J. B. Jones to Frank M. Moore, April 11, 1877, Frontier Battalion Correspondence, Texas Ranger Records, AGR.

61. Parsons and Brice, *Texas Ranger N. O. Reynolds*, 98, citing Jones to Steele, April 12, 1877.

62. W. W. Elliott to J. B. Jones, 1877, Frontier Battalion Correspondence, Texas Ranger Records, AGR; see also Parsons and Brice, *Texas Ranger N. O. Reynolds*, 98. The document is undated but almost certainly must have been delivered to Jones in March or April 1877.

63. Frontier Battalion Monthly Returns, 1877; see also Frank M. Moore to J. B. Jones, March 22, 1877, indicating that J. M. Deaton was wounded in an attempt to rescue Ben Anderson from the Fort McKavett guardhouse about two weeks after he was imprisoned.

64. Fisher, *It Occurred in Kimble*, 216; see also Gillett, *Six Years*, 40; and Johnson, *Mason County "Hoo Doo" War*, 102, 175–77. For data on the Williams family, see "U.S. Federal Census, 1870," in *Families of Kimble County*, 462; and U.S. Federal Census, 1880, Texas, Tom Green County, Fort Concho, Precinct 2, enumerated on June 3, 1880, p. 12, Supervisor's District 4, Enumeration District 119, Dwelling 103, Family 106. Margaret Williams, age twenty-five, and daughter Cora, age three, are living with the family of her married sister, Sarah Kearse, in the 1880 census. This murder has been misinterpreted by David Johnson, who confused the Kimble County Jim Williams with a Llano County man of the same name who had been murdered on September 11, 1876, in Llano County (Johnson, *Mason County "Hoo Doo" War*, 102, 175–77).

## Chapter 7

1. John B. Jones to William Steele, May 6, 1877, Frontier Battalion Correspondence, Texas Ranger Records, AGR; see also Alexander, *Winchester Warriors*, 123.

2. Webb, *Texas Rangers*, 328–33; see also Fisher, *It Occurred in Kimble*, 207–13; and Parsons and Brice, *Texas Ranger N. O. Reynolds*, 94–109.

3. J. B. Jones to William Steele, May 8, 1877, Frontier Battalion Correspondence, Texas Ranger Records, AGR.

4. Fisher, *It Occurred in Kimble*, 211.

5. J. B. Jones to William Steele, May 8, 1877; see also Webb, *Texas Rangers*, 332.

6. Gillett, *Six Years*, 70; see also Wilkins, *Law Comes to Texas*, 128.

7. J. B. Jones to William Steele, May 8, 1877.

8. Webb, *Texas Rangers*, 331.

9. Parsons and Brice, *Texas Ranger N. O. Reynolds*, 102.

10. Bill Allison was Roll Dublin's brother-in-law.

11. Statement of Arrests, Company A, Capt. N. Coldwell, May, 1878, Texas Ranger Records, AGR.

12. John B. Jones to William Steele, May 6, 1877; the murder Jones alluded to was almost certainly the shooting death of Jim Williams by Dell Dublin and Luke Cathey (and probably also Roll Dublin, Bill Allison, and Mack Potter, as accessories) at Williams's ranch on the South Llano River on April 16, just three days before Jones arrived with his Rangers at the forks of the Llano on the first day of the roundup.

13. William Steele to J. C. Sparks, April 27, 1877, Frontier Battalion Correspondence, Texas Ranger Records, AGR.

14. J. B. Jones to W. A. Blackburn, April 23, 1877, Frontier Battalion Correspondence, Texas Ranger Records, AGR.

15. Fisher, *It Occurred in Kimble*, 213.

16. Ibid., 188–89; in an election held after the first term of district court, Kimbleville was succeeded by Junction City as the county seat of Kimble County, after which Kimbleville quickly faded away.

17. Gillett, *Six Years*, 69; see also Wilkins, *Law Comes to Texas*, 128–29.

18. J. B. Jones to William Steele, May 8, 1877. The only known evidence against William Potter was the note from County Hide Inspector J. A. "Black" Burt to Potter, requesting him to instruct confederates to destroy evidence of stolen cattle in advance of the arrival of Richard Tankersley and other Tom Green County cattlemen in February 1877. However, the sudden departure of Richard and Dell Dublin, Mack Potter, and Luke Cathey on the eve of the Kimble County Roundup suggests that Judge Potter, as the senior official in Kimble County, may have gotten wind of the impending operation and advised their immediate departure. On the other hand, the four men may have fled only because of their involvement in Jim Williams's murder.

19. Parsons and Brice, *Texas Ranger N. O. Reynolds*, 102; see also Fisher, *It Occurred in Kimble*, 238; and Alexander, *Winchester Warriors*, 125.

20. Fisher, *It Occurred in Kimble*, 238.

21. Ibid., 212; see also Webb, *Texas Rangers*, 332.

22. John B. Jones to William Steele, May 6, 1877.

**Chapter 8**

1. Frontier Battalion Monthly Returns, 1877.

2. Ibid.

3. Ibid.

4. Ibid.

5. Alexander, *Winchester Warriors*, 128–29; see also Wilkins, *Law Comes to Texas*, 134; see also Roberts, *Rangers and Sovereignty*, 95. Roberts rejoined the Frontier Battalion as a captain in November 1877 and returned to Kimble County with Company D on May 10, 1878.

6. Gillett, *Six Years*, 84; see also Parsons and Brice, *Texas Ranger N. O. Reynolds*, 1, 148.

7. The fact that Company E's Monthly Return for November contains no reference to a Ranger detail escorting Allison eastward to another jail or to state prison suggests that he was acquitted by his Kimble County jury. But Wes Johnson escaped from the hands of the sheriff of Kimble County and was again a fugitive being sought by the Rangers on December 24 (see Frontier Battalion Monthly Returns, 1877).

8. Fisher, *It Occurred in Kimble*, 193; being aware of the remarkable frequency of horse thefts in the South Llano valley and the residence there of the Potter and Dublin boys, it is hard to resist speculating that the theft of Judge Cooley's fine horse may have been an act of ironic revenge designed to let the judge and the community know that the confederation was still alive and functioning.

9. Frontier Battalion Monthly Returns, 1877; Roll Dublin's conspicuously absent name from the Rangers' identified targets implies (a) that he remained in jail, perhaps at Austin, on the origi-

nal charges proffered when he was captured during the Kimble County Roundup, May 1, 1877; (b) that he had temporarily left the area; or (c) that he was temporarily "going straight."

10. Gillett, *Six Years*, 88–89; see also Parsons and Brice, *Texas Ranger N. O. Reynolds*, 166–67.

11. Frontier Battalion Monthly Returns, 1877.

12. Austerman, *Sharps Rifles*, 290–91, 322.

13. Frontier Battalion Monthly Returns, 1877; also Kit Fuller, interview with the author, December 21, 2007. The written arrest record indicates J. K. P. Potter, with the two middle initials merged, as if the writer could not decide whether the prisoner's middle initial was "K" or "P."

14. Parsons and Brice, *Texas Ranger N. O. Reynolds*, 169.

15. Frontier Battalion Monthly Returns, 1878, Texas Ranger Records, AGR.

16. Ibid.

17. Gillett, *Six Years*, 91–92.

18. Frontier Battalion Monthly Returns, 1877; see also Gillett, *Six Years*, 93.

19. Gillett probably refers to Frank and John Potter, then about twenty-four and twenty-two years old, respectively; but also living with Tom Potter, then forty-seven, were four younger sons: Jim, sixteen; Moses, fifteen; William, thirteen; and Tom, Jr., ten.

20. This might also have been Tom, Jr., the youngest Potter son (Parsons and Brice, *Texas Ranger N. O. Reynolds*, 197, citing an article in the *San Antonio Weekly Express Supplement*, January 31, 1878, which reported that a little boy warned Dublin, "Richard, look at the Rangers.").

21. Gillett, *Six Years*, 92–95.

22. Quoted in Parsons and Brice, *Texas Ranger N. O. Reynolds*, 197–98.

23. Parsons and Brice, *Texas Ranger N. O. Reynolds*, 185.

24. D. W. Roberts to J. B. Jones, August 10, 1878, General Correspondence, AGR.

25. D. W. Roberts to J. B. Jones, February 6, 1879, General Correspondence, AGR.

26. Author's review of Frontier Battalion Monthly Returns for Ranger Companies D, E, and F, stationed in the general area for the years 1876–80.

27. D. W. Roberts to J. B. Jones, June 29, 1878, General Correspondence, AGR.

28. N. O. Reynolds to J. B. Jones, January 22, 1878.

29. N. O. Reynolds to J. B. Jones, March 17, 1878, Frontier Battalion Correspondence, Texas Ranger Records, AGR.

30. J. B. Jones to N. O. Reynolds, April 8, 1878, Frontier Battalion Correspondence, Texas Ranger Records, AGR.

31. N. O. Reynolds to J. B. Jones, April 10, 1878, Frontier Battalion Correspondence, Texas Ranger Records, AGR.

32. Wilkins, *Law Comes to Texas*, 191.

33. N. O. Reynolds to J. B. Jones, April 16, 1878, Frontier Battalion Correspondence, Texas Ranger Records, ARG.

34. Fisher, *It Occurred in Kimble*, 218–19.

35. Ranger records are silent with respect to the outcome of Dell Dublin's habeas corpus hearing in Llano in late November of 1877 and also to his subsequent rearrest, but he was in the Austin jail in April 1878 (Frontier Battalion Monthly Returns, 1877). An undated article

in the *Austin Gazette*, as quoted in the March 17 *New York Times*, reported that Dell Dublin was in jail (see n. 22). The most likely scenario is that he was rearrested sometime in early 1878 and carried with other Kimble County outlaws to Austin with the February 21 escort of prisoners.

36. No known relation to Lieutenant N. O. Reynolds.

37. Gillett, *Six Years*, 95–100.

38. Leona Bruce, *Banister Was There* (Fort Worth, TX: Branch-Smith, 1968), 24–26.

39. Frontier Battalion Monthly Returns, 1877.

40. Fisher, *It Occurred in Kimble*, 227–29.

41. Ibid., 238.

42. Frontier Battalion Monthly Returns, 1877.

43. N. C. Patterson, "N. C. Patterson Memoirs," in *Families of Kimble County*, vol. 2 (Junction, TX: Kimble County Historical Commission, 1998), 8; see also Fisher, *It Occurred in Kimble*, 193.

44. Kimble County district court records for 1877 to 1883 are nonexistent, having been incinerated when the county courthouse burned to the ground on April 22, 1884. The fire was probably caused by an arsonist, "there being several cases in the criminal docket . . . and a good deal of litigation in land matters" (*Fort Worth Gazette*, April 27, 1884, from Wyatt, "Newspaper Excerpts"). This absence of Kimble County court records is chiefly responsible for my repeatedly expressed uncertainty as to the outcomes of trials involving the Dublins, Potters, and their confederates.

45. Frontier Battalion Monthly Returns, 1877; and Frontier Battalion Monthly Returns, 1879, Texas Ranger Records, AGR; see also *Results of Operations of State Troops*, vol. 1, AGR.

46. Parsons and Brice, *Texas Ranger N. O. Reynolds*, 204, 207.

47. Ibid., 208, citing correspondence from E. G. Nicholson to William Steele, May 24, 1878; see also typescript copy of letter from May 24, 1878, in Walter P. Webb Papers, Center for American History (University of Texas, Austin).

48. J. B. Jones to N. O. Reynolds, about May 8, 1878, Frontier Battalion Correspondence, Texas Ranger Records, AGR.

49. Frontier Battalion Monthly Returns, 1877.

50. Ibid.; see also Gillett, *Six Years*, 102–3.

51. Gillett, *Six Years*, 98–99.

52. Frontier Battalion Monthly Returns, 1878 and 1879. The returns from May 1878 through March 1879 contain notably few references to the usually mentioned names of the Kimble County confederation.

53. Frontier Battalion Monthly Returns, Company D, October and November, 1878.

54. Menard County District Court Records, cases 257, 264, 265, 324, 325; State of Texas v. Jordan A. Burt, November 4, 1878, 324–25; see also cases 266, 267, 268, State of Texas v. T. H. Potter, November 4, 1878, pp. 326, 352, and 380.

55. D. W. Roberts to J. B. Jones, December 31, 1878, General Correspondence, AGR; the issue was not finally resolved until the spring term of district court, when Judge Blackburn finally ruled that Gorman would retain the sheriff's office for another term (D. W. Roberts to J. B. Jones, April 1, 1879, General Correspondence, AGR). However, Gorman was arrested on

June 19, 1879, for the March 4, 1877, killing of Button Brashear, whereupon John Garland replaced him.

56. Luvenia Conway Roberts, *A Woman's Reminiscences of Six Years in Camp with the Texas Rangers* (1928; repr., Austin, TX: State House Press, 1987), 35–36.

57. H. B. Waddill to Major J. B. Jones, February 27, 1877; see also W. W. Elliott to J. B. Jones, 1877; and Parsons and Brice, *Texas Ranger N. O. Reynolds*, 98.

58. Fisher, *It Occurred in Kimble*, 229–30; see also *Galveston (TX) Daily News*, September 20, 1878, reporting the death of J. M. Deaton, killed by T. Doran on September 12. 1878.

59. Fisher, *It Occurred in Kimble*, 230–32; see also Temple, "John E. Temple," in *Families of Kimble County*, vol. 2 (Junction, TX: Kimble County Historical Commission, 1998), 371.

60. Austerman, *Sharps Rifles*, 322.

61. Carlson, *"Pecos Bill,"* 108–10; see also John G. Johnson, "The Mexican and Indian Raid of '78," *Handbook of Texas Online*, accessed September 26, 2008, http://www.tshaonline.org/handbook/online/articles/MM/btmrv.html.

62. "A Mass Meeting," *Galveston (TX) Daily News*, May 10, 1878.

63. Carlson, *"Pecos Bill,"* 110–12.

64. U.S. Military Division of the Missouri, Record of Engagements, 76–77.

65. Frontier Battalion Monthly Returns, 1878.

66. Ibid.

67. Ibid.

68. Fisher, *It Occurred in Kimble*, 179–80.

69. A. J. Sowell, *Early Settlers and Indian Fighters of Southwest Texas* (1900; repr., Austin, TX: State House Press, 1986), 740–41; see also Gillett, *Six Years*, 129.

## Chapter 9

1. Leo Dowdy, interview with the author, November 11, 1987.

2. LaVere, *Texas Indians*, 177–80.

3. J. Marvin Hunter, ed., *The Trail Drivers of Texas* (1924; repr., Austin: University of Texas Press, 1985), 515–18, 730–34, 923–24.

4. U.S. Federal Census, 1870, Texas, Goliad County, Goliad Post Office, enumerated August 4, 1870, pp. 395 and 396, Dwellings 558 and 564, Families 574 and 580.

5. W. C. (Billy) Dowdy, correspondence with the author, June 12, 2008.

6. H. C. Withers v. John G. and James Dowdy, case 1195, Goliad County, 1878. The location of the Dowdy land is described in the preliminary text of this lawsuit.

7. L. Dowdy, interview; see also U.S. Federal Census, 1870, Texas, Goliad County, Goliad Post Office, enumerated August 4, 1870, p. 395, Dwelling 558, Family 574.

8. U.S. Federal Census, 1870, Texas, Goliad County, Goliad Post Office, enumerated August 4, 1870, p. 396, Dwelling 564, Family 580.

9. Tommie Lee Gardner, "John Gibson Dowdy," in *Kerr County Album*, collected by Kerr County Historical Commission (Dallas: Taylor Publishing, 1986), 226.

10. U.S. Federal Census, 1860, Texas, Goliad County, Goliad Post Office, enumerated July 22, 1860, p. 56, Dwellings 108 and 109, Families 109 and 110; and U.S. Federal Census, 1870,

Texas, Goliad County, Goliad Post Office, enumerated August 4, 1870, pp. 395 and 396, Dwellings 558 and 564, Families 574 and 580.

11. *H. C. Withers v. John G. and James Dowdy.*

12. Ibid.

13. L. Dowdy, interview.

14. Ibid.

15. Nina Dowdy McCall, interview with the author, November 10, 1987.

16. Ibid.

17. Gardner, "John Gibson Dowdy," 226.

18. Johnson Creek, a south-flowing tributary of the Guadalupe River, is not to be confused with the north-flowing Johnson Fork of the Llano River, which heads only about twelve miles west-northwest across a gentle divide. For the location of their homestead, see Sowell, *Early Settlers and Indian Fighters*, 740–41.

19. The 640-acre tract (abstract no. 314, recorded in Kerr County in the Texas State Land Office Archives, Austin, Texas), granted originally to the Socorro Farming Company and patented by Charles Schreiner on December 15, 1877, adjoined two other Schreiner tracts, all together totaling about 1,500 acres.

20. There is some confusion as to when the Dowdys arrived at their new home site on Johnson Creek. However, based on a distillation of sources—including "The Murderous Savages," *San Antonio Daily Express*, October 8, 1878; "The Dowdy Children Massacre," *San Antonio Daily Express*, October 12, 1878; Bob Bennett, *Kerr County, Texas, 1856–1956*, (San Antonio: Naylor, 1956), 186; Nina Harwood, "Murder Details Told by Dowdy Family," *Kerrville (TX) Daily Times*, Hill Country, June 24, 1979; Merrill Doyle interview of Mr. and Mrs. Solon Dowdy, July 11, 1972 (cassette held by the Kerr Regional History Center, Butt-Holdsworth Memorial Library, Kerrville, Texas); Bruce, *Banister Was There*, 39; Gillett, *Six Years*, 129; Sowell, *Early Settlers and Indian Fighters*, 740 (quoting Elizabeth Fessenden); Irene Van Winkle, "Dowdy Murders a Sad Chapter in Kerr History," *West Kerr (TX) Current*, February 9, 2006; Franklin Junior High School Class of 1927–28, "The Dowdy Family," (unpublished manuscript, Butt-Holdsworth Memorial Library, Kerrville, Texas); and "The Dowdy Family, Kerr County: The History," *Kerrville Mountain (TX) Sun*, pamphlet, 1931, 34–35—it appears probable that they arrived in Kerr County about September 20 and were present at the Johnson Creek site by about October 1, 1878.

21. Gillett, *Six Years*, 259.

22. J. B. Jones to W. Steele, December 17, 1878, General Correspondence, AGR; see also R. G. Kimbell, *Ranger Reminiscences*, 1937, AGR; and Gardner, "John Gibson Dowdy," 226.

23. Ned B. Estes, interview with the author, October 23, 1987.

24. Bruce, *Banister Was There*, 39.

25. Estes, interview; see also Franklin Junior High School, "The Dowdy Family," 34; and Van Winkle, "Dowdy Murders a Sad Chapter."

26. J. B. Jones to W. Steele, December 17, 1878.

27. Gillett, *Six Years*, 129.

28. Roquey Jobes, "The Rest of the Story for an Era of Lawlessness," in *Families of Kimble County*, vol. 2 (Junction, TX: Kimble County Historical Commission, 1998), 469.

29. Harwood, "Murder Details," 3; see also Doyle interview of Mr. and Mrs. Solon Dowdy; and W. C. (Billy) Dowdy, interview with the author, May 9, 2008. Dowdy family tradition holds that Alice Dowdy was to marry the unnamed young man within a few days.

30. Doyle interview of Mr. and Mrs. Solon Dowdy; see also Sowell, *Early Settlers and Indian Fighters*, 740.

31. "Dowdy Children Massacre," *San Antonio Daily Express*.

32. Parsons and Brice, *Texas Ranger N. O. Reynolds*, 254.

33. "Dowdy Children Massacre," *San Antonio Daily Express*.

34. In the newspaper reports and written accounts ("Dowdy Children Massacre," *San Antonio Daily Express*, 4; and Sowell, *Early Settlers and Indian Fighters*, 740) there is some confusion as to the names and ages of the murdered Dowdy girls. This can be sorted out by reference to their enumerated records in the 1870 U.S. census records, specifically Texas, Goliad County, Goliad Post Office, Dwelling 558, Family 574. (In 1878, Alice was eighteen; Martha, possibly nicknamed Fanny, was sixteen; and Susan, apparently nicknamed Rilla or Rilly, was fourteen. The eldest Dowdy daughter, Mary, aged twenty-one, remained at home.

35. Billy Dowdy, interview.

36. Ibid.; see also Gillett, *Six Years*, 130.

37. Sowell, *Early Settlers and Indian Fighters*, 740.

38. "Murder Most Foul," *Burnet (TX) Bulletin*, October 26, 1878, quoting B. F. Peppers [*sic*], 4.

39. Parsons and Brice, *Texas Ranger N. O. Reynolds*, 254.

40. Ibid.

41. J. B. Jones to W. Steele, December 17, 1878.

42. "Murderous Savages," *San Antonio Daily Express*, 1.

43. Jasper Moore, interview with the author, December 2, 1987; see also Sowell, *Early Settlers and Indian Fighters*, 74.

44. "Dowdy Children Massacre," *San Antonio Daily Express*, 4.

45. Nina Harwood, "The Truth Will Never Be Known," *Kerrville (TX) Daily Times*, Hill Country, March 25, 1979, 4; see also Sowell, *Early Settlers and Indian Fighters*, 740.

46. Harwood, "The Truth Will Never Be Known"; see also Sowell, *Early Settlers and Indian Fighters*, 740.

47. The graves may still be seen, covered with clam shells embedded in concrete, in the Sunset Cemetery off Texas Highway 27, two miles south of Mountain Home. Many other Dowdy family members are also buried here.

48. Gillett, *Six Years*, 129.

49. Nina Harwood, "Four Dowdy Children's Murder Still Mystery," *Kerrville (TX) Daily Times*, February 22, 1970, 3; it may be that many of the footprints observed clustered around the bodies of the three Dowdy girls were left by their assailants. See also "Our Frontier Enemies," *Galveston (TX) Daily News*, October 8, 1878, 1.

50. J. B. Jones to W. Steele, December 17, 1878.

51. Frederica B. Wyatt, "Junction's Oldest Citizen Lives in Its Oldest House," *San Angelo (TX) Standard Times*, April 2, 1969.

52. Fisher, *It Occurred in Kimble*, 179.

53. Gillett, *Six Years*, 130.

54. J. B. Jones to W. Steele, December 17, 1878.

55. Bruce, *Banister Was There*, 40; see also Gillett, *Six Years*, 129.

56. "Murderous Savages," *San Antonio Daily Express*.

57. J. B. Jones to W. Steele, December 17, 1878. However, Jones also claims (incorrectly) in his report to Steele that "the trail of the murderers . . . had never been followed." This implies that Jones himself, assisted by Nelson, may also have followed the still-visible trail until they lost it.

58. D. W. Roberts to J. B. Jones, October 12, 1878, General Correspondence, AGR.

59. Ibid.

60. Ibid.

61. Parsons and Brice, *Texas Ranger N. O. Reynolds*, 255.

62. "A Bloody Arrow," *San Antonio Daily Express*, October 13, 1878, 2.

63. J. B. Jones to N. O. Reynolds, October 24, 1878, Frontier Battalion Correspondence, Texas Ranger Records, AGR.

64. Ibid.; see also J. B. Jones to N. O. Reynolds, October 25, 1878, Frontier Battalion Correspondence, Texas Ranger Records, AGR; and N. O. Reynolds to J. B. Jones, November 1, 1878, Frontier Battalion Correspondence, Texas Ranger Records, AGR.

65. "Frontier Protection," *San Antonio Daily Express*, November 1, 1878; see also Frontier Battalion Monthly Returns, 1878.

66. Frontier Battalion Monthly Returns, 1878.

67. Gillett, *Six Years*, 130.

68. Bruce, *Banister Was There*, 40; see also Gillett, *Six Years*, 130. At least three of these stone cairns survive, according to Billy Dowdy (interview with the author), although they are not now as tall as Gillett described. The location of the massacre is described by Jobes ("The Rest of the Story"): "0.7 mile west of the yellow light at Mountain Home Post Office on Texas highway 41, on the left [south] of the highway about 200 feet. This is private property which in 1997 was owned by Ms. Laverne Talbert Boles."

69. Frontier Battalion Monthly Returns, 1878 and 1879.

70. Harwood, "Murder Details," 4.

71. Ibid.

72. Billy Dowdy, interview.

73. Ibid. See also the account by L. Carroll Adams, "The Dowdy Massacre," in *Documentation for State Historical Markers* (Austin: Texas Historical Commission, 1978), 1–6; Gardner, "John Gibson Dowdy," 226; and Evelyn M. Carr, "Thomas A. Dowdy," in *Kerr County Album*, collected by Kerr County Historical Commission (Dallas: Taylor Publishing, 1986), 226–27. On January 20, 1880, the Texas General Land Office transferred 640 acres from Survey 1415, held by the T. W. & G. Railroad Company, to James Dowdy. Fifteen months later, on April 23, 1881, Texas Governor Oran Roberts granted patent deed No. 647 on the same 640 acres to James Dowdy.

74. L. Dowdy, interview; see also Doyle interview of Mr. and Mrs. Solon Dowdy.

75. L. Dowdy, interview.

76. Ibid; see also Billy Dowdy interview and Kimbell, *Ranger Reminiscences*. Some accounts of

the Dowdy murders contain claims of some vague prior romantic connection between John Potter and one of the Dowdy young women, either Mary, the surviving eldest daughter, then twenty-one, or Alice, then eighteen. However, the earliest written accounts of the tragedy ("Our Frontier Enemies," *Galveston (TX) Daily News*; "The Murderous Savages," *San Antonio Daily Express*; "The Dowdy Children Massacre," *San Antonio Daily Express*; "A Bloody Arrow," *San Antonio Daily Express*; "Murder Most Foul," *Burnet (TX) Bulletin*; J. B. Jones to W. Steele, December 17, 1878; Sowell, *Early Settlers and Indian Fighters*; Franklin Junior High School, "The Dowdy Family"; and interviews with some first-generation descendants of the surviving siblings [Solon Dowdy and Nina Dowdy McCall]) do not contain such innuendos, which only begin to appear in local newspaper accounts starting in about 1970. Those are based on interviews with various second-generation Dowdy descendants and long-standing area residents. It may be significant that such dark rumors began to surface only after the death of the last Dowdy sibling, Mary Dowdy, in 1945, and may reflect community speculations about her marked reclusive behavior—as a possible sign of guilt—and the apparent disregard of her brothers, Tom, Dick, and George after the massacre. Subsequent events (see chap. 14 and 15) may also have contributed to such speculations. However, the author's 1987 interviews with Myrtle Dowdy, widow of George Dowdy's son Bill, and Leo T. Dowdy, grandson of Tom Dowdy, as well as long-time resident and ex-postmaster of Mountain Home, Ned Estes, all contained differing hints about such a prior Potter-Dowdy romantic connection. Given the very short elapsed time between the Dowdys' arrival on Johnson Creek and the massacre, it is difficult to hypothecate a plausible scenario whereby John Potter would have been able to establish contact with any of the Dowdy daughters. Moreover, it should be acknowledged that any overt contact between an itinerant young cowboy of Indian descent and young southern white women, such as the Dowdy daughters, would have met with the strong disapproval of the Dowdy parents, if not the daughters themselves. However, the claim of Tom Dowdy's wife, Susan, of an earlier encounter with John Potter in Goliad County, in a horse deal gone sour, is tantalizing in this regard. But such a putative romantic encounter would also then require the exceptional coincidence of the Dowdys' move from Goliad County to a Kerr County location not far distant from the Potter home site in adjoining Kimble County, a scenario that is not impossible but highly implausible.

77. Annie May Morriss, *Her Name was Ann* (San Antonio, TX: Naylor Company, 1951), 132–33.

## Chapter 10

1. Wilkins, *Law Comes to Texas*, 175.
2. N. O. Reynolds to J. B. Jones, February 14, 1879, General Correspondence, AGR; see also Gillett, *Six Years*, 133–34.
3. Frontier Battalion Monthly Returns, 1879; see also Wilkins, *Law Comes to Texas*, 189.
4. Wilkins, *Law Comes to Texas*, 189; see also Gillett, *Six Years*, 131–34.
5. Adjutant General files, General Correspondence, February 17, 1879. (This source is a copy of a letter from the officers and citizens of Kimble County to the Texas Legislature requesting the continuation of Ranger pressure against the confederation of Kimble County criminals; it was apparently sent also to the adjutant general's office as a matter of interest.) It is a matter

for speculation whether the support of Will Potter for the continuance of a Ranger presence in Kimble County signifies (1) a change of attitude on Potter's part, (2) that he was in a state of denial regarding the criminal activity of his sons and nephews, (3) that he signed the petition to convince his neighbors of his support for law and order, or (4) that Potter realized he had been a dupe for the Kimble County criminal confederation and was trying to make up for past sins.

6. Frontier Battalion Monthly Returns, 1879; see also *Results of Operations*, AGR.

7. *Results of Operations*, AGR.

8. Robert S. Weddle, "Peg Leg Station on the San Saba River," in *Edwards Plateau Historian*, vol. 3 (Menard, TX: Edwards Plateau Historical Association, 1967), 30–31.

9. Ibid., 28.

10. List of robberies: (1) inferred, last half of 1876 (see chap. 6, n. 41); (2) January 19, 1877; (3) February 2, 1877; (4) December 15, 1877; (5) December 25, 1877: (6) July 6, 1878; see *Burnet (TX) Bulletin*, January 26, 1877; *Burnet (TX) Bulletin*, February 9, 1877; "Topics in the Interior," *Galveston (TX) Daily News*; see also Austerman, *Sharps Rifles*, 290–93, 322, and Alexander, *Winchester Warriors*, 340, which indicates two robberies occurred on February 2, 1877 (which is probably the same one mentioned by the *Burnet Bulletin* on February 9, 1877).

11. Gillett, *Six Years*, 102–5; see also Bruce, *Banister Was There*, 19.

12. D. W. Roberts to J. B. Jones, October 1, 1878, General Correspondence, AGR.

13. J. H. Comstock to J. B. Jones, December 18, 1878, General Correspondence, AGR.

14. J. B. Jones to N. O. Reynolds, December 30, 1878, General Correspondence, AGR.

15. D. W. Roberts to J. B. Jones, January 31, 1879, General Correspondence, AGR.

16. *Results of Operations*, AGR. Allison was arrested in Kimble County on May 27, 1878. How long he remained in custody before being escorted to Austin is not recorded, but it may have been several weeks before Rangers were available for escort duty, inasmuch as Company D sent large detachments out scouting for reported Indians and U.S. Army deserters during the first two weeks of June; transport to Austin would have consumed about four or five days.

17. Gillett, *Six Years*, 102–5.

18. Ibid.

19. Wilkins, *Law Comes to Texas*, 192.

20. Frontier Battalion Monthly Returns, 1879.

21. Frederica B. Wyatt, correspondence with the author, September 1, 2007.

22. Frontier Battalion Monthly Returns, 1879.

23. Ibid.; see also Wyatt, communication with the author: Rube Boyce's wife was the former Adeline Pearl; John and Henry were her brothers. John Boyce was Rube Boyce's brother. Jim Cravens was a twenty-five-year-old settler who lived near Junction City.

24. Frontier Battalion Monthly Returns, 1879; the fugitive Luke Cathey, a previous accomplice of the Dublins in 1876 and early 1877, had been rumored to be back in Kimble County since late March 1879.

25. Frontier Battalion Monthly Returns, 1879.

26. D. W. Roberts to J. B. Jones, August 1, 1879, General Correspondence, AGR.

27. Frederica B. Wyatt, "Dr. William M. Donnan," in *Families of Kimble County*, vol. 2 (Junction, TX: Kimble County Historical Commission, 1998), 121; based on local tradition, Dr. Don-

nan may have been blindfolded while being taken to treat the wounded Dell Dublin and was therefore unable to identify the place where the outlaw was hidden (Evans, interview, March 15, 2010).

28. D. W. Roberts to J. B. Jones, August 1, 1879.

29. D. W. Roberts to J. B. Jones, August 4, 1879, General Correspondence, AGR.

30. D. W. Roberts to J. B. Jones, September 1, 1879, General Correspondence, AGR. The Rangers would certainly have looked for Dell Dublin at his home as well as the nearby homes of William and Tom Potter. They might not have thought to look for the wounded outlaw at James K. P. Potter's remote home in the gloomy rock-walled canyon of Chalk Creek, about five miles distant by wagon road, and about nine miles from Junction City. Wherever Dublin was hidden with his accomplice, Mack Potter, however, the citizens of Kimble County figured it out, and with their sheriff, captured the wounded outlaw.

31. Frontier Battalion Monthly Returns, 1879.

32. Ibid.

33. U.S. District Court, Western District of Texas, official court records 1879 and 1880.

34. Parsons and Brice, *Texas Ranger N. O. Reynolds*, 191, 198; Gillett, *Six Years*, 104.

35. Gillett, *Six Years*, 104–5; Wyatt, communication with the author (see n. 21); traditions of the Boyce and Pearl families hold that the pistol was hidden in a basket of food brought by Adeline to her husband.

36. Frontier Battalion, Monthly Returns, 1880.

37. U.S. District Court, Western District of Texas, official court records, 1882; in January 1882 Boyce was back in the Travis County jail, where he moved for a new trial.

38. U.S. District Court, Western District of Texas, official court records, 1880.

39. Gillett, *Six Years*, 104.

40. *Austin Statesman*, August 26, 1880, "Local and Other Matters," 4.

41. "Texas Highwaymen, Details of the Celebrated Pegleg Stage Robbery," *St. Louis Globe-Democrat*, December 4, 1886, 16.

42. U.S. District Court, Western District of Texas, official court records, 1880.

43. U.S. v. Reuben Boyce, case 13CC (U.S. District Court, Western District of Texas); see also Don H. Biggers, *German Pioneers in Texas* (1925; repr., Fredericksburg, TX: Fredericksburg Publishing, 1983). Allison was placed in the Texas State Penitentiary about September 10, 1880, and released sometime between March 3, 1882, and October 1, 1884, when he and three accomplices murdered saloonkeeper J. W. Braeutigam in Fredericksburg, Texas, during a robbery. Allison died in a fire, perhaps set by himself in an ill-fated escape attempt or by outraged citizens, that burned down the jail in late November 1884.

44. Fisher, *It Occurred in Kimble*, 220; see also Gillett, *Six Years*, 105, and Parsons and Brice, *Texas Ranger N. O. Reynolds*, 191.

45. Adjutant General (Hon. John B. Jones), *Annual Report of the Adjutant General of the State of Texas* (Austin, TX: State Printing Office, December 31, 1880), 27. Jones was including the six convicted Pegleg robbers with at least three other criminals who had been convicted of other offenses in federal district court in San Antonio later in the fall of 1880, including one Tom Moody.

46. See chap. 16 regarding Tom Moody.

## Chapter 11

1. Frontier Battalion Monthly Returns, 1877.
2. Frontier Battalion Monthly Returns, 1878; see also Gillett, *Six Years*, 93–94.
3. Frontier Battalion Monthly Returns, 1877.
4. W. W. Elliott to J. B. Jones, 1877, no date, but almost certainly March or early April (see chap. 6, n. 61); Frontier Battalion Correspondence, Texas Ranger Records, AGR; see also Parsons and Brice, *Texas Ranger N. O. Reynolds*, 98. It is also possible that the third "Potter boy" was James K. P. Potter, except that he would have then been about thirty-one years old, whereas Mack, Bill, and Frank Potter were all in their early to mid twenties.
5. D. W. Roberts to J. B. Jones, August 1, 1880; see also Frontier Battalion Monthly Returns, 1880.
6. C. L. Nevill to J. B. Jones, October 23, 1880, General Correspondence, AGR.
7. D. W. Roberts to J. B. Jones, December 15, 1879, General Correspondence, AGR. Miller's complaint to the Rangers is significant because it demonstrates that the Indian Potter cousins were still taking part in the affairs of the Kimble County confederation, threatening a local settler (Miller) who was to testify against their cousins, Mack and Bill Potter—as well as cronies Roll and Dell Dublin and Matthew Wilkins—in an upcoming trial in federal court in Austin, where they might face long terms in the federal penitentiary if convicted. It is also significant in that a Kimble County citizen (Miller) was willing to testify against a member of the confederation. "Indian Jim" Potter was certainly known and wanted by the spring of 1880, and he was involved in a night-time shoot-out with Rangers in late July 1880 in the South Llano valley (see Frontier Battalion Monthly Returns, 1880; see also D. W. Roberts to J. B. Jones, August 1, 1880).
8. Frontier Battalion Monthly Returns, 1880.
9. D. W. Roberts to J. B. Jones, May 18, 1880.
10. Kimbell, *Ranger Reminiscences*; the memoir of ex-Ranger Corporal R. G. Kimbell, written fifty-seven years after the events he recalled, describes a Ranger scout on the headwaters of the North [South] Llano River in 1880 after "the bunch of men who . . . had massacred the two [three] Dowdy girls and their little brother." This was probably the patrol of July 27, 1880, that fired on "Indian Jim" Potter in unsuccessfully attempting his arrest at the "Potter Waterhole." If Kimbell's memory was correct, and he was not connecting later beliefs concerning John Potter to an earlier encounter, then there were Rangers during the 1878–80 period who believed that the Potters had been involved in the Dowdy murders.
11. Frontier Battalion Monthly Returns, 1877 and 1878; the fact that James K. P. Potter—and Dell Dublin—were not among the five prisoners, including "Black" Burt, who were escorted by the Rangers to jail in Austin after their trials, indicates they were acquitted.
12. Frontier Battalion Monthly Returns, 1879.
13. Frontier Battalion Monthly Returns, 1880.
14. Frontier Battalion Monthly Returns, 1879.
15. U.S. Federal Census, 1860, California, Mendocino County, Ukiah Township, enumerated June 5, 1860, p. 799, Dwelling 43, Family 43; U.S. Federal Census, 1870, California, Mendocino County, Calpellam Township, enumerated July 9, 1870, p. 181A, Dwelling 8, Family 8.
16. "Homicide," *Mendocino (CA) Democrat*, December 19, 1872, 3.

17. "Refused," *Mendocino (CA) Democrat*, February 27, 1873, 3.

18. "Cleveland," *Mendocino (CA) Democrat*, August 8, 1874, 3.

19. Rebecca Potter's first husband was John Gordon, whom she married before September 1852 and divorced sometime between 1856 and 1861. Her second husband, John Hildreth, died in 1876 (Kit Fuller, communication with the author, October 4, 2007, quoting California Court Records, Mendocino County, Marriage Book 2, 458).

20. Fuller, genealogical lists, September 10, 2007; George Cleveland's arrival in Texas may be derived from the fact that Rebecca Potter Gordon Hildreth Cleveland gave birth to her son William Jasper Cleveland on December 12, 1879, in California, so George Cleveland could not have left California for Texas until after mid-April 1879. His first appearance in the Ranger records is July 11, 1879. Allowing for perhaps one or two months for transit, and assuming Cleveland had already been in Kimble County for several weeks before being arrested, suggests that he arrived in late May or June.

21. Frontier Battalion Monthly Returns, 1880.

22. Roberts, *Rangers and Sovereignty*, 131.

23. Ibid., 132–35.

24. Ibid.

25. D. W. Roberts to J. B. Jones, April 8, 1880, General Correspondence, AGR; see also Frontier Battalion Monthly Returns, 1880.

26. "U.S. Federal Census," 1880, in *Families of Kimble County*, 466; see also Frontier Battalion Monthly Returns, 1879; perhaps Corporal Gourley was not aware that James K. P. Potter was to be tried the next day in justice of the peace court, or was not confident that Potter would appear.

27. Frontier Battalion Monthly Returns, 1879.

28. Ibid.

29. D. W. Roberts to J. B. Jones, December 15, 1879.

30. According to the 1879 Frontier Battalion Monthly Returns, on November 16, Captain Roberts and another Ranger made a scout down the San Saba River to the vicinity of Menardville, where they arrested one Peter Robinson, an "escaped U.S. [federal? army deserter?] prisoner," charged with illegally driving cattle from Kimble County; the next day Sergeant E. A. Sieker and four Ranger privates conveyed Robinson to Junction City.

31. Fisher, *It Occurred in Kimble*, 152–54; see also M. B. Sheppard, "John Alexander Miller," in *Families of Kimble County* (Junction, TX: Kimble County Historical Commission, 1985), 250–51.

32. Frontier Battalion Monthly Returns, 1880.

33. Ibid.

34. Ibid. Also, Kimbell, *Ranger Reminiscences*, 4.

35. D. W. Roberts to J. B. Jones, August 1, 1880.

36. Fuller, genealogical lists, September 10, 2007; the woman was probably not Cleveland's wife, Rebecca Potter Gordon Hildreth Cleveland, who would have then been three months pregnant and, in any case, was living in California when Cleveland's son, William Jasper, was born on December 14, 1879. Far more likely is that the woman was James K. P. Potter's wife,

Evaline Hopper Potter, then thirty-one years old, who would have been living with her children in the log house that Potter had built several hundred yards below the outlaws' camp at the "Potter Waterhole" (Evans, interview). The milk pans suggest the presence of young children, who might have been William (then thirteen years old), Frances (ten), Tuck (four), or Lottie Potter (about two).

37. Fuller, correspondence, August 30, 2009, citing *Ukiah City Press*.

38. U.S. Federal Census Mortality Schedule, Kimble County, Texas, for the year ending May 31, 1880.

39. U.S. Federal Census, 1880, Texas, Kimble County, Precinct 1, p. 9, Supervisor's District 6, Enumeration District 95, enumerated June 23, 1880, Dwelling 67, Family 72 (W. Potter family), and "by 72" (Thos. Potter family). Thomas Potter's second son by Molly Metock, Sam, had remained in California when the Potters emigrated to Texas.

40. Kit Fuller, communication with the author, April 25, 2008.

41. Wyatt, communication with the author, November 24, 2009. Wyatt believes that Tom Potter as well as Dick Dublin may be buried in unmarked graves in the Wooten cemetery, located on the south side of Cajac Creek just west of U.S. Highway 377, about fourteen miles south of Junction.

42. D. W. Roberts to J. B. Jones, August 1, 1880.

43. Roberts, *Rangers and Sovereignty*, 120.

44. On July 7, 1885, H. K. Hutchinson and his wife N. A. Hutchinson sold two parcels of land "on the waters of Cajac Creek," surveys 56 and 11, to Mrs. F. I. H. DuPuy; (Kimble County [TX] Courthouse, County Clerk's office, Book A, p. 221). These two tracts encompass the home sites of Will and Tom Potter. No extant record showing any earlier land transfer exists because the Kimble County Courthouse was burned down on April 22, 1884, with all land records destroyed. I suspect the Potters had located on Cajac Creek as squatters, not landowners, which would suggest that Hutchinson filed on the Cajac Creek lands in 1879 or 1880. But Hutchinson had not displaced them from their Cajac Creek location, as he and his wife were living in or near the town of Junction City in June 1880 ("U.S. Federal Census, 1880," in *Families of Kimble County*, 463).

45. Roberts, *Rangers and Sovereignty*, 117; see also Kimbell, *Ranger Reminiscences*, 4, and D. W. Roberts to J. B. Jones, September 30, 1880, General Correspondence, AGR. Roberts's letter (mistakenly dated September 4 but elsewhere designated a semimonthly report, September 30, 1880) indicates the horses were stolen "from Capt. H. K. Hutchinson's rancho on the North Llano."

46. Roberts, *Rangers and Sovereignty*, 117.

47. Frontier Battalion Monthly Returns, 1880.

## Chapter 12

1. Frank C. Rigler, "William Hickman Dunman, Texas Ranger," *The Highlander* (Llano, TX), January 4, 1973, 2B. This Ranger, who was ordinarily known as "Bill" Dunman, will be called "Hick" Dunman here to minimize confusion with another William M. Dunman, also known

as "Bill," who figures prominently in the story later. So far as can be determined, the two men were not closely related; whether they knew each other personally is not known. The list of men under Corporal Kimbell's command is provided in Esther Mueller's "R. C. Roberts as Texas Ranger," *Fredericksburg (TX) Standard*, January 18, 1934, 2. Roberts, a half-brother of Captain D. W. Roberts, related his Ranger adventures, including an extensive account of the chase after the Potter boys, to Esther Mueller fifty-four years after the event, when he was seventy-five years old. See also Roberts, *Rangers and Sovereignty*, 117.

2. Robinson, *Frontier Forts of Texas*, 84; Fort Terrett had been abandoned by the U.S. Army since late 1853; only some stone buildings remained in 1880.

3. Roberts, *Rangers and Sovereignty*, 117.

4. The distance from Fort Terrett to Company D's camp six miles east of Fort McKavett is about thirty miles cross country, a hard five-hour ride. If, by midday of September 24, Merck realized his horses had been stolen (and received confirming reports that morning from neighboring ranchmen), the thefts must have occurred either the night before (September 23) or very early the morning of September 24. If Merck departed Fort Terrett by noon, he could have reached Company D's camp by late afternoon, September 24. Kimbell's squad could have been packed and ready to leave by midmorning September 25, and could have arrived at the scene of the thefts by that evening, in time to find the trail of the thieves, who by then must have had a head start of between thirty-six and forty-eight hours.

5. Kimbell, *Ranger Reminiscences*, 11.

6. The exact route followed by the fleeing horse thieves and Kimbell's following Rangers cannot be known with certainty. However, the probable route can be reconstructed, taking into account (1) the known Indian and outlaw preference for easy traveling on the vacant divides, (2) the locations of conveniently located gently sloping valleys, (3) known watering places in the otherwise dry Edwards Plateau region, (4) information in the memoirs of Kimbell, R. C. Roberts, and Dan W. Roberts, and (5) surviving Ranger correspondence and reports.

7. Austerman, *Sharps Rifles*, 41 and 212; the southern mail route had been abandoned in 1868 because of continual Indian attacks.

8. Mueller, "R. C. Roberts," 2.

9. For details of this historic road, see Austerman, *Sharps Rifles*, 41; see also John C. Reid, *Reid's Tramp, or a Journal of the Incidents of Ten Months Travel through Texas, New Mexico, Arizona, Sonora, and California* (1858; repr., Austin, TX: Steck, 1935), 99, 105–8; see also August Santleben, *A Texas Pioneer: Early Staging and Overland Freighting Days on the Frontiers of Texas and Mexico*, ed. I. D. Affleck (New York: Neale, 1910), 100. For details about Howard's Well, see Gunnar Brune, *Springs of Texas*, vol. 1 (College Station: Texas A&M Press, 1981), 141–42. Howard's Well was a natural spring in the channel of Howard's Draw, just north of its intersection with Government Canyon, in what is now southern Crockett County, about twenty miles southwest of present Ozona. This ephemeral but ordinarily reliable alluvial spring provided the essential water supply for the stage station on the old southern mail route, which had been abandoned in 1868 for the safer northern route. In 1879 the well was "dug down about fifteen feet vertically at one end, approached by a narrow flight of rude stone steps, covered with sand and gravel. The water lies in a little irregular rock basin, and

the supply . . . did not apparently exceed five gallons. But it appears to run in as fast as it is dipped out" (Brune, *Springs of Texas*, 41–42, quoting an 1879 report by Burr Duval). During the 1880s, erosion of adjacent canyon walls related to overgrazing caused the channel to become filled with gravel, covering over the spring. A rock-lined cistern was then dug down into the alluvium, which provided a usually dependable but limited water source for travelers.

10. Thomas B. Hunt, *Journal Showing the Route Taken by the Government Train Accompanying the 15th Regiment, U.S. Infantry from Austin, Texas to Fort Craig, New Mexico and Returning to San Antonio, July–December, 1869* (Washington: U.S. National Archives and Records Service, Office of the Chief of Engineers, Record Group 77, Cartographic Records Section, Civil Works Map File, 1869), 30–32; also author's road log of trips following the old stage route from Beaver Lake to Fort Lancaster, March 2008 and May 2009.

11. Leckie, *Buffalo Soldiers*, 227.

12. Kimbell, *Ranger Reminiscences*, 5; see also Mueller, "R. C. Roberts," 2.

13. Mueller, "R. C. Roberts," 2, documents that they spent the night at Howard's Well. According to Robinson, *Frontier Forts of Texas*, 49–50, Fort Lancaster was last occupied by federal troops in late 1868, but it was used subsequently as an occasional bivouac and gathering point because of its proximity to permanent springs in adjacent Live Oak Draw.

14. Hunt, *Journal Showing the Route*, 30; also author's road logs of March 2008 and May 2009.

15. Kimbell, *Ranger Reminiscences*, 5; see also Mueller, "R. C. Roberts," 2; also author's road logs of March 2008 and May 2009.

16. Mueller, "R. C. Roberts," 2.

17. E. H. Sellards, W. S. Adkins, and F. B. Plummer, *The Geology of Texas*, Vol. 1, *Stratigraphy*, University of Texas Bulletin 3232 (Austin: University of Texas, 1932), 769–70.

18. Bomar, *Texas Weather*, 55.

19. Ramsey, "Camp Melvin," 137–47; see also Loyd M. Uglow, *Standing in the Gap: Army Outposts, Picket Stations, and the Pacification of the Texas Frontier, 1866–1886* (Fort Worth: Texas Christian University Press, 2001), 29, 33, 43, 48–50, and 130. Pecos Station was one of the names given to the crossing of the Pecos that was used by the northern stagecoach line after 1868. The U.S. Army periodically stationed a detachment of troops there to guard the stage station against Indian attacks; that facility was known as Camp Melvin. Army engineers had designed and installed a flexible, floatable pontoon bridge for wheeled vehicles, hence another frequent name for the place was Pontoon Crossing. A small settlement existed on the north bank, where the river meanders close to elevated limestone bluffs, offering protection from occasional Pecos River floods. Telegraph service was available. Pecos Station was located about nine miles northwest of present Iraan and about two miles west of the Texas Highway 349 Pecos River crossing.

20. D. W. Roberts to J. B. Jones, October 9, 1880, General Correspondence, AGR.

21. Ibid.

22. It is tempting to speculate that James K. P. Potter and George Cleveland may have sacrificed the two Indian Potter brothers to save themselves by splitting up and fleeing in a different direction. If so, the ploy worked—apparently, Kimbell and his men were unable to locate

Potter and Cleveland's trail among the more numerous signs of passing traffic on the Fort Stockton road. Also two mature white cowboys driving a few horses on that road would probably have aroused less suspicion than two young Indian cowboys with a small bunch. At any rate, Kimbell's Rangers were able to identify the trail of "Indian Jim" Potter and his brother John and successfully follow it up the Pecos.

23. D. W. Roberts to J. B. Jones, October 9, 1880.

24. Kimbell, *Ranger Reminiscences*, 5.

25. Patrick Dearen, *A Cowboy of the Pecos* (Plano: Republic of Texas Press, 1997), 111–12.

26. R. G. Kimbell, "Fight Between Rangers and Horse-Thieves," *Galveston (TX) Daily News*, November 5, 1880; this is Corporal Kimbell's letter, dated October 27, 1880, reporting on the gunfight with John and Jim Potter near Pope's Crossing on October 8, 1880.

27. Kimbell, *Ranger Reminiscences*, 6.

28. Roberts, *Rangers and Sovereignty*, 120.

29. "The Potters made no attempt to run, but fought until they were both shot down," according to Kimbell's subsequent letter to the *Galveston (TX) Daily News*.

30. Kimbell, *Ranger Reminiscences*, 7. Kimbell telegraphed Captain Roberts on October 13, 1880, from Fort Stockton, so it took him about four days to ride there from the site of the shoot-out. He returned to Dunman, "Guice" [Guyse], and his prisoners about October 16, and Lieutenant Nevill's wagon and men arrived the same day, to transport the wounded John Potter to Fort Davis. For the correct spelling of Buck Guyse's name, see J. Evetts Haley, *Jeff Milton, A Good Man with a Gun* (Norman: University of Oklahoma Press, 1948), 79.

31. This supposition is based on the fact that Kimbell did not arrive at Fort Stockton until either late on October 12 or about midday of October 13—four and a half to five days—whereas his return trip from Stockton to Pope's Crossing took only about three days (October 14–16). The detour to Horsehead Crossing would have added about thirty-five miles—one day's ride—to his journey.

32. Apparently the decision to convey the wounded prisoners to Fort Davis (rather than Fort Stockton) was necessitated because the post surgeon at Fort Stockton refused to treat the wounded Potter brothers. Besides, "it would be as cheap to guard them here as anywhere [and the hospital steward here can kill as quick as any one of the profession]." C. L. Nevill to J. B. Jones, October 16, 1880, General Correspondence, AGR.

33. Kimbell, *Ranger Reminiscences*, 7.

34. Kimbell, "Fight Between Rangers."

35. Kimbell, *Ranger Reminiscences*, 7.

36. Kimbell may have been skeptical of Frank Potter's innocence, as Kimbell was one member of the Ranger squad that was fired upon a little more than two months earlier, when the Rangers attempted to arrest "Indian Jim" Potter at the "Potter Waterhole" fight. The squad speculated that Frank Potter had been the shooter (D. W. Roberts to J. B. Jones, August 1, 1880).

37. Roberts, *Rangers and Sovereignty*, 120; see also Mueller, "R. C. Roberts," 2.

38. C. L. Nevill to J. B. Jones, telegram, October 21, 1880, General Correspondence, AGR.

39. C. L. Nevill to J. B. Jones, October 23, 1880.

40. D. W. Roberts to J. B. Jones, October 13, 1880, General Correspondence, AGR.

## Chapter 13

1. C. L. Nevill to J. B. Jones, October 23, 1880.

2. J. B. Jones to C. L. Nevill, October 21, 1880, General Correspondence, AGR.

3. C. L. Nevill to J. B. Jones, November 17, 1880, General Correspondence, AGR.

4. C. L. Nevill to J. B. Jones, October 23, 1880; see also Company D Muster Rolls, 1877–1881, Texas Ranger Records, AGR. Privates William H. "Hick" Dunman and N. J. Brown received permission to transfer to Lieutenant Nevill's Company E, which had experienced severe difficulty in recruiting qualified new Rangers.

5. Lieutenant C. L. Nevill, Special Order No. 11, March 13, 1881, General Correspondence, AGR: "Frank Potter, Teamster of Co. E is this day discharged the service of the State for good and sufficient reasons to the Company Commander." No reason for Potter's discharge is given, but speculation could be that Nevill discovered Frank Potter's connections to the Potter gang. Buck Guyse enlisted in Lieutenant Nevill's Company E on October 20, 1880, as a private (Texas Ranger Service Records, AGR).

6. Austerman, *Sharps Rifles*, 213–24.

7. D. W. Roberts to J. B. Jones, November 20, 1880, General Correspondence, Frontier Battalion Correspondence, Texas Ranger Records, AGR; see also Mueller, "R. C. Roberts," 2.

8. Austerman, *Sharps Rifles*, 12–13; 220–21.

9. The Toenail Trail was a frontier wagon road and cattle trail running northeast from Fort Mc-Kavett nearly forty miles to the South Concho River at Christoval, so named because it ran through the Toenail Ranch.

10. D. W. Roberts to J. B. Jones, November 20, 1880; see also Mueller, "R. C. Roberts," 2: Roberts reported that several of the five horses recovered from the Potters died on the way back, partly because of very cold weather. The Rangers "were able to deliver only two of the stolen horses to their owner in Kimble County [H. K. Hutchinson]. Their owner, probably thinking that the Rangers had only done their duty [and possibly because of their poor condition] received these horses without a word of thanks."

11. Kimbell, *Ranger Reminiscences*.

12. Mueller, "R. C. Roberts," 2.

13. D. W. Roberts to J. B. Jones, November 26, 1880, General Correspondence, AGR.

14. Mueller, "R. C. Roberts," 2.

15. Frontier Battalion Monthly Returns, 1880.

16. D. W. Roberts to J. B. Jones, May 19, 1881, General Correspondence, AGR; see also "Robbed of His Prisoners," *San Antonio Weekly Express Supplement*, May 19, 1881; see also Fisher, *It Occurred in Kimble*, 217; Roberts, *Rangers and Sovereignty*, 120; Jobes, "The Rest of the Story," 468–69; Wilkins, *Law Comes to Texas*, 209. It is not clear when John Potter was conveyed to San Antonio for safekeeping in the Bexar County jail, but logic suggests that it would have been soon after his return to the custody of the Kimble County sheriff by Corporal Kimbell and his three-man squad on November 22, 1880.

17. Fisher, *It Occurred in Kimble*, 217–18; see also Jobes, "The Rest of the Story," 468–69; see also "Robbed of His Prisoners," *San Antonio Weekly Express Supplement*.

## Chapter 14

1. Fisher, *It Occurred in Kimble*, 224.
2. Ibid., 225; see also State of Texas v. William Dunman, case 572 (Kimble County District Court Records, March 29, 1894).
3. Frontier Battalion Monthly Returns, 1880.
4. Fisher, *It Occurred in Kimble*, 225.
5. Roland S. Jary, interview with the author, November 14, 1987; Mr. Jary provided extensive genealogical data on the Dunman and Reeves families of Texas.
6. Jary, interview.
7. Leroy G. Denman to Governor J. S. Hogg, October 25, 1892, Texas State Prison Records, Texas State Pardons records, Archives and Information Services Division, Texas State Library and Archives Commission. Denman states that Kate Dunman rendered the state important services relevant to several prosecutions for horse theft.
8. Kate Dunman to Texas Governor J. S. Hogg, March 2, 1892, Texas State Prison Records, Texas State Pardons records, Archives and Information Services Division, Texas State Library and Archives Commission. Kate Dunman was asking for a pardon for her son, Dan: "He never knew a father, being only 9 months old when his father died during the Civil War"; see also William M. Dunman letter to his uncle, Mr. Jeptha Williams, April 5, 1896, Texas State Pardons records, at the Confederate Home, Austin, writing that "Judge Williams was the only father I ever knew."
9. Kate Dunman to Texas Governor J. S. Hogg, March 2, 1892; at least six letters are in the pardons files from Kate Dunman during the period January 10, 1892, to April 13, 1896, seeking pardons or clemency for her sons; Texas State Prison Records, Texas State Pardons records, Archives and Information Services Division, Texas State Library and Archives Commission.
10. Frontier Battalion Monthly Returns, 1880.
11. Jary, interview.
12. A letter seems more likely, based on the author's interview of Ned B. Estes. Mr. Estes was then more than ninety years old and had lived in Kerr County since 1922. He claimed to have known Richard (Dick) Dowdy. Mr. Estes said that Bill Dunman wrote a letter from jail to the Dowdys, claiming that John Potter had told him that the eldest Dowdy daughter (Mary, then twenty-one, or Alice, then eighteen) "wouldn't have anything to do with him." Bill Dunman was literate, and his several extant letters are cogent, written in a clear, legible, if somewhat childish script. Moreover, conveying such a revelation by letter had the advantage that it could be passed around among family members.
13. Fisher, *It Occurred in Kimble*, 218; see also "Robbed of His Prisoners," *San Antonio Weekly Express Supplement*, 1, and Jobes, "The Rest of the Story," 468–69; also Estes, interview.
14. Jobes, "The Rest of the Story," 468–69; see also Thomas H. Caffall, "The Joseph Hardin Clements Family," in *Families of Kimble County*, vol. 2 (Junction, TX: Kimble County Historical Commission, 1998), 99. Deputy Jobes, who owned a wagon yard in Junction City, was the owner and driver of the hack used for transporting the prisoners. Joseph Hardin Clements came from a fighting family that had been involved in the infamous Sutton-Taylor feud of DeWitt and Gonzales Counties; the notorious gunman, John Wesley Hardin, was his mater-

nal first cousin and sometime associate. Clements and his wife moved to Kimble County in October 1874 to escape the violence of the Sutton-Taylor feud. Manny Kimbreau was Joe Clements's nephew.

15. Paterson, "I Remember," 80–81; the author's grandmother describes riding in a hack the sixty miles from Kerrville to Junction City in 1890, when they departed at 6:00 a.m. and arrived about 8:30 p.m.

16. The Kerrville–San Antonio road was a well-traveled public thoroughfare on which they would have made better time. "Robbed of His Prisoners," *San Antonio Weekly Express Supplement*.

17. Ibid.

18. Ibid.

19. Ibid.

20. Estes, interview.

21. D. W. Roberts to J. B. Jones, May 19, 1881.

22. Fisher, *It Occurred in Kimble*, 217; the term "cut" may imply that John Potter was castrated by his executioners before being shot to death; however, all other published and oral accounts are silent on this point.

23. L. Dowdy, interview.

24. Ibid.

25. Estes, interview; whether "oldest daughter" refers to Mary Dowdy or the eldest daughter who was killed (Alice) is not clear.

26. Myrtle Dowdy, interview with the author, November 9, 1987.

27. Moore, interview.

28. Doyle interview of Mr. and Mrs. Solon Dowdy.

29. McCall, interview.

30. Franklin Junior High School, "The Dowdy Family."

31. D. W. Roberts to J. B. Jones, October 14, 1879, General Correspondence, AGR: "Five cases for theft have been tried [during this term of district court] at Junction and no convictions, and never will be any until things change."

32. "Robbed of His Prisoners," *San Antonio Weekly Express Supplement*.

33. Dunman's subsequent criminal record casts further doubt on the veracity of his report to his Dowdy cousins.

34. Morriss, *Her Name was Ann*, 132–33.

35. D. W. Roberts to J. B. Jones, October 13, 1880.

**Chapter 15**

1. Wilkins, *Law Comes to Texas*, 227; Webb, *Texas Rangers*, 425.

2. Gillett, *Six Years*, 50.

3. Wilkins, *Law Comes to Texas*, 227.

4. Webb, *Texas Rangers*, 312–24; see also Wilkins, *Law Comes to Texas*, 55–56, 176,189, 236; and Gillett, *Six Years*, 131–34.

5. Company A, under Lieutenant George W. Baylor, arrived in Ysleta in September 1879, and Company E, under Lieutenant Charles Nevill, was sent to Fort Davis in August 1880; see

Wilkins, *Law Comes to Texas*, 194–96, 203–4.

6. N. O. Reynolds to J. B. Jones, February 14, 1879; Frontier Battalion Monthly Returns, 1879; see also *Results of Operations*, AGR.

7. D. W. Roberts to J. B. Jones, July 10, 1881, General Correspondence, AGR; see also Roberts's Company D Muster Roll, 1881, Texas Ranger Records, AGR. In his biography (Roberts, *Rangers and Sovereignty*, 179), the date of his resignation is misstated as 1882.

8. Haley, *Jeff Milton*, 66; see also Wilkins, *Law Comes to Texas*, 227; and Utley, *Lone Star Justice*, 223.

9. L. Dowdy, interview; also Billy Dowdy, interview: the crippled leg may have been congenital, the consequence of childhood polio, or even an old gunshot wound.

10. D. W. Roberts to J. B. Jones, May 19, 1881.

11. "Arrested for Murder, Dick Dowdy, The Killing of Potter and Release of Dunman," *San Antonio Weekly Express Supplement*, June 16, 1881, 1.

12. Records of 24th Judicial District Court (Kerr County), 1883: State of Texas v. Tom Dowdy, case 254 (murder); State of Texas v. R. B. Dowdy, case 255 (murder); State of Texas v. R. B. and Tom Dowdy, case 256 (robbery); State of Texas v. R. B. and Tom Dowdy, case 257 (aiding a prisoner to escape from an officer); State of Texas v. William Dunman, case 258 (murder); State of Texas v. Dan Dunman, case 259 (murder); State of Texas v. William Dunman and Dan Dunman, case 260 (assault and robbery); State of Texas v. Dan Dunman, case 261 (aiding a prisoner to escape from an officer).

13. Ibid.

14. "Robbed of His Prisoners," *San Antonio Weekly Express Supplement*, 1.

15. Kerr County District Court records, 1883; see n. 13.

16. Leo Tarleton was a San Antonio attorney, then about thirty-five years old, with experience in criminal trials. He was not the sitting judge of the 37th Judicial District (Bexar County), San Antonio, nor a retired judge of that or any other judicial district in Texas (Alfred Rodriguez, assistant to clerk of Judicial District 37, San Antonio, Texas, correspondence with the author, April 22, 2008). The appointment of a special judge to preside at the Dowdy trial suggests that it was a "lightning rod" that the elected judge of that judicial district, J. M. Paschal, wanted to avoid, and/or that he was personally close to some of the people involved. In Texas, appointment of special judges must be done by the governor; any attending rationales or justifications would probably have been conveyed by informal correspondence or personal conversation. Although most special judge appointments involve available sitting judges (or retired judges), it was not unheard of to appoint a qualified attorney to serve as a special judge, if both the plaintiff and the defendant agreed (U.S. Federal District Judge Lynn Hughes, correspondence with the author, April 28, 2008; Linda Uecker, clerk of 24th Judicial District, Kerrville, Texas, communication with the author, May 8, 2008).

17. Mike Bowlin, Kerr County Regional History Center, correspondence with the author, July 12 and 13, 2008; Wesley Thigpen was the eldest son of Susan Cassell Dowdy's eldest sister, Martha E., who married John Thigpen in 1849 in Washington Parish, Louisiana. Wesley Thigpen was born in 1851 in Louisiana, but the John Thigpen family moved to Goliad County, Texas, in about 1857. No record has yet been found as to Wesley Thigpen's education or legal credentials.

18. Kerr County District Court records, 1883, case 254.

19. Ibid.

20. Ibid.

21. Kerr County District Court records, 1883, case 255. Dowdy family tradition freely acknowledges that Dick Dowdy killed John Potter with a shotgun after Deputy Clements's prisoners were removed from the hack and the Kimble County law officers drove away (Billy Dowdy, interview); another long-standing question is, who was the fourth man in the group that liberated the prisoners (in addition to Tom and Dick Dowdy, and Dan Dunman)? Billy Dowdy believes that he was James E. Dowdy, father of the murdered young people, as he would have insisted on taking part in the vengeance on Potter. That he was not charged with the murder contributes further to the perception of deep sympathy for the Dowdy parents and acknowledgment of their advanced years.

22. Kerr County District Court records, 1883, cases 256 and 257.

23. Ibid., cases 258, 259, 260, and 261.

**Chapter 16**

1. Billy Dowdy, interview; see also Adams, "The Dowdy Massacre," 1–6.

2. M. Dowdy, interview; see also "Mrs. Susan Cassels [Cassell] Dowdy," *Kerrville (TX) Mountain Sun*, Died, June 21, 1913.

3. Billy Dowdy, interview, May 9, 2008.

4. L. Dowdy, interview; also B. Dowdy, interview.

5. M. Dowdy, interview; also B. Dowdy, interview.

6. "Survivor of Last Indian Massacre in Kerr Dies," *Kerrville (TX) Daily Times*, September 20, 1945, 1.

7. "R. B. Dowdy, 82, Bullet Victim," *Kerrville (TX) Daily Times*, September 8, 1938, 1.

8. Sunset Cemetery, Kerr County, Texas; author's inspection of Lee Ella Dowdy's tombstone.

9. Harwood, "Murder Details," 6.

10. Dan Dunman file, Texas State Prison Records, Texas State Pardons records, Archives and Information Services Division, Texas State Library and Archives Commission.

11. Ibid; see Leroy G. Denman to Governor J. S. Hogg, October 25, 1892; see also LaSalle County citizens' petition to Governor J. S. Hogg, May, 1892; and former Texas Ranger Sergeant H. W. Van Riper's letter to Governor J. S. Hogg, June 16, 1891.

12. William M. Dunman file, Texas State Prison Records, Texas State Pardons records, Archives and Information Services Division, Texas State Library and Archives Commission; see the letters William Dunman to Governor C. A. Culberson, June 2, 1895, and Kate and Maggie Dunman to Texas Board of Pardons, April 13, 1896. "Maggie Dunman" was possibly Maggie E. (Rosson) Dunman, born in 1874, living in 1900 with her parents Joseph and Nelly in Ellis County, not married but having one living child not at home with her (possibly with her mother-in-law, Kate Dunman?) (U.S. Federal Census, 1900, Texas, Ellis County, Precinct 3, p. 47, Dwelling 26, Family 27, enumerated June 2, 1900, Supervisor's District 6, Enumeration District 28).

13. Records of 33rd Judicial District Court (Kimble County), 1894: State of Texas v. William Dunman, case 572, March 29, 1894.

14. *Kimble County (TX) Citizen*, March 15, 1894.

15. Huntsville Prison records, 1894, Texas State Prison Records, Archives and Information Services Division, Texas State Library and Archives Commission.

16. State of Texas v. William Dunman, Kimble County District Court records, October 26, 1895.

17. William Dunman file, Texas State Prison Records, Texas State Pardons records, Archives and Information Services Division, Texas State Library and Archives Commission. It is striking that, in this correspondence, Kate Dunman does not also seek clemency for her younger son, Dan, who was convicted of the same crimes as his brother Bill, received an identical sentence, and was received at Huntsville prison with his brother. But she had already interceded once before for Dan, who now had one more conviction than Bill. Perhaps she was advised against going once too often to the well.

18. Huntsville Prison records, 1901, Texas State Prison Records, Archives and Information Services Division, Texas State Library and Archives Commission.

19. "Mrs. J. R. Dublin to be Feted on Ninetieth Birthday Sunday," *Midland (TX) Reporter-Telegram*, November 2, 1957; see also "Death Claims Area Pioneer," *Midland (TX) Reporter-Telegram*, October 21, 1958.

20. U.S. v. Tom Moody, U.S. District Court, Western District of Texas (San Antonio), 1881, Case 298 (November 8, 1881: guilty as charged—robbery of U.S. mails); see also the following articles in the *San Antonio Daily Express*: "From Brackett, District Court—Arrest for Stage Robbing Commercial Drummers," September 20, 1881; "The Tall Man, He is Safe in our County Jail—Something About Tom Moody and His Deeds," September 22, 1881; "A Stage Robber's Programme," October 4, 1881; and "More Good Work by Joe Sheely," October 25, 1881. Tom Moody was arrested, tried, and convicted on November 8, 1881, in federal court in San Antonio, Texas, of robbing a stagecoach near Sabinal, Texas, on February 13, 1881. Moody, a notorious and daring criminal, received a life sentence. He had been tried in state district court and found not guilty of another stage robbery near Brackettville, Texas, and was arrested immediately after that trial concluded. U.S. Deputy Marshal Joe Sheely was the arresting officer; he later secured physical evidence that provided the compelling basis to convict Moody.

21. "Texas Highwaymen," *St. Louis Globe-Democrat*," December 4, 1886; this extensive article provides much detail about the trials and convictions of the Dublins, Potters, and Matthew Wilkins as well as their fellow inmate in Chester Prison, Tom Moody, who confessed to the stage robbery for which they were wrongly convicted, allowing the State of Texas to pardon and release them. See also *Burnet (TX) Bulletin* (no date—probably early 1887), "The Potters Innocent." My copy is a poor photocopy of one part of a newspaper page attributed to the *Burnet Bulletin*, with no publication date shown (the Potter family was living in Burnet County at this time). Given that the Potter boys were not released from Chester Prison until December 13, 1886, that the *Burnet Bulletin* was a weekly newspaper, and allowing for travel time, it seems likely the article was published in early January 1887.

22. "Mrs. J. R. Dublin to be Feted," *Midland (TX) Reporter-Telegram*; see also "Death Claims Area Pioneer," *Midland (TX) Reporter-Telegram*.

23. Toni Midkiff, correspondence with the author, May 2, 2008, including Dublin family records;

see also U.S. Federal Census, 1900, Texas, Midland County, Precinct 1, p. 12, Dwellings 220–22; Families 231–34, enumerated June 15, 1900, Supervisor's District 4, Enumeration District 110.

24. Unraveling the different Dublin lines is challenging because many of the same first names were given; moreover, the birth dates and locations seem to be unreliable, and the 1880 Kimble County census enumeration may have omitted one or more of the Dublin children. A Charles Albert Dublin was living in the Midland area with his mother, Nancy, in 1900; he was clearly part of the extended Dublin family (he married Roberta Potter). Although he is not shown among the large James Dublin family enumerated in the 1880 federal census in Kimble County, his death certificate indicates he was born in Hamilton County, Texas, in 1867, and his birth date is not inconsistent with the ages of other James Dublin children. The Midkiff descendants consider him a younger brother of Roll and Dell Dublin. Other Dublins who were in the same Midland neighborhood in 1900 may have been cousins, possibly sons of Jimmy Dublin's brother Henry.

25. Toni Midkiff, correspondence.

26. Ibid.

27. "Death Claims Area Pioneer," *Midland (TX) Reporter-Telegram*.

28. "Mrs. J. R. Dublin to be Feted," *Midland (TX) Reporter-Telegram*; see also "Death Claims Area Pioneer," *Midland (TX) Reporter-Telegram*. See also author correspondence with Kit Fuller, September 10 and 25, 2007.

29. *Burnet (TX) Bulletin*, early 1887; see also author correspondence with Kit Fuller, September 10 and 25, 2007, with Potter family genealogical lists.

30. Fuller, correspondence, September 10, 2007, citing U.S. Dept of Interior, Bureau of Pensions correspondence.

31. "Mrs. J. R. Dublin to be Feted," *Midland (TX) Reporter-Telegram*.

32. Fuller, genealogical lists, September 10, 2007.

33. Ibid.

34. Ibid; see also genealogical information from Toni Midkiff, May 2, 2008.

35. C. L. Nevill to J. B. Jones, November 17, 1880.

36. Frontier Battalion Monthly Returns, 1880.

37. Allen A. Erwin, *The Southwest of John H. Slaughter*, 1841–1922 (Glendale, CA: Arthur H. Clark, 1965), 99.

38. James B. Gillett, *Fugitives from Justice: The Notebook of Texas Ranger Sergeant James B. Gillett* (1878; repr., Austin, TX: State House Press, 1977), 4.

39. Erwin, *The Southwest of John H. Slaughter*, 101, 112–13, 115–16, 126.

40. Ben T. Trawick, *That Wicked Little Gringo: The Story of John H. Slaughter* (Tombstone, AZ: Red Marie's Books, 2001), 26–29; 35; 40, 47, 125; also Fuller, genealogical lists, September 10, 2007.

41. Lieutenant C. L. Nevill, Special Order No. 11, memo to record, Company E, Frontier Battalion, Texas Ranger Correspondence, Archives and Information Services Division, Texas State Library and Archives Commission.

42. Kit Fuller, correspondence with the author, June 2, 2008, citing 1893 annual Indian census, Round Valley, Mendocino County, California.

43. Carranco and Beard, *Genocide and Vendetta*, 281.

44. Fuller, genealogical lists, September 10, 2007.

45. Ibid.

46. C. L. Nevill to J. B. Jones, November 17, 1880. Also see Frontier Battalion Monthly Returns, 1880.

47. Fuller, correspondence, October 4, 2007.

48. Fuller, genealogical lists, September 10, 2007.

49. Trawick, *That Wicked Little Gringo*, 58.

50. Fuller, genealogical lists, September 10, 2007.

51. *Galveston (TX) Daily News*, February 28, 1882.

52. "U.S. Federal Census, 1880," in *Families of Kimble County*, 468; U.S. Federal Census, 1900, California, Sonoma County, Analy Township, p. 5B, enumerated June 11, 1900, Dwelling 108, Family 109, Supervisor's District 3, Enumeration District 156; U.S. Federal Census, 1910, California, Sonoma County, Sebastopol, Ward 1, p. 155, enumerated April 15, 1910, Dwelling 1, Family 13, Supervisor's District 2, Enumeration District 138.

53. Mudge, "Ezekiel Kiser Kountz " and "John Cook Kountz," 224–25.

54. Pendergrass, "William Franklin Gilliland Family," 158; see also "U.S. Federal Census, 1880," in *Families of Kimble County*, 468.

55. Fisher, *It Occurred in Kimble*, 152–54; see also Sheppard, "John Alexander Miller," 250–51; and "U.S. Federal Census, 1880," in *Families of Kimble County*, 471; U.S. Federal Census, 1900, Texas, Kimble County, Precinct 3, Dwelling 1, Family 1, p. 1A, Supervisor's District 5, Enumeration District 46; U.S. Federal Census, 1910, Texas, Kimble County, Precinct 8, p. 3A, Dwelling 38, Family 38, Supervisor's District 16, Enumeration District 155; U.S. Federal Census 1920, Texas, Kimble County, Precinct 5, p. 6B, Dwelling 114, Family 117, Supervisors District 16, Enumeration District 132.

56. Patterson, "N. Q. Patterson Family," 290; see also "U.S. Federal Census, 1880," in *Families of Kimble County*, 468.

57. Lee, "Benjamin Franklin Pepper," 294–95; see also "U.S. Federal Census, 1880," in *Families of Kimble County*, 465; U.S. Federal Census, 1900, Texas, Kimble County, Precinct 1, p. 7A, Enumerated June 1, 1900, Dwelling 117, Family 121, Supervisor's District 5, Enumeration District 45; U.S. Federal Census, 1910, California, San Diego County, Ramona Township, p. 1A, enumerated April 15, 1910, Dwelling 10, Family 10, Supervisor's District 8, Enumeration District 135.

58. Temple, "John E. Temple Family," 365; see also "U.S. Federal Census, 1880," in *Families of Kimble County*, 465.

59. T. W. Cutrer, "Daniel W. Roberts," *Handbook of Texas Online*, accessed April 6. 2008, http://www.tshaonline.org/handbook/online/articles/RR/fro11.html.

60. Alice Jack Dolan Shipman, *Taming the Big Bend: A History* (Austin, TX: Von Boeckmann Jones, 1928), 111–13; see also Pat Dolan, unattributed biography contained in service folder, Texas Ranger Museum, Waco, Texas.

61. Parsons and Brice, *Texas Ranger N. O. Reynolds*, 272–342.

62. Gillett, *Six Years*, 81–107, 134.

63. Gillett, *Six Years*, 141–239.

64. Margaret F. Peirce, "James Buchanan Gillett," *Handbook of Texas Online*, accessed on June 6, 2008, http://www.tshaonline.org/handbook/online/articles/GG/fgi25.html.

65. Kimbell, *Ranger Reminiscences*, 1–11.

66. Texas marriage records, Stephens County, October 20, 1881.

67. U.S. Federal Census, 1900, Texas, Limestone County, Precinct 1, p. 10B, Dwelling 173, Family 173, enumerated June 11, 1900, Supervisor's District 9, Enumeration District 51; Emma L. Kimbell is not present in R. G. Kimbell's household, but six children are. Since Kimbell wrote in 1937 that he wanted his remains to be interred next to Emma, who had predeceased him, it seems unlikely that they were divorced or separated.

68. State of Oklahoma, official death certificate, state file no. 000469.

69. Wilkins, *Law Comes to Texas*, 216–20.

70. Parsons and Brice, *Texas Ranger N. O. Reynolds*, 381–83.

71. Mike Bowlin, correspondence with the author, July 20, 2008.

72. Caffall, "The Joseph Hardin Clements Family," 99.

73. Ernest Wallace, *Ranald S. Mackenzie*, 185–95.

74. Edward S. Wallace, "General John Lapham Bullis," 77–85; Ernest Wallace, *Ranald S. Mackenzie*, 98–99; see also Porter, *Black Seminoles*, 207–8, 213, and C. F. Eckhardt, "The Whirlwind: Lt. John Lapham Bullis and the Seminole Negro Scouts," *Texas Escapes Online Magazine*, accessed July 26, 2006, http://www.texasescapes.com/CFEckhardt/Whirlwind-Lt-John-Lapham-Bullis-and-the-Seminole-Negro-Scouts.htm.

75. Tate, "Bullis, John Lapham"; Edward S. Wallace, "General John Lapham Bullis," 77–85.

76. Darrell Debo, "Blackburn," in *Burnet County History*, vol. 1 (Burnet, TX: Burnet County Historical Commission, 1979).

77. U.S. Federal Census 1880, Texas, Bexar County, San Antonio, p. 207C, enumerated June 14, 1880, Dwelling 321, Family 343, Supervisor's District 6, Enumeration District 16; U.S. Federal Census 1900, Texas, Bexar County, San Antonio, Ward 5, p. 3B, enumerated June 2, 1900, Dwelling 45, Family 50, Supervisor's District 5; Enumeration District 97; U.S. Federal Census 1910, Texas Bexar County, San Antonio, Ward 4, p. 6A, enumerated April 21, 1910, Dwelling 92, Family 91, Supervisor's District 14, Enumeration District 21.

78. "Judge Leo Tarleton Dead," *San Antonio Daily Express*, September 21, 1921, 1.

**Chapter 17**

1. Estes, interview; L. Dowdy, interview.

2. D. W. Roberts to J. B. Jones, October 14, 1879.

3. Arthur Herman, *How the Scots Invented the Modern World: The True Story of How Western Europe's Poorest Nation Created Our World and Everything in It* (New York: Three Rivers Press, 2001), 4.

4. Rose, "Regional Perspectives," 5–12.

5. Bil Gilbert, *Westering Man: The Life of Joseph Walker* (Norman: University of Oklahoma Press, 1985), 3–28; and Fehrenbach, *Lone Star*, 81–92. See also James G. Leyburn, *The Scotch-Irish: A Social History* (Chapel Hill: University of North Carolina Press, 1962), 256–72.

6. D. W. Roberts to J. B. Jones, October 14, 1879.

7. "Texas Border Troubles," Misc. Doc. No. 64, House Reports, 201; also Callahan, *American Foreign Policy*, 346–48. Some stolen cattle likely found their way into Texas herds making up for trailing northward to Kansas markets, but intensifying inspections by county hide inspectors during the 1875–82 period gradually shut off this outlet for local cattle rustlers.

8. Gary C. Anderson, *The Conquest of Texas: Ethnic Cleansing in the Promised Land* (Norman: University of Oklahoma Press, 2005), 8, 359. The Rangers themselves did report on several occasions that the women of the Kimble County confederation publicly accused them of abuse of fugitives and prisoners when trying to apprehend their menfolk in the vicinity of their family home sites (see chap. 8). Three comments are relevant here: (1) no physical evidence of such abuse is apparent in the records or news reports; (2) such accusations may be expected from such an entrenched tribal society in the face of state force and in the heat of action; and (3) in such cases, the Rangers were dealing with people of their own ethnicity. Although Anderson's account purports to apply to the full range of Texas Ranger frontier activities, it must also be acknowledged that his history ended with the year 1875, and he does not discuss the Frontier Battalion specifically, even though it was created in 1874.

9. Herman, *How the Scots*, 137.

10. "Stage Robbery Investigation, the Whole Set, Including Witnesses, Hard Cases," *Galveston (TX) Daily News*, August 20, 1879; see also Gillett, *Six Years*, 102–5.

# Bibliography

**Archival Materials**

*Note* : The Adjutant General's Records in the Archives and Information Services Division, Texas State Library and Archives Commission is abbreviated in the notes as AGR.

Archives and Information Services Division, Texas State Library and Archives Commission
 Adjutant General's Records
  Arrest Warrants
  General Correspondence
  *Results of Operations of State Troops*, vol. 1
  R. G. Kimbell, *Ranger Reminiscences*, 1937 (memoirs)
  Texas Ranger Records
   Frontier Battalion Correspondence
   Frontier Battalion Monthly Returns
   Statement of Arrests, Company A, Capt. N. Coldwell, May 1878
 Texas State Pardons Records
 Texas State Prison Records
Butt-Holdsworth Memorial Library, Kerrville, Texas
 Franklin Junior High School Class of 1927–28, "The Dowdy Family" (unpublished manuscript)
 Kerr Regional History Center
  Merrill Doyle interview of Mr. and Mrs. Solon Dowdy, July 11, 1972 (cassette)
Kimble County Land Records, Kimble County Courthouse, Junction, Texas
 Book A
Texas Ranger Museum, Waco, Texas
 Pat Dolan, unattributed biography contained in service folder
Texas State Land Office Archives, Austin, Texas
 Kerr County Land Ownership Map. 1880.
 Kimble County Land Ownership Map, 1879
University of Texas at Austin, Center for American History
 Walter P. Webb Papers
U.S. National Archives and Records Service, Washington, D.C.
 Office of the Chief of Engineers, Record group 77, Cartographic Records Section, Civil Works Map File, 1869
  Thomas B. Hunt, *Journal Showing the Route Taken by the Government Train Accompany-*

*ing the 15th Regiment, U.S. Infantry from Austin, Texas to Fort Craig, New Mexico
and Returning to San Antonio, July–December, 1869.* Washington, D.C.

## Court Records

Goliad County District Court Records, 1878
    H. C. Withers v. John G. and James Dowdy. Case 1195.
Kimble County District Court Records, March 29, 1894
    State of Texas v. William Dunman. Case 572.
Records of 24th Judicial District Court, Kerr County
    State of Texas v. Dan Dunman
        Case 259 (murder)
        Case 261 (aiding a prisoner to escape from an officer)
    State of Texas v. R. B. and Tom Dowdy
        Case 256 (robbery)
        Case 257 (aiding a prisoner to escape from an officer)
    State of Texas v. R. B. Dowdy. Case 255 (murder)
    State of Texas v. Tom Dowdy. Case 254 (murder)
    State of Texas v. William Dunman and Dan Dunman. Case Number 260 (assault and robbery)
    State of Texas v. William Dunman. Case 258 (murder)
U.S. District Court, Western District of Texas (San Antonio), November 8, 1881
    U.S. v. Tom Moody. Case 298 (robbery of U.S. mails—guilty as charged)

## Interviews

Dowdy, Leo. November 11, 1987.
Dowdy, Mrs. Bill (Mabel). November 9, 1987.
Dowdy, Mrs. Myrtle. November 9, 1987.
Dowdy, W. C. (Billy). May 9, 2008.
Estes, Ned B. October 23, 1987.
Evans, Jo Fred Burt. March 15, 2010.
Fuller, Kit. August 28, September 21, and December 21, 2007; April 25–27, 2008.
Jary, Roland S. November 14, 1987.
McCall, Nina Dowdy. November 10, 1987.
Moore, Jasper. December 2, 1987.
Shearer, Wilburn. February 7, 2008.
Wyatt, Frederica B. November 3–4, 2009.

## Newspapers

*Austin Statesman*
*Burnet (TX) Bulletin*
*Fredericksburg (TX) Standard*
*Galveston (TX) Daily News*

*The Highlander* (Llano, TX)

*Kerrville (TX) Daily Times*

*Kerrville (TX) Mountain Sun*

*Kimble County (TX) Citizen*

*Mendocino (CA) Democrat*

*Midland (TX) Reporter-Telegram*

*San Angelo (TX) Standard Times*

*San Antonio Daily Express*

*San Antonio Weekly Express Supplement*

*St. Louis Globe-Democrat*

*West Kerr (TX) Current*

**U.S. Federal Census Records**

California: 1850, 1860, 1870, 1900, 1910

New Mexico Territory: 1870

Texas: 1860, 1870, 1880, 1900, 1910, 1920

**Articles and Books**

Adams, L. Carroll. "The Dowdy Massacre." In *Documentation for State Historical Markers*. Austin: Texas Historical Commission, 1978.

Adjutant General (Hon. John B. Jones). *Annual Report of the Adjutant General of the State of Texas*. Austin: State Printing Office, December 31, 1880.

Alexander, Bob. *Winchester Warriors: Texas Rangers of Company D, 1874–1901*. Denton: University of North Texas Press, 2009.

Alvarez, Elizabeth Cruse, and Robert Plocheck, eds. *Texas Almanac 2008–2009*. Dallas: Dallas Morning News, 2008.

Anderson, Gary C. *The Conquest of Texas: Ethnic Cleansing in the Promised Land*. Norman: University of Oklahoma Press, 2005.

Austerman, Wayne R. *Sharps Rifles and Spanish Mules: The San Antonio–El Paso Mail, 1851–1881*. College Station: Texas A&M University Press, 1985.

Bennett, Bob. *Kerr County, Texas, 1856–1956*. San Antonio, TX: Naylor, 1956.

Biggers, Don H. *German Pioneers in Texas*. 1925. Reprint, Austin, TX: Eakin Press, 1983.

Bomar, George W. *Texas Weather*. Austin: University of Texas Press, 1983.

Bruce, Leona. *Banister Was There*. Fort Worth, TX: Branch-Smith, 1968.

Brune, Gunnar. *Springs of Texas*, vol. 1. College Station: Texas A&M Press, 1981.

Caffall, Thomas H. "The Joseph Hardin Clements Family." In *Families of Kimble County*, vol. 2. Junction, TX: Kimble County Historical Commission, 1998.

Callahan, James M. *American Foreign Policy in Mexican Relations*. New York: Macmillan, 1932.

Carlson, Paul H. *"Pecos Bill": A Military Biography of William R. Shafter*. College Station: Texas A&M University Press, 1989.

Caro, Robert A. *The Path to Power: The Years of Lyndon Johnson*. 1981. Reprint, New York: Random House, 1990.

Carr, Evelyn M. "Thomas A. Dowdy." In *Kerr County Album*, collected by Kerr County Historical Commission. Dallas: Taylor Publishing, 1986.

Carranco, Lynnwood, and Estelle Beard. *Genocide and Vendetta: The Round Valley Wars of Northern California*. Norman: University of Oklahoma Press, 1981.

Carter, Robert G. *On the Border with Mackenzie*. 1935. Reprint, Denton: Texas State Historical Association Press, 2007.

Collins, Michael L. *Texas Devils: Rangers and Regulars in the Lower Rio Grande, 1846–1861*. Norman: University of Oklahoma Press, 2008.

Cox, Mike. *The Texas Rangers: Wearing the Cinco Peso, 1821–1900*. New York: Tom Daugherty Associates / Forge Press, 2008.

Cresap, Bernarr. *Appomattox Commander: The Story of General E. O. C. Ord*. San Diego: A. S. Barnes, 1981.

Cutrer, T. W. "Daniel W. Roberts." *Handbook of Texas Online*. Accessed April 6, 2008. http://www.tshaonline.org/handbook/online/articles/RR/fro11.html.

Dearen, Patrick. *A Cowboy of the Pecos*. Plano: Republic of Texas Press, 1997.

Debo, Darrell. "Blackburn." In *Burnet County History*, vol. 1. Burnet, TX: Burnet County Historical Commission, 1979.

Dobie, J. Frank. *A Vaquero of the Brush Country*. 1929. Reprint, Austin: University of Texas Press, 1981.

Eckhardt, C. F. "The Whirlwind: Lt. John Lapham Bullis and the Seminole Negro Scouts." *Texas Escapes Online Magazine*. Accessed July 26, 2006. http://www.texasescapes.com/CFEckhardt/Whirlwind-Lt-John-Lapham-Bullis-and-the-Seminole-Negro-Scouts.htm.

Erwin, Allen A. *The Southwest of John H. Slaughter, 1841–1922*. Glendale, CA: Arthur H. Clark, 1965.

Fehrenbach, Theodore R. *Comanches: The Destruction of a People*. New York: Knopf, 1989.

———. *Fire and Blood: A History of Mexico*. 1973. Reprint, Cambridge, MA: DaCapo Press, 1995.

———. *Lone Star: A History of Texas and the Texans*. New York: Collier Books, 1968.

Fisher, Ovie C. *It Occurred in Kimble and How: The Story of a Texas County*. 1937. Reprint, San Angelo, TX: Talley Press, 1984.

Fuller, Kit. "Putting the Potters in Perspective." Unpublished paper presented at the annual meeting of the Edwards Plateau Historical Association, April 26, 2008.

Gardner, Tommie Lee. "John Gibson Dowdy." In *Kerr County Album*, collected by Kerr County Historical Commission. Dallas: Taylor Publishing, 1986.

Gibson, A. M. *The Kickapoos: Lords of the Middle Border*. Norman: University of Oklahoma Press, 1963.

Gilbert, Bil. *Westering Man: The Life of Joseph Walker*. Norman: University of Oklahoma Press, 1985.

Gillett, James B. *Fugitives from Justice: The Notebook of Texas Ranger Sergeant James B. Gillett*. Reprint, Austin, TX: State House Press, 1979.

———. *Six Years with the Texas Rangers, 1875–1881*. 1921. Reprint, Lincoln: University of Nebraska Press, 1976.

Goggin, John M. "Mexican Kickapoo Indians." *Southwestern Journal of Anthropology* 7, no. 3 (1951): 314–27.

Gwynne, S. C. *Empire of the Summer Moon: Quanah Parker and the Rise and Fall of the Comanches, the Most Powerful Indian Tribe in American History.* New York: Scribner, 2010.

Haley, J. Evetts. *Jeff Milton: A Good Man with a Gun.* Norman: University of Oklahoma Press, 1948.

Hazlewood, Claudia. "Menard, Texas." *Handbook of Texas Online.* Accessed Aug 17, 2009. http://www.tshaonline.org/handbook/online/articles/hjm12.

Herman, Arthur. *How the Scots Invented the Modern World: The True Story of How Western Europe's Poorest Nation Created Our World and Everything in It.* New York: Three Rivers Press, 2001.

Hill, Dorothy J. "James John Morehead, 1828–1885: A California Pioneer." In *Ripples Along Chico Creek: Perspectives on People and Time.* Chico, CA: Butte County Branch, American League of American Pen Women, 1992.

Hill, Robert T., and T. Wayland Vaughan. "Geology of the Edwards Plateau and Rio Grande Plain Adjacent to Austin and San Antonio, Texas, with Reference to the Occurrence of Underground Waters." *U.S. Geological Survey* 18, no. 2 (1898): 193–321.

Hunter, J. Marvin, ed. *The Trail Drivers of Texas.* 1924. Reprint, Austin: University of Texas Press, 1985.

Jobes, Roquey. "The Rest of the Story for an Era of Lawlessness." In *Families of Kimble County,* vol. 2. Junction, TX: Kimble County Historical Commission, 1998.

Johnson, David. *The Mason County "Hoo Doo" War, 1874–1902.* Denton: University of North Texas Press, 2006.

Johnson, John G. "The Mexican and Indian Raid of '78." *Handbook of Texas Online.* Accessed September 26, 2008. http://www.tshaonline.org/handbook/online/articles/MM/btmrv.html.

LaVere, David. *The Texas Indians.* College Station: Texas A&M University Press, 2004.

Leckie, William H., with Shirley A. Leckie. *The Buffalo Soldiers: A Narrative of the Black Cavalry in the West,* rev. ed. Norman: University of Oklahoma Press, 2003.

Lee, M. P. "Benjamin Franklin Pepper." In *Families of Kimble County.* Junction, TX: Kimble County Historical Commission, 1985.

Leyburn, James G. *The Scotch-Irish: A Social History.* Chapel Hill: University of North Carolina Press, 1962.

McCallum, Henry D., and Frances T. McCallum. *The Wire That Fenced the West.* Norman: University of Oklahoma Press, 1965.

McGuffin, Ray. "Scabtown, U.S.A." In "Interesting Places and Unusual Names" by Anys Whitley Godfrey, 28–32, in *Menard County History: An Anthology.* San Angelo, TX: Anchor, 1982.

Morriss, Annie May. *Her Name Was Ann.* San Antonio, TX: Naylor Company, 1951.

Moungovan, Julia, ed. *The Potter Valley Story.* Ukia, CA: Mendocino County Historical Society, 1972.

Mudge, L. R. "Ezekiel Kiser Kountz and Harriet (Lindamood) Kountz." In *Families of Kimble County.* Junction, TX: Kimble County Historical Commission, 1985.

———. "John Cook Kountz and Laura (Turner) Kountz." In *Families of Kimble County.* Junction, TX: Kimble County Historical Commission, 1985.

Parsons, Chuck, and Donaly E. Brice. *Texas Ranger N. O. Reynolds, the Intrepid.* Honolulu: Talei
    Publishers, 2005.

Pate, J'nell. "United States–Mexican Border Conflicts, 1870–1880." *West Texas Historical As-*
    *sociation Yearbook* 28 (1962): 175–94.

Patterson, H. G. "N. Q. Patterson Family." In *Families of Kimble County.* Junction, TX: Kimble
    County Historical Commission, 1985.

Patterson, N. C. "N. C. Patterson Memoirs." In *Families of Kimble County*, vol. 2. Junction, TX:
    Kimble County Historical Commission, 1998.

Peirce, Margaret F. "James Buchanan Gillett." *Handbook of Texas Online.* Accessed on June 6,
    2008. http://www.tshaonline.org/handbook/online/articles/GG/fgi25.html.

Pendergrass, M. V. "William Franklin Gilliland Family." In *Families of Kimble County.* Junction,
    TX: Kimble County Historical Commission, 1985.

Pool, William C. *A Historical Atlas of Texas.* Austin, TX: Encino Press, 1975.

Porter, Kenneth W. *The Black Seminoles: History of a Freedom-seeking People.* Gainesville: Univer-
    sity Press of Florida, 1996.

Ramsey, Grover C. "Camp Melvin, Crockett County, Texas." *West Texas Historical Association*
    *Yearbook*, 37 (1961): 137–47.

Randolph, Catherine. "Joseph Jackson Ramsey." In *Families of Kimble County.* Junction, TX:
    Kimble County Historical Commission, 1985.

Reid, John C. *Reid's Tramp, or a Journal of the Incidents of Ten Months Travel through Texas, New*
    *Mexico, Arizona, Sonora, and California.* 1858. Reprint, Austin, TX: Steck Company, 1935.

Renfro, H. B., and Dan E. Feray. *Geological Highway Map of Texas.* Tulsa, OK: American Associa-
    tion of Petroleum Geologists, 1979.

Richardson, Rupert N., and Harold B. Simpson. *Frontier Forts of Texas.* Waco, TX: Texian Press,
    1966.

Rippy, J. Fred. *The United States and Mexico.* New York: Knopf, 1926.

Roberts, Dan W. *Rangers and Sovereignty.* 1914. Reprint, Austin, TX: State House Press, 1987.

Roberts, Luvenia Conway. *A Woman's Reminiscences of Six Years in Camp with the Texas Rangers.*
    1928. Facsimile reprint, Austin, TX: State House Press, 1987.

Robinson, Charles M., III. *Frontier Forts of Texas.* Houston: Lone Star Books / Gulf Publishing
    Company, 1986.

Rose, Peter R. "Edwards Group, Surface and Subsurface, Central Texas." In *Report of Investiga-*
    *tions, No. 74.* Austin: Texas Bureau of Economic Geology, 1972.

———. "Regional Perspectives on the Edwards Group of Central Texas: Geology, Geomor-
    phology, Geohydrology, and Their Influence on Settlement History." In *Edwards Water*
    *Resources in Central Texas: Retrospective and Prospective.* Edited by Sue Hovorka, 1–18. Austin:
    Texas Bureau of Economic Geology, 2004. CD-ROM.

———. "Setting the Stage of the Hoo Doo War: Land, People, and History of Settlement."
    In *The Hoo Doo War: Portraits of A Lawless Time*, edited by Peter R. Rose and Elizabeth E.
    Sherry, 11–22. Mason, TX: Mason County Historical Commission, 2003.

Santleben, August. *A Texas Pioneer: Early Staging and Overland Freighting Days on the Frontiers*
    *of Texas and Mexico.* Edited by I. D. Affleck. New York: Neale Publishing Company, 1910.

Schilz, T. F. *Lipan Apaches in Texas*. El Paso: Texas Western Press, 1987.

Sellards, E. H., W. S. Adkins, and F. B. Plummer. *The Geology of Texas*. Vol. 1, *Stratigraphy*. University of Texas Bulletin 3232. Austin: University of Texas, 1932.

Shelton, Delight C. *From Acorns to Oaks*. Willits, CA: Golden Rule Printing, 1986.

Sheppard, M. B. "John Alexander Miller." In *Families of Kimble County*. Junction, TX: Kimble County Historical Commission, 1985.

Shipman, Alice Jack Dolan. *Taming the Big Bend: A History*. Austin, TX: Von Boeckmann Jones, 1928.

Smith, Charles I. *Lower Cretaceous Stratigraphy, Northern Coahuila, Mexico*. Austin: Bureau of Economic Geology, University of Texas, 1970.

Smith, T. F. *From Dominance to Disappearance: The Indians of Texas and the Near Southwest, 1786–1859*. Lincoln: University of Nebraska Press, 2005.

Smyrl, Vivian Elizabeth. "Menard County." *Handbook of Texas Online*. Accessed August 17, 2009. http://www.tshaonline.org/handbook/online/articles/hcm11.

Sowell, A. J. *Early Settlers and Indian Fighters of Southwest Texas*. 1900. Reprint, Austin, TX: State House Press, 1986.

Tate, Michael L. "Bullis, John Lapham." *Handbook of Texas Online*. Accessed April 11, 2008. http://www.tshaonline.org/handbook/online/articles/fbu19.

Temple, R. L. "John E. Temple Family." In *Families of Kimble County*. Junction, TX: Kimble County Historical Commission, 1985.

———. "John E. Temple." In *Families of Kimble County*, vol. 2. Junction, TX: Kimble County Historical Commission, 1998.

"The Texas Border Troubles," Misc. Doc. No. 64, House Reports, 45th Congress, 2nd Session, 1878 (1820).

Thompson, Richard A. *Crossing the Border with the 4th Cavalry: Mackenzie's Raid into Mexico, 1873*. Waco, TX: Texian Press, 1986.

Trawick, Ben T. *That Wicked Little Gringo: The Story of John H. Slaughter*. Tombstone, AZ: Red Marie's Books, 2001.

Uglow, Lloyd M. *Standing in the Gap: Army Outposts, Picket Stations, and the Pacification of the Texas Frontier, 1866–1886*. Fort Worth: Texas Christian University Press, 2001.

"U.S. Federal Census, 1870." In *Families of Kimble County*. Junction, TX: Kimble County Historical Commission, 1985.

"U.S. Federal Census, 1880." In *Families of Kimble County*. Junction, TX: Kimble County Historical Commission, 1985.

U.S. Military Division of the Missouri. *Record of Engagements with Hostile Indians within the Military Division of the Missouri from 1868 to 1882*. Washington, D.C.: Government Printing Office, 1882.

Utley, Robert M. *If These Walls Could Speak: Historic Forts of Texas*. Austin: University of Texas Press, 1990.

———. *Lone Star Justice: The First Century of Texas Rangers*. New York: Oxford University Press, 2002.

———. *The Indian Frontier of the American West, 1846–1890*. Albuquerque: University of New Mexico Press, 1984.

Wallace, Edward S. "General John Lapham Bullis, the Thunderbolt of the Texas Frontier, II." *Southwestern Historical Quarterly* 55 (July 1951): 77–85.

Wallace, Ernest. *Ranald S. Mackenzie on the Texas Frontier.* College Station: Texas A&M University Press, 1993.

Webb, Walter P. *The Great Plains.* 1931. Reprint, Lincoln: University of Nebraska Press / Bison Books, 1981.

———. *The Texas Rangers: A Century of Frontier Defense.* 1935. Reprint, Austin: University of Texas Press, 1977.

Weddle, Robert S. "Peg Leg Station on the San Saba River." In *Edwards Plateau Historian*, vol. 3. Menard, TX: Edwards Plateau Historical Association, 1967.

Wilkins, Frederick. *The Law Comes to Texas: The Texas Rangers, 1870–1901.* Austin, TX: State House Press, 1999.

Wyatt, Frederica B. "Dr. William M. Donnan." In *Families of Kimble County*, vol. 2. Junction, TX: Kimble County Historical Commission, 1998.

———. "Newspaper Excerpts." In *Families of Kimble County*, vol. 2. Junction, TX: Kimble County Historical Commission, 1998.

———. "The Boyce Family." In *Families of Kimble County*. Junction, TX: Kimble County Historical Commission, 1985.

# Index

# About the Author

Peter R. Rose is a fifth-generation Texan and a geologist with more than fifty years of professional experience. The author of the definitive monograph on the Edwards Plateau of West Texas, he is descended from nineteenth-century settlers in Kimble County, where his family maintains ranching operations to the present day. He and his wife, Alice, divide their time between Austin and Telegraph, Texas.